Praise for *Java*

W9-BNR-676

"A comprehensive catalog of computational conundrums that will both perplex and please the perspicacious programmer."

Gilad Bracha, Computational Theologist at Sun Microsystems
and coauthor of *The Java Language Specification*

"*Java Puzzlers* is a must-read for every Java developer, from the neophyte to the master. Written by two acknowledged Java gurus, it shines its explanatory searchlight into every nook and cranny of the Java programming language by presenting almost a hundred programming puzzles, from the most simple to the most profound. Its basic premise is that things are not always as they appear, and it proves that premise time and time again."

Wes Munsil, President, Lexonics, Inc.,
ACM Computing Reviews, September 29, 2005

"Well written, amusing, whimsical, and, above all, informative. Bloch and Gafter have brought us a book that entertains us with corner-cases, one-in-a-million chances, and other happenings that explore the ins, outs, and guts of the Java Programming Language....I enjoyed this book, from start to finish."

Tom Byrne, Slashdot

"I really enjoyed *Java Puzzlers*. It's one of the few Java books I can universally recommend. It will definitely make you a better professional programmer if you take its lessons to heart. As someone who's developed in Java for almost ten years and written a couple of books on it, I can guarantee you'll learn quite a bit from this book. I certainly did."

Jeff Langr, author of *Agile Java*

"There are plenty of books of programmer puzzles and challenges on my shelves, but *Java Puzzlers* does something I find especially useful: It doesn't merely explain why an odd behavior occurs: it also offers suggestions distinctly aimed at Java users in particular and programming language designers in general. Knowing how to use technology when it works correctly is good; knowing how it can fail to work, with what consequences, is also vital."

Peter Coffee, *eWeek*, January 30, 2006

"You think you know the Java language? Try it. (Makes for great interview question fodder, and for that reason alone practicing Java programmers should have a copy on their shelf.)"

Ted Neward, author of *Effective Enterprise Java*
and *Server-Based Java Programming*

Java™ Puzzlers

Traps, Pitfalls, and Corner Cases

Joshua Bloch
Neal Gafter

✦ Addison-Wesley

Upper Saddle River, NJ • Boston • Indianapolis • San Francisco
New York • Toronto • Montreal • London • Munich • Paris • Madrid
Capetown • Sydney • Tokyo • Singapore • Mexico City

The publisher offers excellent discounts on this book when ordered in quantity for bulk purchases or special sales, which may include electronic versions and/or custom covers and content particular to your business, training goals, marketing focus, and branding interests. For more information, please contact:

U.S. Corporate and Government Sales
(800) 382-3419
corpsales@pearsontechgroup.com

For sales outside the U.S., please contact:

International Sales
international@pearsoned.com

Visit us on the Web: www.awprofessional.com

Library of Congress Cataloging-in-Publication Data
Bloch, Joshua.
   Java puzzlers : traps, pitfalls, and corner cases.
      p. cm.
   Includes bibliographical references and index.
   ISBN 0-321-33678-X (pbk. : alk. paper)
   1. Java (Computer program language) I. Gafter, Neal. II. Title.

   QA76.73.J38B58 2005
   005.13'3—dc22

                                             2005015278

ISBN 0-321-33678-X
Text printed in the United States on recycled paper at RR Donnelley in Crawfordsville, Indiana.
Fourth printing, October 2007

To the memory of our fathers:
Fritz W. Bloch (May 2, 1911–May 24, 2003)
Benjamin Abraham Gafter (June 15, 1923–December 14, 2003)

Contents

Preface

Like many books, this one had a long gestation period. We've collected Java puzzles for as long as we've worked with the platform: since mid-1996, in case you're curious. In early 2001, we came up with the idea of doing a talk consisting entirely of Java puzzles. We pitched the idea to Larry Jacobs, then at Oracle, and he bought it hook, line, and sinker.

We gave the first "Java Puzzlers" talk at the Oracle Open World conference in San Francisco in November 2001. To add a bit of pizazz, we introduced ourselves as "Click and Hack, the Type-it Brothers" and stole a bunch of jokes from Tom and Ray Magliozzi of *Car Talk* fame. The presentation was voted best-in-show, and probably would have been even if we hadn't voted for ourselves. We knew we were on to something.

Dressed in spiffy blue mechanic's overalls emblazoned with the "cup and steam" Java logo, we recycled the Oracle talk at JavaOne 2002 to rave reviews—at least from our friends. In the years that followed, we came up with three more "Java Puzzlers" talks and presented them at countless conferences, corporations, and colleges in cities around the globe, from Oslo to Tokyo. The talks were almost universally well liked, and we got very little fruit thrown at us. In the March 2003 issue of *Linux Magazine*, we published an article consisting entirely of Java puzzles and received almost no hate mail. This book contains nearly all the puzzles from our talks and articles and many, many more.

Although this book draws attention to the traps and pitfalls of the Java platform, we do not mean to denigrate it in any way. It is because we love the Java platform that we've devoted nearly a decade of our professional lives to it. Every platform with enough power to do real work has some problems, and Java has far fewer than most. The better you understand the problems, the less likely you are to get hurt by them, and that's where this book comes in.

Most of the puzzles in the book focus on short programs that appear to do one thing but actually do something else. That's why we've chosen to decorate the book with optical illusions—drawings that appear to be one thing but are actually another. Also, you can stare at them while you're trying to figure out what in the world the programs do.

Above all, we wanted this book to be fun. We sincerely hope that you enjoy solving the puzzles as much as we enjoyed writing them and that you learn as much from them as we did.

And by all means, send us your puzzlers! If you have a puzzle that you think belongs in a future edition of this book, write it on the back of a $20 bill and send it to us, or e-mail it to puzzlers@javapuzzlers.com. If we use your puzzle, we'll give you credit.

Last but not least, don't code like my brother.

ACKNOWLEDGMENTS

We thank the whole team at Addison-Wesley for their kindness and professionalism. Early in the life of this project, Ann Sellers was our editor. Her infectious enthusiasm helped get the project off to a good start. When Ann moved on, Greg Doench, executive editor, took over. Greg is a wonderful editor and a perfect gentleman. He accommodated the many demands of this project without batting an eyelash. Greg's editorial assistant is Noreen Regina. Our project editor is Tyrrell Albaugh and our marketing manager is Stephane Nakib. Our cover designer is Chuti Prasertsith and our copy editor is Evelyn Pyle. They all did great work under a tight schedule.

We thank our management at Google for their support. Our director, Prabha Krishna, was unfailingly encouraging. We thank Sergey Brin, Larry Page, and Eric Schmidt for creating the best engineering environment on the planet.

We thank the many Java programmers who submitted bug reports to Sun over the years, especially those who submitted bug reports that turned out not to describe real bugs. Such bug reports were perhaps the richest source of puzzler material: If correct behavior misled programmers into thinking that they had discovered a bug, it probably represents a trap or pitfall. In a similar vein, we thank Sun for having the courage and wisdom to put the entire Java bug database on the Web in 1996 [Bug]. This action was unheard of at the time; even today it is rare.

"Send us your puzzlers," we said at the end of each talk, and send them you did—from all over the world. Special thanks are due Ron Gabor and Mike "madbot" McCloskey for the sheer magnitude of their contributions. Ron contributed Puzzles 28, 29, 30, and 31 and Mike contributed Puzzles 18, 23, 40, 56, and 67. We thank Martin Buchholz for contributing Puzzle 81; Armand Dijamco for contributing Puzzle 14; Prof. Dr. Dominik Gruntz for contributing Puzzles 68 and 69; Kai Huang for contributing Puzzle 77; Jim Hugunin for contributing Puzzle 45; Tim Huske for contributing Puzzle 41; Peter Kessler for contributing Puzzle 35; Michael Klobe for contributing Puzzle 59; Magnus Lundgren for contributing Puzzle 84; Scott Seligman for contributing Puzzle 22; Peter Stout for contributing Puzzle 39; Michael Tennes for contributing Puzzle 70; and Martin Traverso for contributing Puzzle 54.

We thank the dedicated band of reviewers who read the chapters of this book in raw form: Peter von der Ahé, Pablo Bellver, Tracy Bialik, Cindy Bloch, Dan Bloch, Beth Bottos, Joe Bowbeer, Joe Darcy, Bob Evans, Brian Goetz, Tim Halloran, Barry Hayes, Tim Huske, Akiyoshi Kitaoka, Chris Lopez, Mike "madbot" McCloskey, Michael Nielsen, Tim Peierls, Peter Rathmann, Russ Rufer, Steve Schirripa, Yoshiki Shibata, Marshall Spight, Guy Steele, Dean Sutherland, Mark Taylor, Darlene Wallach, and Frank Yellin. They found flaws, suggested improvements, offered encouragement, and hurled invective. Any flaws that remain are the fault of my coauthor.

We thank the queen of the bloggers, Mary Smaragdis, for providing a home for us on her celebrated blog [MaryBlog]. She graciously let us try out the material that became Puzzles 43, 53, 73, 87, and 94 on her readers. We judged the solutions and Mary gave out the prizes. For the record, the winners were Tom Hawtin, Tom Hawtin (again), Bob "Crazybob" Lee, Chris Nokleberg, and the mysterious AT of Odessa, Ukraine. The discussions on Mary's blog contributed greatly to these puzzles.

We thank our many supporters who responded enthusiastically to Java Puzzlers over the years. The members of SDForum Java SIG served as guinea pigs for each talk in its preliminary form. The JavaOne program committee provided a home for the talks. Yuka Kamiya and Masayoshi Okutsu made the "Java Puzzlers" talks a success in Japan, where they took the form of real game shows with onstage contestants. Remarkably, the same person won every single contest: The undisputed Java Puzzler champion of Japan is Yasuhiro Endoh.

We thank James Gosling and the many fine engineers who created the Java platform and improved it over the years. A book like this makes sense only for a platform that is rock solid; without Java, there could be no "Java Puzzlers."

Numerous colleagues at Google, Sun, and elsewhere participated in technical discussions that improved the quality of this book. Among others, Peter von der Ahé, Dan Bloch, and Gilad Bracha contributed useful insights. We give special thanks to Doug Lea, who served as a sounding board for many of the ideas in the book. Once again, Doug was unfailingly generous with his time and knowledge.

We thank Professor Akiyoshi Kitaoka of the Department of Psychology at Ritsumeikan University in Kyoto, Japan, for permission to use some of his optical illusions to decorate this work. Professor Kitaoka's illusions are, quite simply, astonishing. Words cannot do them justice, so you owe it to yourself to take a look. He has two volumes available in Japanese [Kitaoka02, Kitaoka03]. An English translation encompassing both volumes is available [Kitaoka05]. While you wait for your copy to arrive in the mail, pay a visit to Kitaoka's Web site: http://www.ritsumei.ac.jp/~akitaoka/index-e.html. You won't be disappointed.

We thank Tom and Ray Magliozzi of *Car Talk* for providing jokes for us to steal, and we thank their legal counsel of Dewey, Cheetham, and Howe for not suing us.

We thank Josh's wife, Cindy, for helping us with FrameMaker, writing the index, helping us edit the book, and designing the decorative stripe at the beginning of each chapter. Last but not least, we thank our families—Cindy, Tim, and Matt Bloch, and Ricki Lee, Sarah, and Hannah Gafter—for encouraging us to write and for putting up with us while we wrote.

Josh Bloch
Neal Gafter
San Jose, California
May 2005

Introduction

This book is filled with brainteasers about the Java programming language and its core libraries. Anyone with a working knowledge of Java can understand these puzzles, but many of them are tough enough to challenge even the most experienced programmer. Don't feel bad if you can't solve them. They are grouped loosely according to the features they use, but don't assume that the trick to a puzzle is related to its chapter heading; we reserve the right to mislead you.

Most of the puzzles exploit counterintuitive or obscure behaviors that can lead to bugs. These behaviors are known as *traps, pitfalls,* and *corner cases.* Every platform has them, but Java has far fewer than other platforms of comparable power. The goal of the book is to entertain you with puzzles while teaching you to avoid the underlying traps and pitfalls. By working through the puzzles, you will become less likely to fall prey to these dangers in your code and more likely to spot them in code that you are reviewing or revising.

This book is meant to be read with a computer at your side. You'll need a Java development environment, such as Sun's JDK [JDK-5.0]. It should support release 5.0, as some of the puzzles rely on features introduced in this release. You can download the source code for the puzzles from www.javapuzzlers.com. Unless you're a glutton for punishment, we recommend that you do this before solving the puzzles. It's a heck of a lot easier than typing them in yourself.

Most of the puzzles take the form of a short program that appears to do one thing but actually does something else. It's your job to figure out what the program does. To get the most out of these puzzles, we recommend that you take this approach:

1. Study the program and try to predict its behavior without using a computer. If you don't see a trick, keep looking.

2. Once you think you know what the program does, run it. Did it do what you thought it would? If not, can you come up with an explanation for the behavior you observed?

3. Think about how you might fix the program, assuming it is broken.

4. Then and only then, read the solution.

Some of the puzzles require you to write a small amount of code. To get the most out of these puzzles, we recommend that you try—at least briefly—to solve them without using a computer, and then test your solution on a computer. If your code doesn't work, play around with it and see whether you can make it work before reading the solution.

Unlike most puzzle books, this one alternates between puzzles and their solutions. This allows you to read the book without flipping back and forth between puzzles and solutions. The book is laid out so that you must turn the page to get from a puzzle to its solution, so you needn't fear reading a solution accidentally while you're still trying to solve a puzzle.

We encourage you to read each solution, even if you succeed in solving the puzzle. The solutions contain analysis that goes well beyond a simple explanation of the program's behavior. They discuss the relevant traps and pitfalls, and provide lessons on how to avoid falling prey to these hazards. Like most best-practice guidelines, these lessons are not hard-and-fast rules, but you should violate them only rarely and with good reason.

Most solutions contain references to relevant sections of *The Java™ Language Specification, Third Edition* [JLS]. These references aren't essential to understanding the puzzles, but they are useful if you want to delve deeper into the language rules underlying the puzzles. Similarly, many solutions contain references to relevant items in *Effective Java™ Programming Language Guide* [EJ]. These references are useful if you want to delve deeper into best practices.

Some solutions contain discussions of the language or API design decisions that led to the danger illustrated by the puzzle. These "lessons for language designers" are meant only as food for thought and, like other food, should be taken with a grain of salt. Language design decisions cannot be made in isolation. Every language embodies thousands of design decisions that interact in subtle ways. A design decision that is right for one language may be wrong for another.

Many of the traps and pitfalls in these puzzles are amenable to automatic detection by *static analysis*: analyzing programs without running them. Some excellent tools are available for detecting bugs by static analysis, such as Bill Pugh and David Hovemeyer's *FindBugs* [Hovemeyer04]. Some compilers and IDEs, such as Jikes and Eclipse, perform bug detection as well [Jikes, Eclipse]. If you are using one of these compilers, it is especially important that you not compile a puzzle until you've tried to solve it: The compiler's warning messages may give away the solution.

Appendix A of this book is a catalog of the traps and pitfalls in the Java platform. It provides a concise taxonomy of the anomalies exploited by the puzzles, with references back to the puzzles and to other relevant resources. Do not look at the appendix until you're done solving the puzzles. Reading the appendix first would take all the fun out of the puzzles. After you've finished the puzzles, though, this is the place you'll turn to for reference.

Appendix B describes the optical illusions that decorate the book. This appendix explains the nature of each illusion and identifies the inventor, if known. It provides many bibliographic references. This appendix is the place to go if you aren't sure why a given drawing constitutes an illusion, or if you simply want to know more about one of the illusions.

2

Expressive Puzzlers

The puzzles in this chapter are simple. They involve only expression evaluation. But remember, just because they're simple doesn't make them easy.

Puzzle 1: Oddity

The following method purports to determine whether its sole argument is an odd number. Does the method work?

```
public static boolean isOdd(int i) {
    return i % 2 == 1;
}
```

Solution 1: Oddity

An odd number can be defined as an integer that is divisible by 2 with a remainder of 1. The expression i % 2 computes the remainder when i is divided by 2, so it would seem that this program ought to work. Unfortunately, it doesn't; it returns the wrong answer one quarter of the time.

Why one quarter? Because half of all int values are negative, and the isOdd method fails for all negative odd values. It returns false when invoked on any negative value, whether even or odd.

This is a consequence of the definition of Java's remainder operator (%). It is defined to satisfy the following identity for all int values a and all nonzero int values b:

```
(a / b) * b + (a % b) == a
```

In other words, if you divide a by b, multiply the result by b, and add the remainder, you are back where you started [JLS 15.17.3]. This identity makes perfect sense, but in combination with Java's truncating integer division operator [JLS 15.17.2], it implies that **when the remainder operation returns a nonzero result, it has the same sign as its left operand.**

The isOdd method and the definition of the term *odd* on which it was based both assume that all remainders are positive. Although this assumption makes sense for some kinds of division [Boute92], Java's remainder operation is perfectly matched to its integer division operation, which discards the fractional part of its result.

When i is a negative odd number, i % 2 is equal to -1 rather than 1, so the isOdd method incorrectly returns false. To prevent this sort of surprise, **test that your methods behave properly when passed negative, zero, and positive values for each numerical parameter.**

The problem is easy to fix. Simply compare i % 2 to 0 rather than to 1, and reverse the sense of the comparison:

```
public static boolean isOdd(int i) {
    return i % 2 != 0;
}
```

If you are using the isOdd method in a performance-critical setting, you would be better off using the bitwise AND operator (&) in place of the remainder operator:

```
public static boolean isOdd(int i) {
    return (i & 1) != 0;
}
```

The second version may run much faster than the first, depending on what platform and virtual machine you are using, and is unlikely to run slower. As a general rule, the divide and remainder operations are slow compared to other arithmetic and logical operations. **It's a bad idea to optimize prematurely**, but in this case, the faster version is as clear as the original, so there is no reason to prefer the original.

In summary, think about the signs of the operands and of the result whenever you use the remainder operator. The behavior of this operator is obvious when its operands are nonnegative, but it isn't so obvious when one or both operands are negative.

Puzzle 2: Time for a Change

Consider the following word problem:

> Tom goes to the auto parts store to buy a spark plug that costs $1.10, but all he has in his wallet are two-dollar bills. How much change should he get if he pays for the spark plug with a two-dollar bill?

Here is a program that attempts to solve the word problem. What does it print?

```
public class Change {
    public static void main(String args[]) {
        System.out.println(2.00 - 1.10);
    }
}
```

Solution 2: Time for a Change

Naively, you might expect the program to print 0.90, but how could it know that you wanted two digits after the decimal point? If you know something about the rules for converting double values to strings, which are specified by the documentation for Double.toString [Java-API], you know that the program prints the shortest decimal fraction sufficient to distinguish the double value from its nearest neighbor, with at least one digit before and after the decimal point. It seems reasonable, then, that the program should print 0.9. Reasonable, perhaps, but not correct. If you ran the program, you found that it prints 0.8999999999999999.

The problem is that the number 1.1 can't be represented exactly as a double, so it is represented by the closest double value. The program subtracts this value from 2. Unfortunately, the result of this calculation is not the closest double value to 0.9. The shortest representation of the resulting double value is the hideous number that you see printed.

More generally, the problem is that **not all decimals can be represented exactly using binary floating-point.** If you are using release 5.0 or a later release, you might be tempted to fix the program by using the printf facility to set the precision of the output:

```
// Poor solution - still uses binary floating-point!
System.out.printf("%.2f%n", 2.00 - 1.10);
```

This prints the right answer but does not represent a general solution to the underlying problem: It still uses double arithmetic, which is binary floating-point. Floating-point arithmetic provides good approximations over a wide range of values but does not generally yield exact results. **Binary floating-point is particularly ill-suited to monetary calculations**, as it is impossible to represent 0.1—or any other negative power of 10—exactly as a finite-length binary fraction [EJ Item 31].

One way to solve the problem is to use an integral type, such as int or long, and to perform the computation in cents. If you go this route, make sure the integral type is large enough to represent all the values you will use in your program. For this puzzle, int is ample. Here is how the println looks if we rewrite it using int values to represent monetary values in cents. This version prints 90 cents, which is the right answer:

```
System.out.println((200 - 110) + " cents");
```

Another way to solve the problem is to use `BigDecimal`, which performs exact decimal arithmetic. It also interoperates with the SQL `DECIMAL` type via JDBC. There is one caveat: **Always use the `BigDecimal(String)` constructor, never `BigDecimal(double)`.** The latter constructor creates an instance with the *exact* value of its argument: `new BigDecimal(.1)` returns a `BigDecimal` representing 0.1000000000000000055511151231257827021181583404541015625. Using `BigDecimal` correctly, the program prints the expected result of `0.90`:

```java
import java.math.BigDecimal;
public class Change {
    public static void main(String args[]) {
        System.out.println(new BigDecimal("2.00").
                           subtract(new BigDecimal("1.10")));
    }
}
```

This version is not terribly pretty, as Java provides no linguistic support for `BigDecimal`. Calculations with `BigDecimal` are also likely to be slower than those with any primitive type, which might be an issue for some programs that make heavy use of decimal calculations. It is of no consequence for most programs.

In summary, **avoid `float` and `double` where exact answers are required; for monetary calculations, use `int`, `long`, or `BigDecimal`.** For language designers, consider providing linguistic support for decimal arithmetic. One approach is to offer limited support for operator overloading, so that arithmetic operators can be made to work with numerical reference types, such as `BigDecimal`. Another approach is to provide a primitive decimal type, as did COBOL and PL/I.

Puzzle 3: Long Division

This puzzle is called Long Division because it concerns a program that divides two `long` values. The dividend represents the number of microseconds in a day; the divisor, the number of milliseconds in a day. What does the program print?

```java
public class LongDivision {
    public static void main(String[] args) {
        final long MICROS_PER_DAY = 24 * 60 * 60 * 1000 * 1000;
        final long MILLIS_PER_DAY = 24 * 60 * 60 * 1000;
        System.out.println(MICROS_PER_DAY / MILLIS_PER_DAY);
    }
}
```

Solution 3: Long Division

This puzzle seems reasonably straightforward. The number of milliseconds per day and the number of microseconds per day are constants. For clarity, they are expressed as products. The number of microseconds per day is (24 hours/day · 60 minutes/hour · 60 seconds/minute · 1,000 milliseconds/second · 1,000 microseconds/millisecond). The number of milliseconds per day differs only in that it is missing the final factor of 1,000. When you divide the number of microseconds per day by the number of milliseconds per day, all the factors in the divisor cancel out, and you are left with 1,000, which is the number of microseconds per millisecond. Both the divisor and the dividend are of type long, which is easily large enough to hold either product without overflow. It seems, then, that the program must print 1000. Unfortunately, it prints 5. What exactly is going on here?

The problem is that the computation of the constant MICROS_PER_DAY *does* overflow. Although the result of the computation fits in a long with room to spare, it doesn't fit in an int. The computation is performed entirely in int arithmetic, and only after the computation completes is the result promoted to a long. By then, it's too late: The computation has already overflowed, returning a value that is too low by a factor of 200. The promotion from int to long is a *widening primitive conversion* [JLS 5.1.2], which preserves the (incorrect) numerical value. This value is then divided by MILLIS_PER_DAY, which was computed correctly because it does fit in an int. The result of this division is 5.

So why is the computation performed in int arithmetic? Because all the factors that are multiplied together are int values. When you multiply two int values, you get another int value. Java does not have *target typing*, a language feature wherein the type of the variable in which a result is to be stored influences the type of the computation.

It's easy to fix the program by using a long literal in place of an int as the first factor in each product. This forces all subsequent computations in the expression to be done with long arithmetic. Although it is necessary to do this only in the expression for MICROS_PER_DAY, it is good form to do it in both products. Similarly, it isn't always necessary to use a long as the *first* value in a product, but it is good form to do so. Beginning both computations with `long` values makes it clear that they won't overflow. This program prints `1000` as expected:

```
public class LongDivision {
    public static void main(String[] args) {
        final long MICROS_PER_DAY = 24L * 60 * 60 * 1000 * 1000;
        final long MILLIS_PER_DAY = 24L * 60 * 60 * 1000;
        System.out.println(MICROS_PER_DAY / MILLIS_PER_DAY);
    }
}
```

The lesson is simple: **When working with large numbers, watch out for overflow—it's a silent killer.** Just because a variable is large enough to hold a result doesn't mean that the computation leading to the result is of the correct type. When in doubt, perform the entire computation using `long` arithmetic.

The lesson for language designers is that it may be worth reducing the likelihood of silent overflow. This could be done by providing support for arithmetic that does not overflow silently. Programs could throw an exception instead of overflowing, as does Ada, or they could switch to a larger internal representation automatically as required to avoid overflow, as does Lisp. Both of these approaches may have performance penalties associated with them. Another way to reduce the likelihood of silent overflow is to support target typing, but this adds significant complexity to the type system [Modula-3 1.4.8].

Puzzle 4: It's Elementary

OK, so the last puzzle was a bit tricky, but it was about division. Everyone knows that division is tough. This program involves only addition. What does it print?

```
public class Elementary {
    public static void main(String[] args) {
        System.out.println(12345 + 54321);
    }
}
```

Solution 4: It's Elementary

On the face of it, this looks like an easy puzzle—so easy that you can solve it without pencil or paper. The digits of the left operand of the plus operator ascend from 1 to 5, and the digits of the right operand descend. Therefore, the sums of corresponding digits remain constant, and the program must surely print 66666. There is only one problem with this analysis: When you run the program, it prints 17777. Could it be that Java has an aversion to printing such a beastly number? Somehow this doesn't seem like a plausible explanation.

Things are seldom what they seem. Take this program, for instance. It doesn't say what you think it does. Take a careful look at the two operands of the + opera-tor. We are adding the `int` value 12345 to the `long` value 54321. Note the subtle difference in shape between the digit 1 at the beginning of the left operand and the lowercase letter *el* at the end of the right operand. The digit 1 has an acute angle between the horizontal stroke, or *arm*, and the vertical stroke, or *stem*. The lower-case letter *el*, by contrast, has a right angle between the arm and the stem.

Before you cry "foul," note that this issue has caused real confusion. Also note that the puzzle's title contained a hint: It's El-ementary; get it? Finally, note that there is a real lesson here. **Always use a capital *el* (L) in `long` literals, never a lowercase *el* (1).** This completely eliminates the source of confusion on which the puzzle relies:

```
System.out.println(12345 + 5432L);
```

Similarly, **avoid using a lone *el* (1) as a variable name.** It is difficult to tell by looking at this code snippet whether it prints the list 1 or the number 1:

```
// Bad code - uses el (1) as a variable name
List<String> 1 = new ArrayList<String>();
1.add("Foo");
System.out.println(1);
```

In summary, the lowercase letter *el* and the digit 1 are nearly identical in most typewriter fonts. To avoid confusing the readers of your program, never use a low-ercase *el* to terminate a `long` literal or as a variable name. Java inherited much from the C programming language, including its syntax for `long` literals. It was probably a mistake to allow `long` literals to be written with a lowercase *el*.

Puzzle 5: The Joy of Hex

The following program adds two hexadecimal, or "hex," literals and prints the result in hex. What does the program print?

```
public class JoyOfHex {
    public static void main(String[] args) {
        System.out.println(
            Long.toHexString(0x100000000L + 0xcafebabe));
    }
}
```

Solution 5: The Joy of Hex

It seems obvious that the program should print 1cafebabe. After all, that is the sum of the hex numbers 100000000_{16} and $cafebabe_{16}$. The program uses long arithmetic, which permits 16 hex digits, so arithmetic overflow is not an issue. Yet, if you ran the program, you found that it prints cafebabe, with no leading 1 digit. This output represents the low-order 32 bits of the correct sum, but somehow the thirty-third bit gets lost. It is as if the program were doing int arithmetic instead of long, or forgetting to add the first operand. What's going on here?

Decimal literals have a nice property that is not shared by hexadecimal or octal literals: Decimal literals are all positive [JLS 3.10.1]. To write a negative decimal constant, you use the unary negation operator (-) in combination with a decimal literal. In this way, you can write any int or long value, whether positive or negative, in decimal form, and **negative decimal constants are clearly identifiable by the presence of a minus sign.** Not so for hexadecimal and octal literals. They can take on both positive and negative values. **Hex and octal literals are negative if their high-order bit is set.** In this program, the number 0xcafebabe is an int constant with its high-order bit set, so it is negative. It is equivalent to the decimal value -889275714.

The addition performed by the program is a *mixed-type computation*: The left operand is of type long, and the right operand is of type int. To perform the computation, Java promotes the int value to a long with a *widening primitive conversion* [JLS 5.1.2] and adds the two long values. Because int is a signed integral type, the conversion performs *sign extension*: It promotes the negative int value to a numerically equal long value.

The right operand of the addition, 0xcafebabe, is promoted to the long value 0xffffffffcafebabeL. This value is then added to the left operand, which is 0x100000000L. When viewed as an int, the high-order 32 bits of the sign-extended right operand are -1, and the high-order 32 bits of the left operand are 1. Add these two values together and you get 0, which explains the absence of the leading 1 digit in the program's output. Here is how the addition looks when done in longhand. (The digits at the top of the addition are carries.)

```
    1111111
    0xffffffffcafebabeL
+   0x0000000100000000L
    0x00000000cafebabeL
```

Fixing the problem is as simple as using a `long` hex literal to represent the right operand. This avoids the damaging sign extension, and the program prints the expected result of `1cafebabe`:

```
public class JoyOfHex {
    public static void main(String[] args) {
        System.out.println(
            Long.toHexString(0x100000000L + 0xcafebabeL));
    }
}
```

The lesson of this puzzle is that mixed-type computations can be confusing, more so given that hex and octal literals can take on negative values without an explicit minus sign. To avoid this sort of difficulty, **it is generally best to avoid mixed-type computations.** For language designers, it is worth considering support for unsigned integral types, which eliminate the possibility of sign extension. One might argue that negative hex and octal literals should be prohibited, but this would likely frustrate programmers, who often use hex literals to represent values whose sign is of no significance.

Puzzle 6: Multicast

Casts are used to convert a value from one type to another. This program uses three casts in succession. What does it print?

```
public class Multicast {
    public static void main(String[] args) {
        System.out.println((int) (char) (byte) -1);
    }
}
```

Solution 6: Multicast

This program is confusing any way you slice it. It starts with the int value -1, then casts the int to a byte, then to a char, and finally back to an int. The first cast narrows the value from 32 bits down to 8, the second widens it from 8 bits to 16, and the final cast widens it from 16 bits back to 32. Does the value end up back where it started? If you ran the program, you found that it does not. It prints 65535, but why?

The program's behavior depends critically on the sign extension behavior of casts. Java uses two's-complement binary arithmetic, so the int value -1 has all 32 bits set. The cast from int to byte is straightforward. It performs a *narrowing primitive conversion* [JLS 5.1.3], which simply lops off all but the low-order 8 bits. This leaves a byte value with all 8 bits set, which (still) represents −1.

The cast from byte to char is trickier because byte is a signed type and char unsigned. It is usually possible to convert from one integral type to a wider one while preserving numerical value, but it is impossible to represent a negative byte value as a char. Therefore, the conversion from byte to char is not considered a *widening primitive conversion* [JLS 5.1.2], but a *widening and narrowing primitive conversion* [JLS 5.1.4]: The byte is converted to an int and the int to a char.

All of this may sound a bit complicated. Luckily, there is a simple rule that describes the sign extension behavior when converting from narrower integral types to wider: **Sign extension is performed if the type of the original value is signed; zero extension if it is a char, regardless of the type to which it is being converted**. Knowing this rule makes it easy to solve the puzzle.

Because byte is a signed type, sign extension occurs when converting the byte value −1 to a char. The resulting char value has all 16 bits set, so it is equal to $2^{16} − 1$, or 65,535. The cast from char to int is also a widening primitive conversion, so the rule tells us that zero extension is performed rather than sign extension. The resulting int value is 65535, which is just what the program prints.

Although there is a simple rule describing the sign extension behavior of widening primitive conversions between signed and unsigned integral types, it is best not to write programs that depend on it. If you are doing a widening conversion to or from a char, which is the only unsigned integral type, it is best to make your intentions explicit.

If you are converting from a char value c to a wider type and you don't want sign extension, consider using a bit mask for clarity, even though it isn't required:

```
int i = c & 0xffff;
```

Alternatively, write a comment describing the behavior of the conversion:

```
int i = c;  // Sign extension is not performed
```

If you are converting from a char value c to a wider integral type and you want sign extension, cast the char to a short, which is the same width as a char but signed. Given the subtlety of this code, you should also write a comment:

```
int i = (short) c;  // Cast causes sign extension
```

If you are converting from a byte value b to a char and you don't want sign extension, you must use a bit mask to suppress it. This is a common idiom, so no comment is necessary:

```
char c = (char) (b & 0xff);
```

If you are converting from a byte to a char and you want sign extension, write a comment:

```
char c = (char) b;  // Sign extension is performed
```

The lesson is simple: **If you can't tell what a program does by looking at it, it probably doesn't do what you want.** Strive for clarity. Although a simple rule describes the sign extension behavior of widening conversions involving signed and unsigned integral types, most programmers don't know it. If your program depends on it, make your intentions clear.

Puzzle 7: Swap Meat

This program uses the compound assignment operator for exclusive OR. The technique that it illustrates is part of the programming folklore. What does it print?

```
public class CleverSwap {
    public static void main(String[] args) {
        int x = 1984;  // (0x7c0)
        int y = 2001;  // (0x7d1)
        x ^= y ^= x ^= y;
        System.out.println("x = " + x + "; y = " + y);
    }
}
```

Solution 7: Swap Meat

As its name implies, this program is supposed to swap the values of the variables x and y. It you ran it, you found that it fails miserably, printing x = 0; y = 1984.

The obvious way to swap two variables is to use a temporary variable:

```
int tmp = x;
x = y;
y = tmp;
```

Long ago, when central processing units had few registers, it was discovered that one could avoid the use of a temporary variable by taking advantage of the property of the exclusive OR operator (^) that (x ^ y ^ x) == y:

```
// Swaps variables without a temporary - Don't do this!
x = x ^ y;
y = y ^ x;
x = y ^ x;
```

Even back in those days, this technique was seldom justified. Now that CPUs have many registers, it is never justified. Like most "clever" code, it is far less clear than its naive counterpart and far slower. Still, some programmers persist in using it. Worse, they complicate matters by using the idiom illustrated in this puzzle, which combines the three exclusive OR operations into a single statement.

This idiom was used in the C programming language and from there made its way into C++ but is not guaranteed to work in either of these languages. It is guaranteed *not* to work in Java. The Java language specification says that **operands of operators are evaluated from left to right** [JLS 15.7]. To evaluate the expression x ^= *expr*, the value of x is sampled before *expr* is evaluated, and the exclusive OR of these two values is assigned to the variable x [JLS 15.26.2]. In the CleverSwap program, the variable x is sampled twice—once for each appearance in the expression—but both samplings occur before any assignments.

The following code snippet describes the behavior of the broken swap idiom in more detail and explains the output that we observed:

```
// The actual behavior of x ^= y ^= x ^= y in Java
int tmp1 = x;       // First appearance of x in the expression
int tmp2 = y;       // First appearance of y
int tmp3 = x ^ y;   // Compute x ^ y
x = tmp3;           // Last assignment: Store x ^ y in x
y = tmp2 ^ tmp3;    // 2nd assignment: Store original x value in y
x = tmp1 ^ y;       // First assignment: Store 0 in x
```

In C and C++, the order of expression evaluation is not specified. When compiling the expression x ^= *expr*, many C and C++ compilers sample the value of x after evaluating *expr*, which makes the idiom work. Although it may work, it runs afoul of the C/C++ rule that you must not modify a variable repeatedly between successive sequence points [ISO-C]. Therefore, the behavior of this idiom is undefined even in C and C++.

For what it's worth, it is possible to write a Java expression that swaps the contents of two variables without using a temporary. It is both ugly and useless:

```
// Rube Goldberg would approve, but don't ever do this!
y = (x ^= (y ^= x)) ^ y;
```

The lesson is simple: **Do not assign to the same variable more than once in a single expression.** Expressions containing multiple assignments to the same variable are confusing and seldom do what you want. Even expressions that assign to multiple variables are suspect. More generally, **avoid clever programming tricks.** They are bug-prone, difficult to maintain, and often run more slowly than the straightforward code they replace [EJ Item 37].

Language designers might consider prohibiting multiple assignments to the same variable in one expression, but it would not be feasible to enforce this prohibition in the general case, because of aliasing. For example, consider the expression x = a[i]++ - a[j]++. Does it increment the same variable twice? That depends on the values of i and j at the time the expression is evaluated, and there is no way for the compiler to determine this in general.

Puzzle 8: Dos Equis

This puzzle tests your knowledge of the *conditional operator*, better known as the "question mark colon operator." What does the following program print?

```
public class DosEquis {
    public static void main(String[] args) {
        char x = 'X';
        int i = 0;
        System.out.print(true  ? x : 0);
        System.out.print(false ? i : x);
    }
}
```

Solution 8: Dos Equis

The program consists of two variable declarations and two `print` statements. The first `print` statement evaluates the conditional expression (`true ? x : 0`) and prints the result. The result is the value of the char variable x, which is `'X'`. The second `print` statement evaluates the conditional expression (`false ? i : x`) and prints the result. Again the result is the value of x, which is still `'X'`, so the program ought to print XX. If you ran the program, however, you found that it prints X88. This behavior seems strange. The first `print` statement prints X and the second prints 88. What accounts for their different behavior?

The answer lies in a dark corner of the specification for the conditional operator [JLS 15.25]. Note that the types of the second and third operands are different from each other in both of the conditional expressions: x is of type char, whereas 0 and i are both of type int. As mentioned in the solution to Puzzle 5, **mixed-type computation can be confusing. Nowhere is this more apparent than in conditional expressions.** You might think that the result types of the two conditional expressions in this program would be identical, as their operand types are identical, though reversed, but it isn't so.

The rules for determining the result type of a conditional expression are too long and complex to reproduce in their entirety, but here are three key points.

1. If the second and third operands have the same type, that is the type of the conditional expression. In other words, you can avoid the whole mess by steering clear of mixed-type computation.

2. If one of the operands is of type *T* where *T* is byte, short, or char and the other operand is a constant expression of type int whose value is representable in type *T*, the type of the conditional expression is *T*.

3. Otherwise, binary numeric promotion is applied to the operand types, and the type of the conditional expression is the promoted type of the second and third operands.

Points 2 and 3 are the key to this puzzle. In both of the two conditional expressions in the program, one operand is of type char and the other is of type int. In both expressions, the value of the int operand is 0, which is representable as a char. Only the int operand in the first expression, however, is constant (0); the int operand in the second expression is variable (i). Therefore, point 2 applies to the first expression and its return type is char. Point 3 applies to the second conditional expression, and its return type is the result of applying binary numeric promotion to int and char, which is int [JLS 5.6.2].

The type of the conditional expression determines which overloading of the print method is invoked. For the first expression, PrintStream.print(char) is invoked; for the second, PrintStream.print(int). The former overloading prints the value of the variable x as a Unicode character (X), whereas the latter prints it as a decimal integer (88). The mystery is solved.

Putting the final modifier on the declaration for i would turn i into a constant expression, causing the program to print XX, but it would still be confusing. To eliminate the confusion, it is best to change the type of i from int to char, avoiding the mixed-type computation.

In summary, it is generally best to **use the same type for the second and third operands in conditional expressions.** Otherwise, you and the readers of your program must have a thorough understanding of the complex specification for the behavior of these expressions.

For language designers, perhaps it is possible to design a conditional operator that sacrifices some flexibility for increased simplicity. For example, it might be reasonable to demand that the second and third operands be of the same type. Alternatively, the conditional operator could be defined without special treatment for constants. To make these alternatives more palatable to programmers, a syntax could be provided for expressing literals of all primitive types. This may be a good idea in its own right, as it adds to the consistency and completeness of the language and reduces the need for casts.

Puzzle 9: Tweedledum

Now it's your turn to write some code. On the bright side, you have to write only two lines for this puzzle and two lines for the next. How hard could that be? Provide declarations for the variables x and i such that this is a legal statement:

```
x += i;
```

but this is not:

```
x = x + i;
```

Solution 9: Tweedledum

Many programmers think that the first statement in this puzzle (x += i) is simply a shorthand for the second (x = x + i). This isn't quite true. Both of these statements are *assignment expressions* [JLS 15.26]. The second statement uses the *simple assignment operator* (=), whereas the first uses a *compound assignment operator*. (The compound assignment operators are +=, -=, *=, /=, %=, <<=, >>=, >>>=, &=, ^=, and |=.) The Java language specification says that the compound assignment *E1 op= E2* is equivalent to the simple assignment *E1 = (T) ((E1) op (E2))*, where *T* is the type of *E1*, except that *E1* is evaluated only once [JLS 15.26.2].

In other words, **compound assignment expressions automatically cast the result of the computation they perform to the type of the variable on their left-hand side.** If the type of the result is identical to the type of the variable, the cast has no effect. If, however, the type of the result is wider than that of the variable, the compound assignment operator performs a silent *narrowing primitive conversion* [JLS 5.1.3]. Attempting to perform the equivalent simple assignment would generate a compilation error, with good reason.

To make this concrete and to provide a solution to the puzzle, suppose that we precede the puzzle's two assignment expressions with these declarations:

```
short x = 0;
int i = 123456;
```

The compound assignment compiles without error:

```
x += i;  // Contains a hidden cast!
```

You might expect the value of x to be 123,456 after this statement executes, but it isn't; it's −7,616. The int value 123456 is too big to fit in a short. The automatically generated cast silently lops off the two high-order bytes of the int value, which is probably not what you want.

The corresponding simple assignment is illegal because it attempts to assign an int value to a short variable, which requires an explicit cast:

```
x = x + i;  // Won't compile - "possible loss of precision"
```

It should be apparent that compound assignment expressions can be danger-ous. To avoid unpleasant surprises, **do not use compound assignment operators on variables of type byte, short, or char.** When using compound assignment operators on variables of type `int`, ensure that the expression on the right-hand side is not of type `long`, `float`, or `double`. When using compound assignment operators on variables of type `float`, ensure that the expression on the right-hand side is not of type `double`. These rules are sufficient to prevent the compiler from generating dangerous narrowing casts.

In summary, compound assignment operators silently generate a cast. If the type of the result of the computation is wider than that of the variable, the generated cast is a dangerous narrowing cast. Such casts can silently discard precision or magnitude. For language designers, it is probably a mistake for compound assignment operators to generate invisible casts; compound assignments where the variable has a narrower type than the result of the computation should probably be illegal.

Puzzle 10: Tweedledee

Contrariwise, provide declarations for the variables x and i such that this is a legal statement:

```
x = x + i;
```

but this is not:

```
x += i;
```

At first glance, this puzzle might appear to be the same as the previous one. Rest assured, it's different. The two puzzles are opposite in terms of which statement must be legal and which must be illegal.

Solution 10: Tweedledee

Like the previous puzzle, this one depends on the details of the specification for compound assignment operators. That is where the similarity ends. Based on the previous puzzle, you might think that compound assignment operators are less restrictive than the simple assignment operator. This is generally true, but the simple assignment operator is more permissive in one area.

Compound assignment operators require both operands to be primitives, such as int, or boxed primitives, such as Integer, with one exception: The += operator allows its right-hand operand to be of any type if the variable on the left-hand side is of type String, in which case the operator performs string concatenation [JLS 15.26.2, 15.8.1]. The simple assignment operator (=) is much less picky when it comes to allowing object reference types on the left-hand side: You can use them to your heart's content so long as the expression on the right-hand side is *assignment compatible* with the variable on the left [JLS 5.2].

You can exploit this difference to solve the puzzle. To perform string concatenation with the += operator, you must declare the variable on its left-hand side to be of type String. Using the simple assignment operator, the results of a string concatenation can be stored in a variable of type Object.

To make this concrete and to provide a solution to the puzzle, suppose that we precede the puzzle's two assignment expressions with these declarations:

```
Object x = "Buy ";
String i = "Effective Java!";
```

The simple assignment is legal because x + i is of type String, and String is assignment compatible with Object:

```
x = x + i;
```

The compound assignment is illegal because the left-hand side has an object reference type other than String:

```
x += i;
```

This puzzle has little in the way of a lesson for programmers. For language designers, the compound assignment operator for addition could allow the left-hand side to be of type Object if the right-hand side were of type String. This change would eliminate the counterintuitive behavior illustrated by this puzzle.

3

Puzzlers with Character

This chapter contains puzzles that concern strings, characters, and other textual data.

Puzzle 11: The Last Laugh

What does the following program print?

```java
public class LastLaugh {
    public static void main(String args[]) {
        System.out.print("H" + "a");
        System.out.print('H' + 'a');
    }
}
```

Solution 11: The Last Laugh

If you are like most people, you thought that the program would print HaHa. It looks as though it concatenates H to a in two ways, but looks can be deceiving. If you ran the program, you found that it prints Ha169. Now why would it do a thing like that?

As expected, the first call to System.out.print prints Ha: Its argument is the expression "H" + "a", which performs the obvious string concatenation. The second call to System.out.print is another story. Its argument is the expression 'H' + 'a'. The problem is that 'H' and 'a' are char literals. Because neither operand is of type String, the + operator performs addition rather than string concatenation.

The compiler evaluates the constant expression 'H' + 'a' by promoting each of the char-valued operands ('H' and 'a') to int values through a process known as *widening primitive conversion* [JLS 5.1.2, 5.6.2]. Widening primitive conversion of a char to an int zero extends the 16-bit char value to fill the 32-bit int. In the case of 'H', the char value is 72 and in the case of 'a', it is 97, so the expression 'H' + 'a' is equivalent to the int constant 72 + 97, or 169.

From a linguistic standpoint, the resemblance between char values and strings is illusory. As far as the language is concerned, a char is an unsigned 16-bit primitive integer—nothing more. Not so for the libraries. They contain many methods that take char arguments and treat them as Unicode characters.

So how do you concatenate characters? You could use the libraries. For example, you could use a string buffer:

```
StringBuffer sb = new StringBuffer();
sb.append('H');
sb.append('a');
System.out.println(sb);
```

This works, but it's ugly. There are ways to avoid the verbosity of this approach. You can force the + operator to perform string concatenation rather than addition by ensuring that at least one of its operands is a string. The common idiom is to begin a sequence of concatenations with the empty string (""), as follows:

```
System.out.print("" + 'H' + 'a');
```

This idiom ensures that subexpressions are converted to strings. Although useful it is a bit ungainly and can lead to some confusion itself.

Can you guess what the following statement prints? If you aren't sure, try it:

```
System.out.println("2 + 2 = " + 2+2);
```

As of release 5.0, you also have the option of using the `printf` facility:

```
System.out.printf("%c%c", 'H', 'a');
```

In summary, use the string concatenation operator with care. **The + operator performs string concatenation if and only if at least one of its operands is of type `String`;** otherwise, it performs addition. If none of the values to be concatenated are strings, you have several choices: prepend the empty string; convert the first value to a string explicitly, using `String.valueOf`; use a string buffer; or if you are using release 5.0, use the `printf` facility.

This puzzle also contains a lesson for language designers. Operator overloading, even to the limited extent that it is supported in Java, can be confusing. It may have been a mistake to overload the + operator for string concatenation.

Puzzle 12: ABC

This puzzle asks the musical question, What does this program print?

```
public class Abc {
    public static void main(String[] args) {
        String letters = "ABC";
        char[] numbers = { '1', '2', '3' };
        System.out.println(letters + " easy as " + numbers);
    }
}
```

Solution 12: ABC

One would hope that the program prints ABC easy as 123. Unfortunately, it does not. If you ran it, you found that it prints something like ABC easy as [C@16f0472. Why is the output so ugly?

Although char is an integral type, many libraries treat it specially, because char values usually represent characters rather than integers. For example, passing a char value to println prints a Unicode character rather than its numerical code. Character arrays get similar special treatment: The char[] overloading of println prints all of the characters contained in the array, and the char[] overloadings of String.valueOf and StringBuffer.append behave analogously.

The string concatenation operator, however, is not defined in terms of these methods. It is defined to perform *string conversion* on both of its operands and then to concatenate the resulting strings. String conversion for object references, which include arrays, is defined as follows [JLS 15.18.1.1]:

> If the reference is null, it is converted to the string "null". Otherwise, the conversion is performed as if by an invocation of the toString method of the referenced object with no arguments; but if the result of invoking the toString method is null, then the string "null" is used instead.

So what is the behavior of invoking toString on a non-null char array? Arrays inherit the toString method from Object [JLS 10.7], whose specification says, "Returns a string consisting of the name of the class of which the object is an instance, the at-sign character '@', and the unsigned hexadecimal representation of the hash code of the object" [Java-API]. The specification for Class.getName says that the result of invoking this method on the class object for char[] is the string "[C". Putting it all together gives the ugly string printed by our program.

There are two ways to fix it. You can explicitly convert the array to a string before invoking string concatenation:

```
System.out.println(letters + " easy as " +
                   String.valueOf(numbers));
```

Alternatively, you can break the System.out.println invocation in two to make use of the char[] overloading of println:

```
System.out.print(letters + " easy as ");
System.out.println(numbers);
```

Note that these fixes work only if you invoke the correct overloading of the `valueOf` or `println` method. In other words, they depend critically on the compile-time type of the array reference. The following program illustrates this dependency. It looks as though it incorporates the second fix described, but it produces the same ugly output as the original program because it invokes the `Object` overloading of `println` instead of the `char[]` overloading:

```
// Broken - invokes the wrong overloading of println!
class Abc {
    public static void main(String[] args) {
        String letters = "ABC";
        Object numbers = new char[] { '1', '2', '3' };
        System.out.print(letters + " easy as ");
        System.out.println(numbers); // Invokes println(Object)
    }
}
```

To summarize, char arrays are not strings. **To convert a char array to a string, invoke `String.valueOf(char[])`.** Some library methods do provide stringlike support for `char` arrays, typically having one overloading for `Object` and another for `char[]`; only the latter has the desired behavior.

The lesson for language designers is that the `char[]` type should probably have overridden `toString` to return the characters contained in the array. More generally, the array types should probably have overridden `toString` to return a string representation of the contents of the array.

Puzzle 13: Animal Farm

Readers of George Orwell's *Animal Farm* may remember old Major's pronouncement that "all animals are equal." The following Java program attempts to test this pronouncement. What does it print?

```
public class AnimalFarm {
    public static void main(String[] args) {
        final String pig = "length: 10";
        final String dog = "length: " + pig.length();
        System.out.println("Animals are equal: "
                           + pig == dog);
    }
}
```

Solution 13: Animal Farm

A superficial analysis of the program might suggest that it should print `Animals are equal: true`. After all, `pig` and `dog` are both final `String` variables initialized to the character sequence `"length: 10"`. In other words, the strings referred to by `pig` and `dog` are and will forever remain equal to each other. The `==` operator, however, does not test whether two objects are equal; it tests whether two object references are *identical*. In other words, it tests whether they refer to precisely the same object. In this case, they do not.

You may be aware that compile-time constants of type `String` are *interned* [JLS 15.28]. In other words, any two *constant expressions* of type `String` that designate the same character sequence are represented by identical object references. If initialized with constant expressions, both `pig` and `dog` would indeed refer to the same object, but `dog` is not initialized with a constant expression. The language constrains which operations are permitted to appear in a constant expression [JLS 16.28], and method invocation is not among them. Therefore the program should print `Animals are equal: false`, right?

Well, no, actually. If you ran the program, you found that it prints `false` and nothing else. It doesn't print `Animals are equal: `. How could it not print this string literal, which is right there in black and white? The solution to Puzzle 11 contains a hint: The `+` operator, whether used for addition or string concatenation, binds more tightly than the `==` operator. Therefore, the parameter of the `println` method is evaluated like this:

```
System.out.println(("Animals are equal: " + pig) == dog);
```

The value of the `boolean` expression is, of course, `false`, and that is exactly what the program prints. There is one surefire way to avoid this sort of difficulty: **When using the string concatenation operator, always parenthesize nontrivial operands.** More generally, when you are not sure whether you need parentheses, err on the side of caution and include them. If you parenthesize the comparison in the `println` statement as follows, it will produce the expected output of `Animals are equal: false`:

```
System.out.println("Animals are equal: " + (pig == dog));
```

Arguably, the program is still broken. **Your code should rarely, if ever, depend on the interning of string constants.** Interning was designed solely to reduce the memory footprint of the virtual machine, not as a tool for programmers. As this puzzle demonstrates, it isn't always obvious which expressions will result in string constants. Worse, if your code depends on interning for its correct operation, you must carefully keep track of which fields and parameters must be interned. The compiler can't check these invariants for you, because interned and noninterned strings are represented by the same type (String). The bugs that result from the failure to intern a string are typically quite difficult to detect.

When comparing object references, you should **use the equals method in preference to the == operator** unless you need to compare object identity rather than value. Applying this lesson to our program, here is how the println statement should look. It is clear that the program prints true when it is fixed in this fashion:

```
System.out.println("Animals are equal: " + pig.equals(dog));
```

This puzzle has two lessons for language designers. The natural precedence of string concatenation might not be the same as that of addition. This implies that it is problematic to overload the + operator to perform string concatenation, as mentioned in Puzzle 11. Also, reference equality is more confusing than value equality for immutable types, such as String. Perhaps the == operator should perform value comparisons when applied to immutable reference types. One way to achieve this would be to make the == operator a shorthand for the equals method, and to provide a separate method to perform reference identity comparison, akin to System.identityHashCode.

Puzzle 14: Escape Rout

The following program uses two *Unicode escapes*, which represent Unicode characters by their hexadecimal numeric codes. What does the program print?

```
public class EscapeRout {
  public static void main(String[] args) {
    // \u0022 is the Unicode escape for double quote (")
    System.out.println("a\u0022.length() + \u0022b".length());
  }
}
```

Solution 14: Escape Rout

A naive analysis of the program suggests that it should print 26 because there are 26 characters between the quotation marks that bound the string `"a\u0022.length() + \u0022b"`. A deeper analysis suggests that the program should print 16, as each of the two Unicode escapes requires six characters in the source file but represents only one character in the string. The string is therefore ten characters shorter than it appears. Running the program tells a different story. It prints neither 26 nor 16 but 2.

The key to understanding this puzzle is that **Java provides no special treatment for Unicode escapes within string literals.** The compiler translates Unicode escapes into the characters they represent before it parses the program into tokens, such as strings literals [JLS 3.2]. Therefore, the first Unicode escape in the program closes a one-character string literal (`"a"`), and the second one opens a one-character string literal (`"b"`). The program prints the value of the expression `"a".length() + "b".length()`, or 2.

If the author of the program had actually wanted this behavior, it would have been much clearer to say:

```
System.out.println("a".length() + "b".length());
```

More likely, the author wanted to put the two double quote characters into the string literal. You can't do this with Unicode escapes, but you can do it with *escape sequences* [JLS 3.10.6]. The escape sequence representing a double quote is a backslash followed by a double quote (`\"`). If the Unicode escapes in the original program are replaced with this escape sequence, it will print 16 as expected:

```
System.out.println("a\".length() + \"b".length());
```

There are escape sequences for many characters, including the single quote (`\'`), linefeed (`\n`), tab (`\t`), and backslash (`\\`). You can use escape sequences in character literals as well as in string literals. In fact, you can put any ASCII character into a string literal or a character literal by using a special kind of escape sequence called an *octal escape*, but it is preferable to use normal escape sequences where possible. Both normal escape sequences and octal escapes are far preferable to Unicode escapes because unlike Unicode escapes, escape sequences are processed after the program is parsed into tokens.

All the programs in this book are written using the ASCII subset of Unicode. ASCII is the lowest common denominator of character sets. ASCII has only 128 characters, but Unicode has more than 65,000. A Unicode escape can be used to insert any Unicode character into a program using only ASCII characters. A Unicode escape means exactly the same thing as the character that it represents.

Unicode escapes are designed for use when a programmer needs to insert a character that can't be represented in the source file's character set. They are used primarily to put non-ASCII characters into identifiers, string literals, character literals, and comments. Occasionally, a Unicode escape adds to the clarity of a program by positively identifying one of several similar-looking characters.

In summary, **prefer escape sequences to Unicode escapes in string and character literals.** Unicode escapes can be confusing because they are processed so early in the compilation sequence. **Do not use Unicode escapes to represent ASCII characters.** Inside of string and character literals, use escape sequences; outside of these literals, insert ASCII characters directly into the source file.

Puzzle 15: Hello Whirled

The following program is a minor variation on an old chestnut. What does it print?

```
/**
 * Generated by the IBM IDL-to-Java compiler, version 1.0
 * from F:\TestRoot\apps\a1\units\include\PolicyHome.idl
 * Wednesday, June 17, 1998 6:44:40 o'clock AM GMT+00:00
 */
public class Test {
    public static void main(String[] args) {
        System.out.print("Hell");
        System.out.println("o world");
    }
}
```

Solution 15: Hello Whirled

This puzzle looks fairly straightforward. The program contains two statements. The first prints `Hell` and the second prints `o world` on the same line, effectively concatenating the two strings. Therefore, you might expect the program to print `Hello world`. You would be sadly mistaken. In fact, it doesn't compile.

The problem is in the third line of the comment, which contains the characters `\units`. These characters begin with a backslash (\) followed by the letter u, which denotes the start of a Unicode escape. Unfortunately, these characters are not followed by four hexadecimal digits, so the Unicode escape is ill-formed, and the compiler is required to reject the program. **Unicode escapes must be well formed, even if they appear in comments.**

It is legal to place a well-formed Unicode escape in a comment, but there is rarely a reason to do so. Programmers sometimes use Unicode escapes in Javadoc comments to generate special characters in the documentation:

```
// Questionable use of Unicode escape in Javadoc comment

/**
 * This method calls itself recursively, causing a
 * <tt>StackOverflowError</tt> to be thrown.
 * The algorithm is due to Peter von der Ah\u00E9.
 */
```

This technique represents an unnecessary use of Unicode escapes. **Use HTML entity escapes instead of Unicode escapes in Javadoc comments**:

```
/**
 * This method calls itself recursively, causing a
 * <tt>StackOverflowError</tt> to be thrown.
 * The algorithm is due to Peter von der Ah&eacute;.
 */
```

Either of the preceding comments should cause the name to appear in the documentation as "Peter von der Ahé," but the latter comment is also understandable in the source file.

In case you were wondering, the comment in this puzzle was derived from an actual bug report. The program was machine generated, which made it difficult to track the problem down to its source, an IDL-to-Java compiler. To avoid placing other programmers in this position, **tools must not put Windows filenames into**

comments in generated Java source files without first processing them to eliminate backslashes.

In summary, ensure that the characters \u do not occur outside the context of a valid Unicode escape, even in comments. Be particularly wary of this problem in machine-generated code.

Puzzle 16: Line Printer

The *line separator* is the name given to the character or characters used to separate lines of text, and varies from platform to platform. On Windows, it is the CR character (carriage return) followed by the LF character (linefeed). On UNIX, it is the LF character alone, often referred to as the newline character. The following program passes this character to `println`. What does it print? Is its behavior platform dependent?

```
public class LinePrinter {
    public static void main(String[] args) {
        // Note: \u000A is Unicode representation of linefeed (LF)
        char c = 0x000A;
        System.out.println(c);
    }
}
```

Solution 16: Line Printer

The behavior of this program is platform independent: It won't compile on any platform. If you tried to compile it, you got an error message that looks something like this:

```
LinePrinter.java:3: ';' expected
    // Note: \u000A is Unicode representation of linefeed (LF)
                 ^
1 error
```

If you are like most people, this message did not help to clarify matters.

The key to this puzzle is the comment on the third line of the program. Like the best of comments, this one is true. Unfortunately, this one is a bit too true. The compiler not only translates Unicode escapes into the characters they represent before it parses a program into tokens (Puzzle 14), but it does so before discarding comments and white space [JLS 3.2].

This program contains a single Unicode escape (\u000A), located in its sole comment. As the comment tells you, this escape represents the linefeed character, and the compiler duly translates it before discarding the comment. Unfortunately, this linefeed character is the first *line terminator* after the two slash characters that begin the comment (//) and so terminates the comment [JLS 3.4]. The words following the escape (is Unicode representation of linefeed (LF)) are therefore not part of the comment; nor are they syntactically valid.

To make this more concrete, here is what the program looks like after the Unicode escape has been translated into the character it represents:

```
public class LinePrinter {
    public static void main(String[] args) {
        // Note:
 is Unicode representation of linefeed (LF)
        char c = 0x000A;
        System.out.println(c);
    }
}
```

The easiest way to fix the program is to remove the Unicode escape from the comment, but a better way is to initialize c with an escape sequence instead of a hex integer literal, obviating the need for the comment:

```java
public class LinePrinter {
    public static void main(String[] args) {
        char c = '\n';
        System.out.println(c);
    }
}
```

Once this has been done, the program will compile and run, but it's still a questionable program. It is platform dependent for exactly the reason suggested in the puzzle. On certain platforms, such as UNIX, it will print two complete line separators; on others, such as Windows, it won't. Although the output may look the same to the naked eye, it could easily cause problems if it were saved in a file or piped to another program for subsequent processing.

If you want to print two blank lines, you should invoke println twice. As of release 5.0, you can use printf instead of println, with the format string "%n%n". Each occurrence of the characters %n will cause printf to print the appropriate platform-specific line separator.

Hopefully, the last three puzzles have convinced you that Unicode escapes can be thoroughly confusing. The lesson is simple: **Avoid Unicode escapes except where they are truly necessary.** They are rarely necessary.

Puzzle 17: Huh?

Is this a legal Java program? If so, what does it print?

```
\u0070\u0075\u0062\u006c\u0069\u0063\u0020\u0020\u0020\u0020
\u0063\u006c\u0061\u0073\u0073\u0020\u0055\u0067\u006c\u0079
\u007b\u0070\u0075\u0062\u006c\u0069\u0063\u0020\u0020\u0020
\u0020\u0020\u0020\u0020\u0073\u0074\u0061\u0074\u0069\u0063
\u0076\u006f\u0069\u0064\u0020\u006d\u0061\u0069\u006e\u0028
\u0053\u0074\u0072\u0069\u006e\u0067\u005b\u005d\u0020\u0020
\u0020\u0020\u0020\u0020\u0061\u0072\u0067\u0073\u0029\u007b
\u0053\u0079\u0073\u0074\u0065\u006d\u002e\u006f\u0075\u0074
\u002e\u0070\u0072\u0069\u006e\u0074\u006c\u006e\u0028\u0020
\u0022\u0048\u0065\u006c\u006c\u006f\u0020\u0077\u0022\u002b
\u0022\u006f\u0072\u006c\u0064\u0022\u0029\u003b\u007d\u007d
```

Solution 17: Huh?

Of course it's a legal Java program! Isn't it obvious? It prints Hello world. Well, maybe it isn't so obvious. In fact, the program is totally incomprehensible. Each time you use a Unicode escape unnecessarily, you make your program a bit less comprehensible, and this program takes the concept to its logical extreme. In case you are curious, here is what the program looks like after the Unicode escapes are translated to the characters they represent:

```
public
class Ugly
{public
    static
void main(
String[]
    args){
System.out
.println(
"Hello w"+
"orld");}}
```

Here is how it looks after cleaning up the formatting:

```
public class Ugly {
    public static void main(String[] args) {
        System.out.println("Hello w" + "orld");
    }
}
```

The lesson of this puzzle is: Just because you can doesn't mean you should. Alternatively, If it hurts when you do it, don't do it! More seriously, this puzzle serves to reinforce the lessons of the previous three: **Unicode escapes are essential when you need to insert characters that can't be represented in any other way into your program. Avoid them in all other cases.** Unicode escapes reduce program clarity and increase the potential for bugs.

For language designers, perhaps it should be illegal to use Unicode escapes to represent ASCII characters. This would make the programs in Puzzles 14, 15, and 17 (this puzzle) invalid, eliminating a great deal of confusion. This restriction would cause no great hardship to programmers.

Puzzle 18: String Cheese

This program creates a string from a sequence of bytes, then iterates over the characters in the string and prints them as numbers. Describe the sequence of numbers that the program prints:

```java
public class StringCheese {
    public static void main(String[] args) {
        byte[] bytes = new byte[256];
        for(int i = 0; i < 256; i++)
            bytes[i] = (byte)i;
        String str = new String(bytes);
        for(int i = 0, n = str.length(); i < n; i++)
            System.out.print((int)str.charAt(i) + " ");
    }
}
```

Solution 18: String Cheese

First, the `byte` array is initialized with every possible `byte` value from 0 to 255. Then these `byte` values are translated into `char` values by the `String` constructor. Finally, the `char` values are cast to `int` values and printed. The printed values are guaranteed to be nonnegative, because `char` values are unsigned, so you might expect the program to print the integers from 0 to 255 in order.

If you ran the program, maybe you saw this sequence. Then again, maybe you didn't. We ran it on four machines and saw four different sequences, including the one described previously. This program isn't even guaranteed to terminate normally, much less to print any particular sequence. Its behavior is completely unspecified.

The culprit here is the `String(byte[])` constructor. Its specification says: "Constructs a new `String` by decoding the specified `byte` array using the platform's default charset. The length of the new `String` is a function of the charset, and hence may not be equal to the length of the `byte` array. The behavior of this constructor when the given bytes are not valid in the default charset is unspecified" [Java-API].

What exactly is a charset? Technically, it is "the combination of a coded character set and a character-encoding scheme" [Java-API]. In other words, a charset is a bunch of characters, the numerical codes that represent them, and a way to translate back and forth between a sequence of character codes and a sequence of bytes. The translation scheme differs greatly among charsets. Some have a one-to-one mapping between characters and bytes; most do not. The only default charset that will make the program print the integers from 0 to 255 in order is ISO-8859-1, more commonly known as Latin-1 [ISO-8859-1].

A J2SE Runtime Environment's default charset depends on the underlying operating system and locale. If you want to know your JRE's default charset and you are using release 5.0 or a later release, you can find out by invoking `java.nio.charset.Charset.defaultCharset()`. If you are using an earlier release, you can find out by reading the system property `"file.encoding"`.

Luckily, you are not forced to put up with the vagaries of default charsets. **When translating between `char` sequences and `byte` sequences, you can and usually should specify a charset explicitly.** A `String` constructor that takes a charset name in addition to a `byte` array is provided for this purpose. If you replace the `String` constructor invocation in the original program with the one that follows, the program is guaranteed to print the integers from 0 to 255 in order, regardless of the default charset:

```
String str = new String(bytes, "ISO-8859-1");
```

This constructor is declared to throw UnsupportedEncodingException, so you must catch it or, preferably, declare the main method to throw it, or the program won't compile. The program won't actually throw the exception, though. The specification for Charset mandates that every implementation of the Java platform support certain charsets, and ISO-8859-1 is among them.

The lesson of this puzzle is that **every time you translate a byte sequence to a String, you are using a charset, whether you specify it explicitly or not.** If you want your program to behave predictably, specify a charset each time you use one. For API designers, perhaps it was not such a good idea to provide a String(byte[]) constructor that depends on the default charset.

Puzzle 19: Classy Fire

The following program uses a method to classify characters. What does the program print? In case you are not familiar with the String.indexOf(char) method, it returns the index of the first occurrence of the specified character in the string, or −1 if the string doesn't contain the character:

```
public class Classifier {
    public static void main(String[] args) {
        System.out.println(
            classify('n') + classify('+') + classify('2'));
    }
    static String classify(char ch) {
        if ("0123456789".indexOf(ch) >= 0)
            return "NUMERAL ";
        if ("abcdefghijklmnopqrstuvwxyz".indexOf(ch) >= 0)
            return "LETTER ";
/* (Operators not supported yet)
        if ("+-*/&|!=".indexOf(ch) >= 0)
            return "OPERATOR ";
 */
        return "UNKNOWN ";
    }
}
```

Solution 19: Classy Fire

If you guessed that this program prints LETTER UNKNOWN NUMBER, you fell for the trap. The program doesn't even compile. Let's take another look at the relevant section, this time highlighting the block comment in boldface:

```
        if ("abcdefghijklmnopqrstuvwxyz".indexOf(ch) >= 0)
            return "LETTER ";
/* (Operators not supported yet)
        if ("+-*/&||!=".indexOf(ch) >= 0)
            return "OPERATOR ";
 */
        return "UNKNOWN ";
    }
}
```

As you can see, the comment ends inside the string, which quite naturally contains the characters */. The resulting program is syntactically invalid. Our attempt to comment out a section of the program failed because **string literals are not treated specially within comments.**

More generally, the text inside of comments is not treated specially in any way [JLS 3.7]. Therefore, **block comments do not nest.** Consider the following code snippet:

```
/* Add the numbers from 1 to n */
int sum = 0;
for (int i = 1; i <= n; i++)
    sum += i;
```

Now suppose that we try to comment out the snippet with a block comment. Again, we highlight the entire comment in boldface:

```
/*
    /* Add the numbers from to 1 to n */
    int sum = 0;
    for (int i = 1; i <= n; i++)
        sum += i;
 */
```

As you can see, we failed to comment out the original snippet. On the bright side, the resulting code contains a syntax error, so the compiler will tell us that we have a problem.

You may occasionally see a section of code that is disabled with an `if` statement whose `boolean` expression is the constant `false`:

```
// Code commented out with an if statement - doesn't always work!
if (false) {
    /* Add the numbers from 1 to n */
    int sum = 0;
    for (int i = 1; i <= n; i++)
        sum += i;
}
```

The language specification recommends this as a technique for conditional compilation [JLS 14.21], but it is not well suited to commenting out code. It can't be used unless the code to be disabled is a sequence of valid statements.

The best way to comment out a section of code is to use a sequence of single-line comments. Most IDEs automate this process:

```
// Code commented out with a sequence of single-line comments
//     /* Add the numbers from 1 to n */
//     int sum = 0;
//     for (int i = 1; i <= n; i++)
//         sum += i;
```

In summary, **a block comment does not reliably comment out a section of code.** Use a sequence of single-line comments instead. For language designers, note that nestable block comments are not a good idea. They force the compiler to parse the text inside block comments, which causes more problems than it solves.

Puzzle 20: What's My Class?

This program was designed to print the name of its class file. In case you aren't familiar with class literals, `Me.class.getName()` returns the fully qualified name of the class Me, or `"com.javapuzzlers.Me"`. What does the program print?

```
package com.javapuzzlers;
public class Me {
    public static void main(String[] args) {
        System.out.println(
            Me.class.getName().replaceAll(".", "/") + ".class");
    }
}
```

Solution 20: What's My Class?

The program appears to obtain its class name ("com.javapuzzlers.Me"), replace all occurrences of the string "." with "/", and append the string ".class". You might think that the program would print com/javapuzzlers/Me.class, which is the class file from which it was loaded. If you ran the program, you found that it actually prints //////////////////.class. What's going on here? Are we a victim of the slasher?

The problem is that **String.replaceAll takes a regular expression as its first parameter,** not a literal sequence of characters. (Regular expressions were added to the Java platform in release 1.4.) The regular expression "." matches any single character, and so every character of the class name is replaced by a slash, producing the output we saw.

To match only the period character, the period in the regular expression must be *escaped* by preceding it with a backslash (\). Because the backslash character has special meaning in a string literal—it begins an escape sequence—the backslash itself must be escaped with a second backslash. This produces an escape sequence that generates a backslash in the string literal. Putting it all together, the following program prints com/javapuzzlers/Me.class as expected:

```
package com.javapuzzlers;

public class Me {
    public static void main(String[] args) {
        System.out.println(
            Me.class.getName().replaceAll("\\.", "/") + ".class");
    }
}
```

To solve this kind of problem, release 5.0 provides the new static method java.util.regex.Pattern.quote. It takes a string as a parameter and adds any necessary escapes, returning a regular expression string that matches the input string exactly. Here is how the program looks when modified to make use of this method:

```
package com.javapuzzlers;
import java.util.regex.Pattern;

public class Me {
    public static void main(String[] args) {
        System.out.println(Me.class.getName().
            replaceAll(Pattern.quote("."), "/") + ".class");
    }
}
```

Another problem with this program is that the correct behavior is platform dependent. Not all file systems use the slash character to separate hierarchical file-name components. To get a valid filename for the platform on which you are running, you should use the correct platform-dependent separator character in place of the slash. That is exactly what the next puzzle does.

Puzzle 21: What's My Class, Take 2

This program does exactly what the one in the previous puzzle did, but doesn't assume that the slash character is used to separate filename components. Instead, the program uses java.io.File.separator, which is a public String field specified to contain the platform-specific filename separator. Does the program print the correct platform-specific name of the class file from which it was loaded?

```
package com.javapuzzlers;
import java.io.File;

public class MeToo {
    public static void main(String[] args) {
    System.out.println(MeToo.class.getName().
        replaceAll("\\.", File.separator) + ".class");
  }
}
```

Solution 21: What's My Class, Take 2

The program displays one of two behaviors depending on the underlying platform. If the file separator is a slash, as it is on UNIX, the program prints com/javapuzzlers/MeToo.class, which is correct. If, however, the file separator is a backslash, as it is on Windows, the program prints something like this:

```
Exception in thread "main"
StringIndexOutOfBoundsException: String index out of range: 1
 at java.lang.String.charAt(String.java:558)
 at java.util.regex.Matcher.appendReplacement(Matcher.java:696)
 at java.util.regex.Matcher.replaceAll(Matcher.java:806)
 at java.lang.String.replaceAll(String.java:2000)
 at com.javapuzzlers.MeToo.main(MeToo.java:6)
```

Although this behavior *is* platform dependent, it isn't exactly what we were looking for. What went wrong on Windows? It turns out that the second parameter of String.replaceAll is a not an ordinary string but a *replacement string,* as defined in the java.util.regex specification [Java-API]. A backslash appearing in a replacement string escapes the following character, causing it to be treated literally. When you run the program on Windows, the replacement string is a lone backslash character, which is invalid. Admittedly, the exception could be a little more informative.

So how do you solve this problem? Release 5.0 provides not one but two new methods that solve it. One is java.util.regex.Matcher.quoteReplacement, which translates a string into the corresponding replacement string. Here is how to fix the program by using this method:

```
System.out.println(MeToo.class.getName().replaceAll(
    "\\.", Matcher.quoteReplacement(File.separator))
        + ".class");
```

The second method introduced in release 5.0 provides an even better solution. This method, String.replace(CharSequence, CharSequence), does the same thing as String.replaceAll, but treats both the pattern and the replacement as literal strings. Here is how to fix the program by using this method:

```
System.out.println(MeToo.class.getName().
    replace(".", File.separator) + ".class");
```

But what if you are using an earlier Java release? Unfortunately, there is no easy way to generate the replacement string. It is easier to dispense with regular expressions entirely and to use `String.replace(char, char)`:

```
System.out.println(MeToo.class.getName().
    replace('.', File.separatorChar) + ".class");
```

The main lesson of this puzzle and the previous one is: **Be careful when using unfamiliar library methods.** When in doubt, consult the Javadoc. Also, regular expressions are tricky: Problems tend to show up at run time rather than compile time.

For API designers, it is important to use a method-naming scheme that distinguishes methods whose behavior differs in significant ways. Java's `String` class is not perfect in this regard. For many programmers, it is not easy to remember which string-replacement methods use literal strings and which ones use regular expressions or replacement strings.

Puzzle 22: Dupe of URL

This puzzle takes advantage of a little-known feature of the Java programming language. What does this program do?

```
public class BrowserTest {
    public static void main(String[] args) {
        System.out.print("iexplore:");
        http://www.google.com;
        System.out.println(":maximize");
    }
}
```

Solution 22: Dupe of URL

This is a bit of a trick question. The program doesn't do anything special. It simply prints iexplore::maximize. The URL that appears in the middle of the program is a *statement label* [JLS 14.7] followed by an *end-of-line comment* [JLS 3.7]. Labels are rarely needed in Java, which thankfully lacks a goto statement. The "little-known feature of the Java programming language" to which the puzzle refers is that you are allowed to put a label on any statement. This program labels an *expression statement*, which is legal but useless.

For what it's worth, this would be a more reasonable way to format the program, assuming that you really want to include the label:

```java
public class BrowserTest {
    public static void main(String[] args) {
        System.out.print("iexplore:");

    http:    // www.google.com;
        System.out.println(":maximize");
    }
}
```

That said, there is no earthly reason to include the label or the comment, which has nothing to do with the program.

The lesson of this puzzle is that misleading comments and extraneous code cause confusion. **Write comments carefully and keep them up to date. Excise dead code.** Also, if something seems too strange to be true, it's probably false.

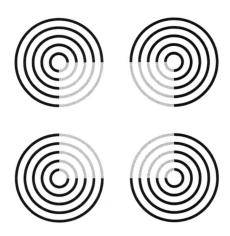

Puzzle 23: No Pain, No Gain

This program prints a word, using a random number generator to select the first character. Describe the behavior of the program:

```java
import java.util.Random;

public class Rhymes {
    private static Random rnd = new Random();

    public static void main(String[] args) {
        StringBuffer word = null;
        switch(rnd.nextInt(2)) {
            case 1:  word = new StringBuffer('P');
            case 2:  word = new StringBuffer('G');
            default: word = new StringBuffer('M');
        }
        word.append('a');
        word.append('i');
        word.append('n');
        System.out.println(word);
    }
}
```

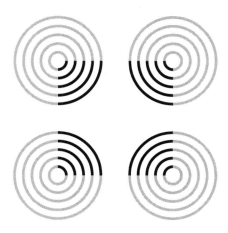

Solution 23: No Pain, No Gain

At first glance, this program might appear to print out the words Pain, Gain, and Main with equal likelihood, varying from run to run. It appears to choose the first letter of the word, depending on the value chosen by the random number generator: M for 0, P for 1, and G for 2. The puzzle's title might have provided you with a clue that it doesn't actually print Pain or Gain. Perhaps more surprisingly, it doesn't print Main either, and its behavior doesn't vary from run to run. It always prints ain.

Three bugs conspire to cause this behavior. Did you spot them all? The first bug is that the random number is chosen so the switch statement can reach only two of its three cases. The specification for Random.nextInt(int) says: "Returns a pseudorandom, uniformly distributed int value between 0 (inclusive) and the specified value (exclusive)" [Java-API]. This means that the only possible values of the expression rnd.nextInt(2) are 0 and 1. The switch statement will never branch to case 2, which suggests that the program will never print Gain. The parameter to nextInt should have been 3 rather than 2.

This is a fairly common source of problems, known as a *fencepost error*. The name comes from the common but incorrect answer of 10 to the question, If you build a fence 100 feet long with posts 10 feet apart, how many posts do you need? Both 11 and 9 are correct answers, depending on whether there are posts at the ends of the fence, but 10 is wrong. **Watch out for fencepost errors.** Whenever you are working with lengths, ranges, or moduli, be careful to determine which endpoints should be included, and make sure that your code behaves accordingly.

The second bug is that there are no break statements between the cases. Whatever the value of the switch expression, the program will execute that case and all subsequent cases [JLS 14.11]. Each case assigns a value to the variable word, and the last assignment wins. The last assignment will always be the one in the final case (default), which is new StringBuffer('M'). This suggests that the program will never print Pain or Gain but always Main.

The absence of break statements in switch cases is a common error that tools can help you catch. As of release 5.0, javac provides the -Xlint:fallthrough flag to generate warnings when you forget a break between one case and the next. **Don't fall through from one nonempty case to another.** It's bad style because it's unusual and therefore confusing to the reader. Nine times out of ten, it indicates an error. If Java had not been modeled after C, its switch statement would probably not require breaks. The lesson for language designers is to consider providing a structured `switch` statement.

The last and most subtle bug is that the expression `new StringBuffer('M')` probably does not do what you think it does. You may not be familiar with the `StringBuffer(char)` constructor, and with good reason: It does not exist. There is a parameterless constructor, one that takes a `String` indicating the initial contents of the string buffer and one that takes an `int` indicating its initial capacity. In this case, the compiler selects the `int` constructor, applying a *widening primitive conversion* to convert the `char` value `'M'` into the `int` value 77 [JLS 5.1.2]. In other words, `new StringBuffer('M')` returns an empty string buffer with an initial capacity of 77. The remainder of the program appends the characters a, i, and n to the empty string buffer and prints out its contents, which are always `ain`.

To avoid this kind of problem, **use familiar idioms and APIs whenever possible. If you must use unfamiliar APIs, read the documentation carefully.** In this case, the program should have used the common `StringBuffer` constructor that takes a `String`.

This corrected version of the program fixes all three bugs, printing `Pain`, `Gain`, and `Main` with equal likelihood:

```
import java.util.Random;

public class Rhymes {
    private static Random rnd = new Random();

    public static void main(String[] args) {
        StringBuffer word = null;
        switch(rnd.nextInt(3)) {
          case 1:
            word = new StringBuffer("P");
            break;
          case 2:
            word = new StringBuffer("G");
            break;
          default:
            word = new StringBuffer("M");
            break;
        }
        word.append('a');
        word.append('i');
        word.append('n');
        System.out.println(word);
    }
}
```

Although this program fixes the bugs, it is overly verbose. Here is a more elegant version:

```java
import java.util.Random;

public class Rhymes {
    private static Random rnd = new Random();
    public static void main(String args[]) {
        System.out.println("PGM".charAt(rnd.nextInt(3)) + "ain");
    }
}
```

Better still is the following version. Although slightly longer, it is more general. It does not depend on the fact that the possible outputs differ only in their first characters:

```java
import java.util.Random;

public class Rhymes {
    public static void main(String args[]) {
        String a[] = {"Main", "Pain", "Gain"};
        System.out.println(randomElement(a));
    }

    private static Random rnd = new Random();
    private static String randomElement(String[] a) {
        return a[rnd.nextInt(a.length)];
    }
}
```

To summarize: First, be careful of fencepost errors. Second, remember to put a break after each case in switch statements. Third, use common idioms and APIs, and consult the documentation when you stray from the well-worn path. Fourth, a char is not a String but is more like an int. Finally, watch out for sneaky puzzlers.

Loopy Puzzlers

All the puzzles in this chapter concern loops.

Puzzle 24: A Big Delight in Every Byte

This program loops through the byte values, looking for a certain value. What does the program print?

```java
public class BigDelight {
    public static void main(String[] args) {
        for (byte b = Byte.MIN_VALUE; b < Byte.MAX_VALUE; b++) {
            if (b == 0x90)
                System.out.print("Joy!");
        }
    }
}
```

Solution 24: A Big Delight in Every Byte

The loop iterates over all the byte values except Byte.MAX_VALUE, looking for 0x90. This value fits in a byte and is not equal to Byte.MAX_VALUE, so you might think that the loop would hit it once and print Joy! on that iteration. Looks can be deceiving. If you ran the program, you found that it prints nothing. What happened?

Simply put, 0x90 is an int constant that is outside the range of byte values. This is counterintuitive because 0x90 is a two-digit hexadecimal literal. Each hex digit takes up 4 bits, so the entire value takes up 8 bits, or 1 byte. The problem is that byte is a signed type. The constant 0x90 is a positive int value of 8 bits with the highest bit set. Legal byte values range from −128 to +127, but the int constant 0x90 is equal to +144.

The comparison of a byte to an int is a *mixed-type comparison.* If you think of byte values as apples and int values as oranges, the program is comparing apples to oranges. Consider the expression ((byte)0x90 == 0x90). Appearances notwithstanding, it evaluates to false. To compare the byte value (byte)0x90 to the int value 0x90, Java promotes the byte to an int with a widening primitive conversion [JLS 5.1.2] and compares the two int values. Because byte is a signed type, the conversion performs *sign extension,* promoting negative byte values to numerically equal int values. In this case, the conversion promotes (byte)0x90 to the int value -112, which is unequal to the int value 0x90, or +144.

Mixed-type comparisons are always confusing because the system is forced to promote one operand to match the type of the other. The conversion is invisible and may not yield the results that you expect. There are several ways to avoid mixed-type comparisons. To pursue our fruit metaphor, you can choose to compare apples to apples or oranges to oranges. You can cast the int to a byte, after which you will be comparing one byte value to another:

```
if (b == (byte)0x90)
    System.out.println("Joy!");
```

Alternatively, you can convert the byte to an int, suppressing sign extension with a mask, after which you will be comparing one int value to another:

```
if ((b & 0xff) == 0x90)
    System.out.println("Joy!");
```

Either of these solutions works, but the best way to avoid this kind of problem is to move the constant value outside the loop and into a constant declaration.

Here is a first attempt:

```
public class BigDelight {
    private static final byte TARGET = 0x90;    // Broken!
    public static void main(String[] args) {
        for (byte b = Byte.MIN_VALUE; b < Byte.MAX_VALUE; b++)
            if (b == TARGET)
                System.out.print("Joy!");
    }
}
```

Unfortunately, it doesn't compile. The constant declaration is broken, and the compiler will tell you the problem: `0x90` is not a valid value for the type `byte`. If you fix the declaration as follows, the program will work fine:

```
private static final byte TARGET = (byte)0x90;
```

To summarize: **Avoid mixed-type comparisons, because they are inherently confusing** (Puzzle 5). To help achieve this goal, **use declared constants in place of "magic numbers."** You already knew that this was a good idea; it documents the meanings of constants, centralizes their definitions, and eliminates duplicate definitions. Now you know that it also forces you to give each constant a type appropriate for its use, eliminating one source of mixed-type comparisons.

The lesson for language designers is that sign extension of `byte` values is a common source of bugs and confusion. The masking that is required in order to suppress sign extension clutters programs, making them less readable. Therefore, the byte type should be unsigned. Also, consider providing literals for all primitive types, reducing the need for error-prone type conversions (Puzzle 27).

Puzzle 25: Inclement Increment

This program increments a variable repeatedly and then prints its value. What is it?

```
public class Increment {
    public static void main(String[] args) {
        int j = 0;
        for (int i = 0; i < 100; i++)
            j = j++;
        System.out.println(j);
    }
}
```

Solution 25: Inclement Increment

At first glance, the program might appear to print 100. After all, it does increment j 100 times. Perhaps surprisingly, it does not print 100 but 0. All that incrementing gets us nowhere. Why?

As the puzzle's title suggests, the problem lies in the statement that does the increment:

```
j = j++;
```

Presumably, the author of the statement meant for it to add 1 to the value of j, which is what the expression j++ does. Unfortunately, the author inadvertently assigned the value of this expression back to j. When placed after a variable, the ++ operator functions as the *postfix increment operator* [JLS 15.14.2]: The value of the expression j++ is the original value of j before it was incremented. Therefore, the preceding assignment first saves the value of j, then sets j to its value plus 1, and, finally, resets j back to its original value. In other words, the assignment is equivalent to this sequence of statements:

```
int tmp = j;
j = j + 1;
j = tmp;
```

The program repeats this process 100 times, after which the value of j is exactly what it was before the loop, or 0.

Fixing the program is as simple as removing the extraneous assignment from the loop, leaving:

```
for (int i = 0; i < 100; i++)
    j++;
```

With this modification, the program prints 100 as expected.

The lesson is this the same as in Puzzle 7: **Do not assign to the same variable more than once in a single expression.** An expression containing multiple assignments to the same variable is confusing and seldom does what you want.

Puzzle 26: In the Loop

The following program counts the number of iterations of a loop and prints the count when the loop terminates. What does it print?

```java
public class InTheLoop {
    public static final int END = Integer.MAX_VALUE;
    public static final int START = END - 100;

    public static void main(String[] args) {
        int count = 0;
        for (int i = START; i <= END; i++)
            count++;
        System.out.println(count);
    }
}
```

Solution 26: In the Loop

If you don't look at the program very carefully, you might think that it prints 100; after all, END is 100 more than START. If you look a bit more carefully, you will see that the program doesn't use the typical loop idiom. Most loops continue as long as the loop index is less than the end value, but this one continues as long as the index is less than *or equal to* the end value. So it prints 101, right? Well, no. If you ran the program, you found that it prints nothing at all. Worse, it keeps running until you kill it. It never gets a chance to print count, because it's stuck in an infinite loop.

The problem is that the loop continues as long as the loop index (i) is less than or equal to Integer.MAX_VALUE, but *all* int variables are *always* less than or equal to Integer.MAX_VALUE. It is, after all, defined to be the highest int value in existence. When i gets to Integer.MAX_VALUE and is incremented, it silently wraps around to Integer.MIN_VALUE.

If you need a loop that iterates near the boundaries of the int values, you are better off using a long variable as the loop index. Simply changing the type of the loop index from int to long solves the problem, causing the program to print 101 as expected:

```
for (long i = START; i <= END; i++)
```

More generally, the lesson here is that ints are not integers. **Whenever you use an integral type, be aware of the boundary conditions.** What happens if the value underflows or overflows? Often it is best to use a larger type. (The integral types are byte, char, short, int, and long.)

It is possible to solve this problem without resorting to a long index variable, but it's not pretty:

```
int i = START;
do {
    count++;
} while (i++ != END);
```

Given the paramount importance of clarity and simplicity, it is almost always better to use a long index under these circumstances, with perhaps one exception: If you are iterating over all (or nearly all) the int values, it's about twice as fast to stick with an `int`. Here is an idiom to apply a function `f` to all four billion `int` values:

```
// Apply the function f to all four billion int values
int i = Integer.MIN_VALUE;
do {
    f(i);
} while (i++ != Integer.MAX_VALUE);
```

The lesson for language designers is the same as that of Puzzle 3: It may be worth considering support for arithmetic that does not overflow silently. Also, it may be worth providing support for loops designed specifically to iterate over ranges of integral values, as many languages do.

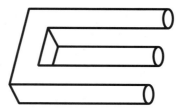

Puzzle 27: Shifty i's

Like the program in the Puzzle 26, this one contains a loop that keeps track of how many iterations it takes to terminate. Unlike that program, this one uses the left-shift operator (`<<`). As usual, your job is to figure out what the program prints. When you read it, remember that Java uses two's-complement binary arithmetic, so the representation of −1 in any signed integral type (`byte`, `short`, `int`, or `long`) has all its bits set:

```
public class Shifty {
    public static void main(String[] args) {
        int i = 0;
        while (-1 << i != 0)
            i++;
        System.out.println(i);
    }
}
```

Solution 27: Shifty i's

The constant -1 is the `int` value with all 32 bits set (0xffffffff). The left-shift operator shifts zeroes in from the right to fill the low-order bits vacated by the shift, so the expression (-1 << i) has its rightmost i bits set to 0 and the remaining 32 - i bits set to 1. Clearly, the loop completes 32 iterations, as -1 << i is unequal to 0 for any i less than 32. You might expect the termination test to return `false` when i is 32, causing the program to print 32, but it doesn't print 32. In fact, it doesn't print anything but goes into an infinite loop.

The problem is that (-1 << 32) is equal to −1 rather than 0, because **shift operators use only the five low-order bits of their right operand as the shift distance,** or six bits if the left operand is a `long` [JLS 15.19]. This applies to all three shift operators: <<, >>, and >>>. The shift distance is always between 0 and 31, or 0 and 63 if the left operand is a `long`. It is calculated mod 32, or mod 64 if the left operand is a `long`. Attempting to shift an `int` value 32 bits or a `long` value 64 bits just returns the value itself. There is no shift distance that discards all 32 bits of an `int` value or all 64 bits of a `long` value.

Luckily, there is an easy way to fix the problem. Instead of repeatedly shifting -1 by a different shift distance, save the result of the previous shift operation and shift it one more bit to the left on each iteration. This version of the program prints 32 as expected:

```
public class Shifty {
    public static void main(String[] args) {
        int distance = 0;
        for (int val = -1; val != 0; val <<= 1)
            distance++;
        System.out.println(distance);
    }
}
```

The fixed program illustrates a general principle: **Shift distances should, if possible, be constants**. If the shift distance is staring you in the face, you are much less likely to exceed 31 or, if the left operand is a `long`, 63. Of course, it isn't always possible to use a constant shift distance. When you must use a nonconstant shift distance, make sure that your program can cope with this problematic case or does not encounter it.

There is another surprising consequence of the aforementioned behavior of shift operators. Many programmers expect a right-shift operator with a negative shift distance to function as a left shift and vice-versa. This is not the case. A right shift always functions as a right shift, and a left shift always functions as a left shift. Negative shift distances are made positive by lopping off all but the five low-order bits—six bits if the left operand is a `long`. So, for example, shifting an `int` to the left with a shift distance of −1 has the effect of shifting it 31 bits to the left.

In summary, shift distances are calculated mod 32 or, if the left operand is a `long`, mod 64. It is therefore impossible to shift away an entire value by using any shift operator or distance. Also, it is impossible to perform a left shift with a right-shift operator or vice-versa. Use a constant shift distance if possible, and exercise care if the shift distance can't be made constant.

Language designers should perhaps consider restricting shift distances to the range from 0 to the type size in bits and changing the semantics of shifting a value by the type size to return 0. Although this would avoid the confusion illustrated by this puzzle, it could have negative performance consequences; Java's semantics for the shift operators are those of the shift instructions on many processors.

Puzzle 28: Looper

This puzzle and the five that follow turn the tables on you. Instead of showing some code and asking what it does, they make *you* write the code, albeit in small amounts. These puzzles are called *loopers*. You will be shown a loop that looks as though it ought to terminate quickly, and it will be your job to come up with a variable declaration that makes it loop indefinitely, when placed immediately above the loop. For example, consider this `for` loop:

```
for (int i = start; i <= start + 1; i++) {
}
```

It looks as though it should run for only two iterations, but it can be made to loop indefinitely by taking advantage of the overflow behavior illustrated in Puzzle 26. The following declaration does the trick:

```
int start = Integer.MAX_VALUE - 1;
```

Now it's your turn. What declaration turns this loop into an infinite loop?

```
while (i == i + 1) {
}
```

Solution 28: Looper

Looking at the `while` loop, it really seems as though it ought to terminate immediately. A number is never equal to itself plus 1, right? Well, what if the number is infinity? Java mandates the use of IEEE 754 floating-point arithmetic [IEEE-754], which lets you represent infinity as a `double` or `float`. As we learned in school, infinity plus 1 is still infinity. If `i` is initialized to infinity before the loop starts, the termination test (`i == i + 1`) evaluates to `true`, and the loop never terminates.

You can initialize `i` with any floating-point arithmetic expression that evaluates to infinity; for example:

```
double i = 1.0 / 0.0;
```

Better yet, you can take advantage of a constant that is provided for you by the standard libraries:

```
double i = Double.POSITIVE_INFINITY;
```

In fact, you don't have to initialize `i` to infinity to make the loop spin forever. Any sufficiently large floating-point value will do; for example:

```
double i = 1.0e40;
```

This works because the larger a floating-point value, the larger the distance between the value and its successor. This distribution of floating-point values is a consequence of their representation with a fixed number of significant bits. Adding 1 to a floating-point value that is sufficiently large will not change the value, because it doesn't "bridge the gap" to its successor.

Floating-point operations return the floating-point value that is closest to their exact mathematical result. Once the distance between adjacent floating-point values is greater than 2, adding 1 to a floating-point value will have no effect, because the half-way point between values won't be reached. For the `float` type, the least magnitude beyond which adding 1 will have no effect is 2^{25}, or 33,554,432; for the `double` type, it is 2^{54}, or approximately 1.8×10^{16}.

The distance between adjacent floating-point values is called an *ulp*, which is an acronym for unit in the last place. In release 5.0, the `Math.ulp` method was introduced to calculate the ulp of a `float` or `double` value.

In summary, **it is possible to represent infinity as a double or a float**. Most people find this somewhat surprising the first time they hear of it, perhaps because you can't represent infinity by using any of the integral types. Second, **adding a small floating-point value to a large one will not change the large value**. This too may be counterintuitive, as it isn't true for the real numbers. It is worth remembering that **binary floating-point arithmetic is only an approximation to real arithmetic**.

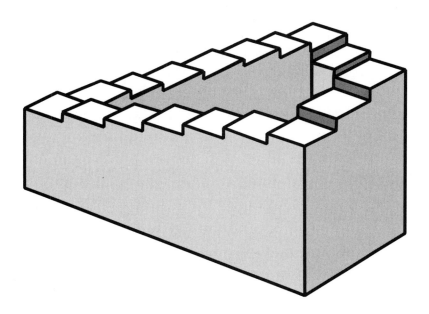

Puzzle 29: Bride of Looper

Provide a declaration for i that turns this loop into an infinite loop:

```
while (i != i) {
}
```

Solution 29: Bride of Looper

This looper is perhaps even more puzzling than the previous one. It really seems that it ought to terminate immediately, no matter what declaration precedes it. A number is always equal to itself, right?

Right, but IEEE 754 floating-point arithmetic reserves a special value to represent a quantity that is not a number [IEEE-754]. This value, known as *NaN* (short for "Not a Number"), is the value of all floating-point computations that do not have well-defined numeric values, such as `0.0 / 0.0`. The specification says that **NaN is not equal to any floating-point value,** *including itself* [JLS 15.21.1]. Therefore, if i is initialized to NaN before the loop starts, the termination test (i != i) evaluates to `true`, and the loop never terminates. Strange but true.

You can initialize i with any floating-point arithmetic expression that evaluates to NaN; for example:

```
double i = 0.0 / 0.0;
```

Once again, you can add clarity by using a constant that is provided for you by the standard libraries:

```
double i = Double.NaN;
```

NaN holds other similar surprises. **Any floating-point operation evaluates to NaN if one or more of its operands are NaN.** This rule is perfectly reasonable, but it has strange consequences. For example, this program prints `false`:

```
class Test {
    public static void main(String[] args) {
        double i = 0.0 / 0.0;
        System.out.println(i - i == 0);
    }
}
```

The principle underlying the rules for computing with NaN is that **once it generates NaN, a computation is damaged, and no further computation can repair the damage.** The NaN value is intended to allow a damaged computation to proceed to a point where it is convenient to deal with the situation.

In summary, the `float` and `double` types have a special NaN value to represent a quantity that is not a number. The rules for computations involving NaN are simple and sensible, but the consequences of these rules can be counterintuitive.

Puzzle 30: Son of Looper

Provide a declaration for i that turns this loop into an infinite loop:

```
while (i != i + 0) {
}
```

Unlike previous loopers, you must not use floating-point in your answer. In other words, you must not declare i to be of type double or float.

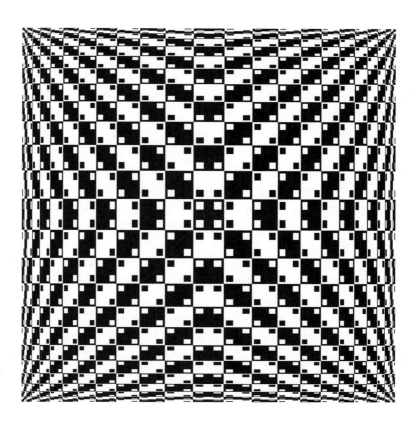

Solution 30: Son of Looper

Like the previous puzzle, this one seems impossible at first glance. After all, a number is always equal to itself plus 0, and you were forbidden from using floating-point, so you can't use NaN. There is no NaN equivalent for the integral types. What gives?

The inescapable conclusion is that the type of i must be non-numeric, and therein lies the solution. The only non-numeric type for which the + operator is defined is String. The + operator is *overloaded*: For the String type, it performs not addition but string concatenation. If one operand in the concatenation is of some type other than String, that operand is converted to a string prior to concatenation [JLS 15.18.1].

In fact, i can be initialized to *any* value so long as it is of type String; for example:

```
String i = "Buy seventeen copies of Effective Java!";
```

The int value 0 is converted to the String value "0" and appended to the blatant plug. The resulting string is not equal to the original as computed by the equals method, so it certainly can't be identical, as computed by the == operator. Therefore, the boolean expression (i != i + 0) evaluates to true and the loop never terminates.

In summary, **operator overloading can be very misleading**. The plus sign in the puzzle looks like addition, but it is made to perform string concatenation by choosing the correct type for the variable i, which is String. The puzzle is made even more misleading because the variable is named i, a name that is usually reserved for integer variables. **Good variable, method, and class names are at least as important to program readability as good comments.**

The lesson for language designers is the same as in Puzzles 11 and 13. Operator overloading can be confusing. Perhaps the + operator should not have been overloaded for string concatenation. It may well be worth providing a string concatenation operator, but it doesn't have to be +.

Puzzle 31: Ghost of Looper

Provide a declaration for i that turns this loop into an infinite loop:

```
while (i != 0)
    i >>>= 1;
```

Recall that >>>= is the assignment operator corresponding to the unsigned right-shift operator. Zeros are shifted in from the left to fill bits vacated by the shift, even if the value being shifted is negative.

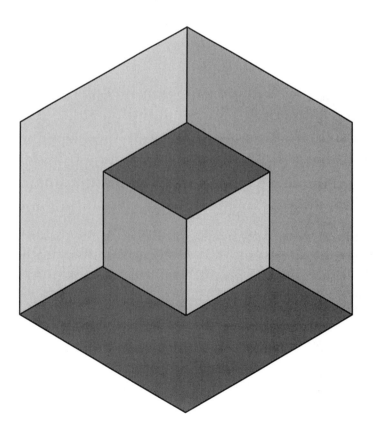

Solution 31: Ghost of Looper

This looper is a bit more complex than the three that preceded it, as the loop has a nonempty body. In the body, the value of i is replaced by its value shifted right by one bit position. For the shift to be legal, i must be of an integral type (byte, char, short, int, or long). The unsigned right-shift operator shifts zeros in from the left, so it might seem that the loop could perform only as many iterations as the number of bits in the largest integral type, which is 64. This is indeed what would happen if you preceded the loop with this declaration:

```
long i = -1; // -1L has all 64 bits set
```

How could you possibly turn this into an infinite loop? The key to solving this puzzle is that >>>= is a *compound assignment operator*. (The compound assignment operators are *=, /=, %=, +=, -=, <<=, >>=, >>>=, &=, ^=, and |=.) An unfortunate fact about the compound assignment operators is that they can silently perform *narrowing primitive conversions* [JLS 15.26.2], which are conversions from one numeric type to a less expressive numeric type. **Narrowing primitive conversions can lose information about the magnitude or precision of numeric values** [JLS 5.1.3].

To make this concrete, suppose that you precede the loop with the following declaration:

```
short i = -1;
```

Because the initial value of i ((short)0xffff) is nonzero, the body of the loop is executed. The first step in the execution of the shift operation is that the value of i is promoted to an int. All arithmetic operations do this to operands of type short, byte, or char. This promotion is a *widening* primitive conversion, so no information is lost. This promotion performs sign extension, so the resulting int value is 0xffffffff. This value is then shifted to the right by one bit without sign extension to yield the int value 0x7fffffff. Finally, this value is stored back into i. In order to store the int value into the short variable, Java performs the dreaded narrowing primitive conversion, which simply lops off the high-order 16 bits of the value. This leaves (short)0xffff, and we are back where we started. The second and successive iterations of the loop behave identically, so the loop never terminates.

Similar behavior occurs if you declare i to be a short or byte variable initialized to any negative value. You will not get an infinite loop if you declare i to be a char, as char values are unsigned, so the widening primitive conversion that occurs prior to the shift doesn't perform sign extension.

In summary, **do not use compound assignment operators on short, byte, or char variables**. Such expressions perform mixed-type arithmetic, which can be confusing in and of itself. Far worse, they perform an implicit narrowing cast, which can discard information. The results can be disastrous.

The lesson for language designers is that languages should not perform narrowing conversions silently. One could well argue that Java should have disallowed the use of compound assignment operators on short, byte, and char variables.

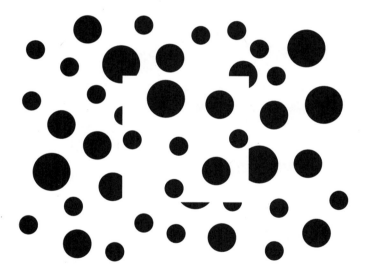

Puzzle 32: Curse of Looper

Provide declarations for i and j that turn this loop into an infinite loop:

```
while (i <= j && j <= i && i != j) {
}
```

Solution 32: Curse of Looper

Oh, no, not another seemingly impossible looper! If `i <= j` and `j <= i`, surely `i` must equal `j`? This property certainly holds for the real numbers. In fact, it is so important that it has a name: The ≤ relation on the real numbers is said to be *antisymmetric*. Java's `<=` operator used to be antisymmetric before release 5.0, but no longer.

Until release 5.0, Java's *numerical comparison operators* (`<`, `<=`, `>`, and `>=`) required both of their operands to be of a primitive numeric type (`byte`, `char`, `short`, `int`, `long`, `float`, or `double`) [JLS2 15.20.1]. In release 5.0, the specification was changed to say that the type of each operand must be *convertible to* a primitive numeric type [JLS 15.20.1, 5.1.8]. Therein lies the rub.

In release 5.0, autoboxing and auto-unboxing were added to the language. If you are unfamiliar with them see: http://java.sun.com/j2se/5.0/docs/guide/language/autoboxing.html [Boxing]. The `<=` operator is still antisymmetric on the set of primitive numeric values, but now it applies to operands of *boxed numeric types* as well. (The boxed numeric types are `Byte`, `Character`, `Short`, `Integer`, `Long`, `Float`, and `Double`.) The `<=` operator is not antisymmetric on operands of these types, because Java's *equality operators* (`==` and `!=`) perform reference identity comparison rather than value comparison when applied to object references.

To make this concrete, the following declarations give the expression (`i <= j && j <= i && i != j`) the value `true`, turning the loop into an infinite loop:

```
Integer i = new Integer(0);
Integer j = new Integer(0);
```

The first two subexpressions (`i <= j` and `j <= i`) perform *unboxing conversions* [JLS 5.1.8] on `i` and `j` and compare the resulting `int` values numerically. Both `i` and `j` represent 0, so both of these subexpressions evaluate to `true`. The third subexpression (`i != j`) performs an identity comparison on the object references `i` and `j`. The two variables refer to distinct objects, as each was initialized to a new `Integer` instance. Therefore, the third subexpression also evaluates to `true`, and the loop spins forever.

You might wonder why the language specification wasn't changed to make the equality operators perform value comparisons when applied to boxed numeric types. The answer is simple: compatibility. When a language is widely used, it is unacceptable to change the behavior of existing programs in ways that violate existing specifications. The following program was always guaranteed to print false, and so it must remain:

```
public class ReferenceComparison {
    public static void main(String[] args) {
        System.out.println(new Integer(0) == new Integer(0));
    }
}
```

The equality operators do perform numerical comparison when only one of their two operands is of a boxed numeric type and the other is of a primitive type. Because this was illegal prior to release 5.0, there are no compatibility problems. To make this concrete, the following program was illegal in release 1.4 and prints true in release 5.0:

```
public class ValueComparison {
    public static void main(String[] args) {
        System.out.println(new Integer(0) == 0);
    }
}
```

In summary, **there is a fundamental difference in the way numerical comparison operators and equality operators behave when both operands are of boxed numeric types: Numerical comparison operators perform value comparisons, while equality operators perform reference identity comparisons**.

For language designers, life might have been simpler and more pleasant if the equality operators had always performed value comparisons (Puzzle 13). Perhaps the real lesson is that language designers should acquire high-quality crystal balls in order to predict the future of the language and make all design decisions accordingly. More seriously, designers should think about how the language might evolve and should attempt to minimize constraints on evolution.

Puzzle 33: Looper Meets the Wolfman

Provide a declaration for i that turns this loop into an infinite loop. This one doesn't require the use of any release 5.0 features:

```
while (i == -i && i != 0) {
}
```

Solution 33: Looper Meets the Wolfman

Yet another puzzling looper. In the `boolean` expression (`i == -i && i != 0`), the unary minus operator is applied to `i`, which implies that its type must be numeric: It is illegal to apply the unary minus operator to a non-numeric operand. Therefore, we are looking for a nonzero numeric value that is equal to its own negation. NaN does not satisfy this property, as it is not equal to any value, so `i` must represent an actual number. Surely there is no number with this property?

Well, there is no real number with this property, but none of Java's numeric types model the real numbers perfectly. Floating-point values are represented with a sign bit; a significand, informally known as the *mantissa*; and an exponent. No floating-point value other than 0 is equal to itself with the sign bit flipped, so the type of `i` must be integral.

The signed integral types use *two's-complement arithmetic*: To negate a value, you flip every bit and add 1 to the result [JLS 15.15.4]. One big advantage of two's-complement arithmetic is that there is a unique representation for 0. If you negate the `int` value 0, you get `0xffffffff + 1`, which is 0. There is, however, a corresponding disadvantage. There exist an even number of `int` values—2^{32} to be precise—and one of these values is used to represent 0. That leaves an odd number of `int` values to represent positive and negative integers, which means that there must be a different number of positive and negative `int` values. This in turn implies that there is at least one `int` value whose negation cannot be correctly represented as an `int` value.

In fact, there is exactly one such `int` value, and it is `Integer.MIN_VALUE`, or -2^{31}. Its hexadecimal representation is `0x8000000`. The sign bit is 1, and all the other bits are 0. If we negate this value, we get `0x7fffffff + 1`, which is `0x8000000`, or `Integer.MIN_VALUE`! In other words, **`Integer.MIN_VALUE` is its own negation**, as is `Long.MIN_VALUE`. Negating either of these values causes an overflow, but Java ignores overflows in integer computations. The results are well defined, even if they are not always what you want them to be.

This declaration will make the `boolean` expression (`i == -i && i != 0`) evaluate to `true`, causing the loop to spin indefinitely:

```
int i = Integer.MIN_VALUE;
```

So will this one:

```
long i = Long.MIN_VALUE;
```

In case you're familiar with modular arithmetic, it's worth pointing out that this puzzle can be solved algebraically. Java's `int` arithmetic is actually arithmetic mod 2^{32}, so the puzzle requires a nonzero solution to this linear congruence:

$$i \equiv -i \pmod{2^{32}}$$

Adding i to both sides, we get:

$$2i \equiv 0 \pmod{2^{32}}$$

The nonzero solution to this congruence is $i = 2^{31}$. Although this value is not representable as an `int`, it is congruent to -2^{31}, which is `Integer.MIN_VALUE`.

In summary, Java uses two's-complement arithmetic, which is asymmetric. The signed integral types (`int`, `long`, `byte`, and `short`) each have one more negative value than positive, which is always the minimum value representable in the type. Negating `Integer.MIN_VALUE` doesn't change its value, and the same holds true for `Long.MIN_VALUE`. Negating `Short.MIN_VALUE` and casting the resulting `int` value back to a `short` returns the original value (`Short.MIN_VALUE`). A similar result holds for `Byte.MIN_VALUE`. More generally, **watch out for overflow: Like the Wolfman, it's a killer**.

The lesson for language designers is the same as in Puzzle 26. Consider providing linguistic support for some form of integer arithmetic where overflow does not happen silently.

Puzzle 34: Down for the Count

Like the programs in Puzzles 26 and 27, this program has a single loop, keeps track of the number of iterations, and prints that number when the loop terminates. What does the program print?

```java
public class Count {
    public static void main(String[] args) {
        final int START = 2000000000;
        int count = 0;
        for (float f = START; f < START + 50; f++)
            count++;
        System.out.println(count);
    }
}
```

Solution 34: Down for the Count

A superficial analysis might suggest that this program would print 50. After all, the loop variable (f) is initialized to 2,000,000,000, the final value is 50 more than the initial value, and the loop has the traditional "half-open" form: It uses the < operator, which causes it to include the initial value but not the final value.

This analysis, however, misses a key point: The loop variable is a float rather than the traditional int. Remember back to Puzzle 28; it is apparent that the increment (f++) will not work. The initial value of f is close to Integer.MAX_VALUE, so it requires 31 bits to express precisely, and the float type provides only 24 bits of precision. Incrementing such a large float value will not change it. Therefore, it would appear that this program should loop indefinitely, with f never getting any closer to its terminal value. If, however, you ran the program, you found that it doesn't loop indefinitely; in fact, it terminates immediately, printing 0. What gives?

The problem is that the termination test fails in much the same way that the increment does. The loop runs only so long as the loop index f is less than (float)(START + 50). The promotion from int to float is performed automatically when comparing an int to a float [JLS 15.20.1]. Unfortunately, this promotion is one of the three widening primitive conversions that can result in loss of precision [JLS 5.1.2]. (The others are long to float and long to double.)

The initial value of f is so large that adding 50 to it and converting the result to a float produces the same value as simply converting f to a float. In other words, (float)2000000000 == 2000000050, so the expression f < START + 50 is false before the loop body has executed even once, and the loop body never gets a chance to run.

Fixing this program is as simple as changing the type of the loop variable from a float to an int. This avoids all the imprecision associated with floating-point computation:

```
for (int i = START; i < START + 50; i++)
    count++;
```

Without using a computer, how could you possibly have known that 2,000,000,050 has the same float representation as 2,000,000,000? The key is to observe that 2,000,000,000 has ten factors of 2: It begins with a 2 and has nine factors of 10, each of which is 5 × 2. This means that the binary representation of 2,000,000,000 ends in ten 0s. The binary representation of 50 requires only six bits, so adding 50 to 2,000,000,000 doesn't influence any bit higher than the sixth from the right. In particular, the seventh and eighth bits from the right are still 0. Promoting this 31-bit int to a float with 24 bits of precision rounds between the seventh and eighth bits, which simply discards the rightmost seven bits. The rightmost six bits are the only ones on which 2,000,000,000 and 2,000,000,050 differ, so their float representations are identical.

The moral of this puzzle is simple: **Do not use floating-point loop indices,** because it can lead to unpredictable behavior. If you need a floating-point value in the body of a loop, take the int or long loop index and convert it to a float or double. **You may lose precision when converting an int or long to a float or a long to a double**, but at least it will not affect the loop itself. **When you use floating-point, use double rather than float** unless you are certain that float provides enough precision *and* you have a compelling performance need to use float. The times when it's appropriate to use float rather than double are few and far between.

The lesson for language designers, yet again, is that silent loss of precision can be very confusing to programmers. See Puzzle 31 for further discussion.

Puzzle 35: Minute by Minute

The following program simulates a simple clock. Its loop variable represents a millisecond counter that goes from 0 to the number of milliseconds in an hour. The body of the loop increments a minute counter at regular intervals. Finally, the program prints the minute counter. What does it print?

```
public class Clock {
    public static void main(String[] args) {
        int minutes = 0;
        for (int ms = 0; ms < 60*60*1000; ms++)
            if (ms % 60*1000 == 0)
                minutes++;
        System.out.println(minutes);
    }
}
```

Solution 35: Minute by Minute

The loop in this program is the standard idiomatic for loop. It steps the millisecond counter (ms) from 0 to the number of milliseconds in an hour, or 3,600,000, including the former but not the latter. The body of the loop appears to increment the minute counter (minutes) each time the millisecond counter is a multiple of 60,000, which is the number of milliseconds in a minute. This happens 3,600,000 / 60,000, or 60 times in the lifetime of the loop, so you might expect the program to print 60, which is, after all, the number of minutes in an hour. Running the program, however, tells a different story: It prints 60000. Why does it increment minutes so often?

The problem lies in the boolean expression (ms % 60*1000 == 0). You might think that this expression is equivalent to (ms % 60000 == 0), but it isn't. The remainder and multiplication operators have the same precedence [JLS 15.17], so the expression ms % 60*1000 is equivalent to (ms % 60) * 1000. This expression is equal to 0 if (ms % 60) is 0, so the loop increments minutes every 60 iterations. This accounts for the final result being off by a factor of a thousand.

The easiest way to fix the program is to insert a pair of parentheses into the boolean expression to force the correct order of evaluation:

```
if (ms % (60 * 1000) == 0)
    minutes++;
```

There is, however, a much better way to fix the program. **Replace all magic numbers with appropriately named constants**:

```
public class Clock {
    private static final int MS_PER_HOUR   = 60 * 60 * 1000;
    private static final int MS_PER_MINUTE = 60 * 1000;
    public static void main(String[] args) {
        int minutes = 0;
        for (int ms = 0; ms < MS_PER_HOUR; ms++)
            if (ms % MS_PER_MINUTE == 0)
                minutes++;
        System.out.println(minutes);
    }
}
```

The expression ms % 60*1000 in the original program was laid out to fool you into thinking that multiplication has higher precedence than remainder. The compiler, however, ignores this white space, so **never use spacing to express grouping; use parentheses**. Spacing can be deceptive, but parentheses never lie.

Exceptional Puzzlers

The puzzles in this chapter concern exceptions and the closely related `try-finally` statement. A word of caution: Puzzle 44 is exceptionally difficult.

Puzzle 36: Indecision

This poor little program can't quite make up its mind. The `decision` method returns `true`. But it also returns `false`. What does it print? Is it even legal?

```java
public class Indecisive {
    public static void main(String[] args) {
        System.out.println(decision());
    }

    static boolean decision() {
        try {
            return true;
        } finally {
            return false;
        }
    }
}
```

Solution 36: Indecision

You might think that this program is illegal. After all, the decision method can't return both true and false. If you tried it, you found that it compiles without error and prints false. Why?

The reason is that **in a try-finally statement, the finally block is always executed when control leaves the try block** [JLS 14.20.2]. This is true whether the try block completes normally or *abruptly*. Abrupt completion of a statement or block occurs when it throws an exception, executes a break or continue to an enclosing statement, or executes a return from the method as in this program. These are called abrupt completions because they prevent the program from executing the next statement in sequence.

When both the try block and the finally block complete abruptly, the reason for the abrupt completion in the try block is discarded, and the whole try-finally statement completes abruptly for the same reason as the finally block. In this program, the abrupt completion caused by the return statement in the try block is discarded, and the try-finally statement completes abruptly because of the return statement in the finally block. Simply put, the program tries to return true but finally it returns false.

Discarding the reason for abrupt completion is almost never what you want, because the original reason for abrupt completion might be important to the behavior of a program. It is especially difficult to understand the behavior of a program that executes a break, continue, or return statement in a try block only to have the statement's behavior vetoed by a finally block.

In summary, every finally block should complete normally, barring an unchecked exception. **Never exit a finally block with a return, break, continue, or throw, and never allow a checked exception to propagate out of a finally block.**

For language designers, finally blocks should perhaps be required to complete normally in the absence of unchecked exceptions. Toward this end, a try-finally construct would require that the finally block *can complete normally* [JLS 14.21]. A return, break, or continue statement that transfers control out of a finally block would be disallowed, as would any statement that could cause a checked exception to propagate out of the finally block.

Puzzle 37: Exceptionally Arcane

This puzzle tests your knowledge of the rules for declaring exceptions thrown by methods and caught by catch blocks. What does each of the following three programs do? Don't assume that all of them compile:

```java
import java.io.IOException;
public class Arcane1 {
    public static void main(String[] args) {
        try {
            System.out.println("Hello world");
        } catch (IOException e) {
            System.out.println("I've never seen println fail!");
        }
    }
}
```

```java
public class Arcane2 {
    public static void main(String[] args) {
        try {
            // If you have nothing nice to say, say nothing
        } catch (Exception e) {
            System.out.println("This can't happen");
        }
    }
}
```

```java
interface Type1 {
    void f() throws CloneNotSupportedException;
}
interface Type2 {
    void f() throws InterruptedException;
}
interface Type3 extends Type1, Type2 {
}
public class Arcane3 implements Type3 {
    public void f() {
        System.out.println("Hello world");
    }
    public static void main(String[] args) {
        Type3 t3 = new Arcane3();
        t3.f();
    }
}
```

Solution 37: Exceptionally Arcane

The first program, Arcane1, illustrates a basic principle of checked exceptions. It may look as though it should compile: The try clause does I/O, and the catch clause catches IOException. But the program does not compile because the println method isn't declared to throw any checked exceptions, and IOException is a checked exception. The language specification says that **it is a compile-time error for a catch clause to catch a checked exception type _E_ if the corresponding try clause can't throw an exception of some subtype of _E_** [JLS 11.2.3].

By the same token, the second program, Arcane2, may look as though it shouldn't compile, but it does. It compiles because its sole catch clause checks for Exception. Although the JLS is not terribly clear on this point, **catch clauses that catch Exception or Throwable are legal regardless of the contents of the corresponding try clause**. Although Arcane2 is a legal program, the contents of its catch clause will never be executed; the program prints nothing.

The third program, Arcane3, also looks as though it shouldn't compile. Method f is declared to throw checked exception CloneNotSupportedException in interface Type1 and to throw checked exception InterruptedException in interface Type2. Interface Type3 inherits from Type1 and Type2, so it would seem that invoking f on an object whose static type is Type3 could potentially throw either of these exceptions. A method must either catch each checked exception its body can throw, or declare that it throws the exception. The main method in Arcane3 invokes f on an object whose static type is Type3 but does neither of these things for CloneNotSupportedException or InterruptedException. Why does the program compile?

The flaw in this analysis is the assumption that Type3.f can throw either the exception declared on Type1.f or the one declared on Type2.f. This simply isn't true. Each interface limits the set of checked exceptions that method f can throw. **The set of checked exceptions that a method can throw is the intersection of the sets of checked exceptions that it is declared to throw in all applicable types**, not the union. As a result, the f method on an object whose static type is Type3 can't throw any checked exceptions at all. Therefore, Arcane3 compiles without error and prints Hello world.

In summary, the first program illustrates the basic requirement that catch clauses for checked exceptions are permitted only when the corresponding try clause can throw the exception in question. The second program illustrates a corner case where this requirement does not apply. The third program illustrates the interaction of multiple inherited `throws` clauses, which reduces rather than increases the number of exceptions that a method is permitted to throw. The behaviors illustrated by this puzzle don't generally cause subtle bugs, but they can be a bit surprising the first time you see them.

Puzzle 38: The Unwelcome Guest

The program in this puzzle models a system that attempts to read a user ID from its environment, defaulting to a guest user if the attempt fails. The author of the program was faced with a situation whereby the initializing expression for a static field could throw an exception. Because Java doesn't allow static initializers to throw checked exceptions, the initialization must be wrapped in a `try-finally` block. What does the program print?

```java
public class UnwelcomeGuest {
    public static final long GUEST_USER_ID = -1;

    private static final long USER_ID;
    static {
        try {
            USER_ID = getUserIdFromEnvironment();
        } catch (IdUnavailableException e) {
            USER_ID = GUEST_USER_ID;
            System.out.println("Logging in as guest");
        }
    }

    private static long getUserIdFromEnvironment()
            throws IdUnavailableException {
        throw new IdUnavailableException(); // Simulate an error
    }

    public static void main(String[] args) {
        System.out.println("User ID: " + USER_ID);
    }
}

class IdUnavailableException extends Exception {
    IdUnavailableException() { }
}
```

Solution 38: The Unwelcome Guest

This program seems straightforward. The call to `getUserIdFromEnvironment` appears to throw an exception, causing the program to assign the value of `GUEST_USER_ID` (-1L) to `USER_ID` and to print `Logging in as guest`. Then the `main` method executes, causing the program to print `User ID: -1`. Once again, appearances are deceiving. The program doesn't compile. If you tried to compile it, you saw an error message that looked something like this:

```
UnwelcomeGuest.java:9:
    variable USER_ID might already have been assigned
            USER_ID = GUEST_USER_ID;
            ^
```

What's the problem? The `USER_ID` field is a *blank final*, which is a final field whose declaration lacks an initializer [JLS 4.12.4]. It is clear that the exception can be thrown in the `try` block only if the assignment to `USER_ID` fails, so it is perfectly safe to assign to `USER_ID` in the `catch` block. Any execution of the static initializer block will cause exactly one assignment to `USER_ID`, which is just what is required for blank finals. Why doesn't the compiler know this?

Determining whether a program can perform more than one assignment to a blank final is a hard problem. In fact, it's impossible. It is equivalent to the classic *halting problem*, which is known to be unsolvable in general [Turing36]. To make it possible to write a Java compiler, the language specification takes a conservative approach to this issue. **A blank final field can be assigned only at points in the program where it is *definitely unassigned*.** The specification goes to great lengths to provide a precise but conservative definition for this term [JLS 16]. Because it is conservative, **there are some provably safe programs that the compiler must reject.** This puzzle illustrates one such program.

Luckily, you do not have to learn the gory details of definite assignment to write Java programs. Usually the definite assignment rules don't get in the way. If you happen to write a program that really can assign to a blank final more than once, the compiler will helpfully point this out to you. Only rarely, as in this puzzle, will you write a program that is safe but does not satisfy the formal requirements of the specification. The compiler will complain just as if you had written an unsafe program, and you will have to modify your program to satisfy it.

The best way to solve this kind of problem is to turn the offending field from a blank final into an ordinary final, replacing the static initializer block with a static field initializer. This is best done by refactoring the code in the static block into a helper method:

```
public class UnwelcomeGuest {
    public static final long GUEST_USER_ID = -1;
    private static final long USER_ID = getUserIdOrGuest();
    private static long getUserIdOrGuest() {
        try {
            return getUserIdFromEnvironment();
        } catch (IdUnavailableException e) {
            System.out.println("Logging in as guest");
            return GUEST_USER_ID;
        }
    }
    ... // The rest of the program is unchanged
}
```

This version of the program is clearly correct and is more readable than the original because it adds a descriptive name for the field value computation, where the original version had only an anonymous static initializer block. With this change to the program, it works as expected.

In summary, most programmers do not need to learn the details of the definite assignment rules. Usually the rules just do the right thing. **If you must refactor a program to eliminate a compilation error caused by the definite assignment rules, consider adding a new method.** Besides solving the definite assignment problem, it may offer an opportunity to make the program more readable.

Puzzle 39: Hello, Goodbye

This program adds an unusual twist to the usual Hello world program. What does it print?

```
public class HelloGoodbye {
    public static void main(String[] args) {
        try {
            System.out.println("Hello world");
            System.exit(0);
        } finally {
            System.out.println("Goodbye world");
        }
    }
}
```

Solution 39: Hello, Goodbye

The program contains two `println` statements: one in a `try` block and the other in the corresponding `finally` block. The `try` block executes its `println` and finishes execution prematurely by calling `System.exit`. At this point, you might expect control to transfer to the `finally` block. If you tried the program, though, you found that it never can say goodbye: It prints only `Hello world`. Doesn't this violate the principle explained in Puzzle 36?

It is true that a `finally` block is executed when a `try` block completes execution whether normally or abruptly. In this program, however, the `try` block does not complete execution at all. **The `System.exit` method halts the execution of the current thread and all others dead in their tracks.** The presence of a `finally` clause does not give a thread special permission to continue executing.

When `System.exit` is called, the virtual machine performs two cleanup tasks before shutting down. First, it executes all *shutdown hooks* that have been registered with `Runtime.addShutdownHook`. This is useful to release resources external to the VM. **Use shutdown hooks for behavior that must occur before the VM exits.** The following version of the program demonstrates this technique, printing both `Hello world` and `Goodbye world`, as expected:

```
public class HelloGoodbye {
    public static void main(String[] args) {
        System.out.println("Hello world");
        Runtime.getRuntime().addShutdownHook(
            new Thread() {
                public void run() {
                    System.out.println("Goodbye world");
                }
            });
        System.exit(0);
    }
}
```

The second cleanup task performed by the VM when `System.exit` is called concerns finalizers. If either `System.runFinalizersOnExit` or its evil twin `Runtime.runFinalizersOnExit` has been called, the VM runs the finalizers on all objects that have not yet been finalized. These methods were deprecated a long time ago and with good reason. **Never call `System.runFinalizersOnExit` or `Runtime.runFinalizersOnExit` for any reason: They are among the most dangerous methods in the Java libraries** [ThreadStop]. Calling these methods can result in finalizers being run on live objects while other threads are concurrently manipulating them, resulting in erratic behavior or deadlock.

In summary, `System.exit` stops all program threads immediately; it does not cause `finally` blocks to execute, but it does run shutdown hooks before halting the VM. Use shutdown hooks to terminate external resources when the VM shuts down. It is possible to halt the VM without executing shutdown hooks by calling `Runtime.halt`, but this method is rarely used.

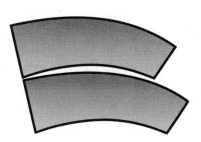

Puzzle 40: The Reluctant Constructor

Although it is common to see a `throws` clause on a method declaration, it is less common to see one on a constructor declaration. The following program has such a declaration. What does it print?

```java
public class Reluctant {
    private Reluctant internalInstance = new Reluctant();

    public Reluctant() throws Exception {
        throw new Exception("I'm not coming out");
    }

    public static void main(String[] args) {
        try {
            Reluctant b = new Reluctant();
            System.out.println("Surprise!");
        } catch (Exception ex) {
            System.out.println("I told you so");
        }
    }
}
```

Solution 40: The Reluctant Constructor

The `main` method invokes the `Reluctant` constructor, which throws an exception. You might expect the `catch` clause to catch this exception and print `I told you so`. A closer look at the program reveals that the `Reluctant` instance contains a second internal instance, and its constructor also throws an exception. Whichever exception gets thrown, it looks as though the `catch` clause in `main` should catch it, so it seems a safe bet that the program will print `I told you so`. But if you tried running it, you found that it does nothing of the sort: It throws a `StackOverflowError`. Why?

Like most programs that throw a `StackOverflowError`, this one contains an infinite recursion. When you invoke a constructor, the **instance variable initializers run before the body of the constructor** [JLS 12.5]. In this case, the initializer for the variable `internalInstance` invokes the constructor recursively. That constructor, in turn, initializes its own `internalInstance` field by invoking the `Reluctant` constructor again and so on, ad infinitum. These recursive invocations cause a `StackOverflowError` before the constructor body ever gets a chance to execute. Because `StackOverflowError` is a subtype of `Error` rather than `Exception`, the `catch` clause in `main` doesn't catch it.

It is not uncommon for an object to contain instances of its own type. This happens, for example, in linked list nodes, tree nodes, and graph nodes. You must initialize such contained instances carefully to avoid a `StackOverflowError`.

As for the nominal topic of this puzzle—constructors declared to throw exceptions—note that **a constructor must declare any checked exceptions thrown by its instance initializers.** This program, which illustrates a common service-provider pattern, won't compile, because it violates this rule:

```
public class Car {
    private static Class engineClass = ... ; // Service provider
    private Engine engine = (Engine) engineClass.newInstance();
    public Car() { }  // Throws two checked exceptions!
}
```

Although it has no body, the constructor throws two checked exceptions: `InstantiationException` and `IllegalAccessException`. They are thrown by `Class.newInstance`, which is called when initializing the `engine` field. The best way to fix this is to create a private static helper method that computes the initial value of the field and handles exceptions appropriately. In this case, let's assume that the `Class` object referred to by `engineClass` was chosen to guarantee that it is both accessible and instantiable. The following version of `Car` compiles without error:

```
// Fixed - instance initializers don't throw checked exceptions
public class Car {
    private static Class engineClass = ... ;
    private Engine engine = newEngine();
    private static Engine newEngine() {
        try {
            return (Engine) engineClass.newInstance();
        } catch (IllegalAccessException e) {
            throw new AssertionError(e);
        } catch (InstantiationException e) {
            throw new AssertionError(e);
        }
    }
    public Car() { }
}
```

In summary, instance initializers run before constructor bodies. Any exceptions thrown by instance initializers propagate to constructors. If initializers throw checked exceptions, constructors must be declared to throw them too, but this should be avoided, because it is confusing. Finally, beware of infinite recursion when designing classes whose instances contain other instances of the same class.

Puzzle 41: Field and Stream

This method copies one file to another and was designed to close every stream it creates, even if it encounters I/O errors. Unfortunately, it doesn't always do this. Why not, and how can you fix it?

```
static void copy(String src, String dest) throws IOException {
    InputStream in = null;
    OutputStream out = null;
    try {
        in = new FileInputStream(src);
        out = new FileOutputStream(dest);
        byte[] buf = new byte[1024];
        int n;
        while ((n = in.read(buf)) >= 0)
            out.write(buf, 0, n);
    } finally {
        if (in != null) in.close();
        if (out != null) out.close();
    }
}
```

Solution 41: Field and Stream

This program seems to have all the bases covered. The stream fields (`in` and `out`) are initialized to `null` and set to the new streams as soon as they are created. The `finally` block closes the stream referred to by each field if it is non-null. An error during the copy would cause an `IOException`, but the `finally` block would still execute before the method returns. What could go wrong?

The problem is in the `finally` block itself. The `close` method can throw an `IOException` too. If this happens when `in.close` is called, the exception prevents `out.close` from getting called, and the output stream remains open.

Note that this program violates the advice of Puzzle 36: The calls to `close` can cause the `finally` block to complete abruptly. Unfortunately, the compiler doesn't help you find the problem, because `close` throws the same exception type as `read` and `write`, and the enclosing method (copy) is declared to propagate it.

The solution is to wrap each call to `close` in a nested `try` block. The following version of the `finally` block is guaranteed to invoke `close` on both streams:

```
} finally {
    if (in != null) {
        try {
            in.close();
        } catch (IOException ex) {
            // There is nothing we can do if close fails
        }
    }

    if (out != null) {
        try {
            out.close();
        } catch (IOException ex) {
            // Again, there is nothing we can do if close fails
        }
    }
}
```

As of release 5.0, you can refactor the code to take advantage of the `Closeable` interface:

```
} finally {
    closeIgnoringException(in);
    closeIgnoringException(out);
}
```

```
private static void closeIgnoringException(Closeable c) {
    if (c != null) {
        try {
            c.close();
        } catch (IOException ex) {
            // There is nothing we can do if close fails
        }
    }
}
```

In summary, when you call the close method in a finally block, protect it
with a nested try-catch to prevent propagation of the IOException. More generally, **handle any checked exception that can be thrown within a finally block
rather than letting it propagate.** This is a special case of the lesson in Puzzle 36,
and the same lessons for language designers apply.

Puzzle 42: Thrown for a Loop

The following program loops through a sequence of int arrays and keeps track of
how many of the arrays satisfy a certain property. What does the program print?

```
public class Loop {
    public static void main(String[] args) {
        int[][] tests = { { 6, 5, 4, 3, 2, 1 }, { 1, 2 },
                          { 1, 2, 3 }, { 1, 2, 3, 4 }, { 1 } };
        int successCount = 0;

        try {
            int i = 0;
            while (true) {
                if (thirdElementIsThree(tests[i++]))
                    successCount++;
            }
        } catch (ArrayIndexOutOfBoundsException e) {
            // No more tests to process
        }
        System.out.println(successCount);
    }

    private static boolean thirdElementIsThree(int[] a) {
        return a.length >= 3 & a[2] == 3;
    }
}
```

Solution 42: Thrown for a Loop

The program tests each element of the array `tests` with the `thirdElementIsThree` method. The loop through this array is certainly not traditional: Rather than terminating when the loop index is equal to the array length, the loop terminates when it attempts to access an array element that isn't there. Although nontraditional, this loop ought to work. The `thirdElementIsThree` method returns `true` if its argument has three or more elements and the third element is equal to 3. This is true for two of the five `int` arrays in `tests`, so it looks as though the program should print 2. If you ran it, you found that it prints 0. Surely there must be some mistake?

In fact, there are two mistakes. The first mistake is that the program uses the hideous loop idiom that depends on an array access throwing an exception. This idiom is not only unreadable but also extremely slow. **Do not use exceptions for loop control; use exceptions only for exceptional conditions** [EJ Item 39]. To correct this mistake, replace the entire `try-finally` block with the standard idiom for looping over an array:

```
for (int i = 0; i < tests.length; i++)
    if (thirdElementIsThree(tests[i]))
        successCount++;
```

If you are using release 5.0 or a later release, you can use the for-each construct instead:

```
for (int[] test : tests)
    if (thirdElementIsThree(test))
        successCount++;
```

As bad as the first mistake is, it alone is not sufficient to account for the observed behavior. Fixing this mistake will, however, help us to find the real bug, which is more subtle. If we fix the first mistake and run the program again, it fails with this stack trace:

```
Exception in thread "main"
java.lang.ArrayIndexOutOfBoundsException: 2
    at Loop.thirdElementIsThree(Loop.java:19)
    at Loop.main(Loop.java:13)
```

Clearly, there is a bug in the `thirdElementIsThree` method: It is throwing an `ArrayIndexOutOfBoundsException`. This exception was previously masquerading as the end of the hideous exception-based loop.

The `thirdElementIsThree` method does return `true` if its argument has three or more elements and the third element is equal to 3. The problem is what it does when these conditions do not hold. If you look closely at the `boolean` expression whose value it returns, you'll see that it is a bit different from most `boolean` AND operations. The expression is `a.length >= 3 & a[2] == 3`. Usually, you see the `&&` operator used under these circumstances. This expression uses the `&` operator. Isn't that the bitwise AND operator?

It turns out that the `&` operator has another meaning. In addition to its common use as the bitwise AND operator for integral operands, it is overloaded to function as the *logical AND operator* when applied to `boolean` operands [JLS 15.22.2]. This operator differs from the more commonly used *conditional AND operator* (`&&`) in that the `&` operator always evaluates both of its operands, whereas the `&&` operator does not evaluate its right operand if its left operand evaluates to `false` [JLS 15.23]. Therefore, the `thirdElementIsThree` method attempts to access the third element of its array argument even if it has fewer than three elements. Fixing this method is as simple as replacing the `&` operator with the `&&` operator. With this change, the program prints 2 as expected:

```
private static boolean thirdElementIsThree(int[] a) {
    return a.length >= 3 && a[2] == 3;
}
```

Just as there is a logical AND operator to go with the more commonly used conditional AND operator, there is a logical OR operator (`|`) to go with the conditional OR operator (`||`) [JLS 15.22.2, 15.24]. The `|` operator always evaluates both of its operands, whereas the `||` operator does not evaluate its right operand if its left operand evaluates to `true`. It is easy to use the logical operator rather than conditional operator by accident. Unfortunately, the compiler won't help you find this error. Intentional uses of the logical operators are so rare that all uses are suspect; if you really want to use one of these operators, make your intentions clear with a comment.

In summary, do not use the hideous loop idiom where an exception is used in preference to an explicit termination test; this idiom is unclear, slow, and masks other bugs. **Be aware of the existence of the logical AND and OR operators, and do not fall prey to unintentional use.** For language designers, this is another example where operator overloading is confusing. It is not clear that there is a case for providing the logical AND and OR operators in addition to their conditional counterparts. If these operators are to be supported, they should be visually distinct from their conditional counterparts.

Puzzle 43: Exceptionally Unsafe

In JDK 1.2, Thread.stop, Thread.suspend, and a few other thread-related methods were deprecated because they are unsafe [ThreadStop]. The following method demonstrates one of the horrible things you could do with Thread.stop:

```
// Don't do this - circumvents exception checking!
public static void sneakyThrow(Throwable t) {
    Thread.currentThread().stop(t); // Deprecated!!
}
```

This nasty little method does exactly what the throw statement does, except that it bypasses all exception checking by the compiler. You can (sneakily) throw any exception, checked or otherwise, from any point in your code, and the compiler won't bat an eyelash.

It is possible to write a method that is functionally equivalent to sneakyThrow without using any deprecated methods. In fact, there are at least two ways to do it. One of them works only in release 5.0 and later releases. Can you write such a method? It must be written in Java, not in JVM bytecode. You must not change the method after its clients are compiled. Your method doesn't have to be perfect: It is acceptable if it can't throw one or two subclasses of Exception.

Solution 43: Exceptionally Unsafe

One solution to this puzzle takes advantage of a design deficiency in the `Class.newInstance` method, which instantiates a class reflectively. To quote from the documentation for this method [Java-API]: "Note that this method propagates any exception thrown by the nullary [in other words, parameterless] constructor, including a checked exception. Use of this method effectively bypasses the compile-time exception checking that would otherwise be performed." Once you know this, it's not too hard to write a `sneakyThrow` equivalent:

```
// Don't do this either - circumvents exception checking!
public class Thrower {
    private static Throwable t;

    private Thrower() throws Throwable {
        throw t;
    }

    public static synchronized void sneakyThrow(Throwable t) {
        Thrower.t = t;
        try {
            Thrower.class.newInstance();
        } catch (InstantiationException e) {
            throw new IllegalArgumentException();
        } catch (IllegalAccessException e) {
            throw new IllegalArgumentException();
        } finally {
            Thrower.t = null; // Avoid memory leak
        }
    }
}
```

A few subtle things are going on in this solution. The exception to be thrown during constructor execution can't be passed to the constructor as a parameter, because `Class.newInstance` invokes a class's parameterless constructor. Therefore, the `sneakyThrow` method stashes this exception in a static variable. To make the method thread-safe, it must be synchronized. This causes concurrent invocations to take turns using the static `t` field.

Note that the `t` field is nulled out in a `finally` block: Just because the method is sneaky doesn't mean it should also be leaky. If this field weren't nulled out, it would prevent the exception from being garbage collected. Finally, note that the method will fail with an `IllegalArgumentException` if you ask it to throw an

InstantiationException or IllegalAccessException. This is an inherent limitation of the technique.

The documentation for Class.newInstance goes on to say that "the Constructor.newInstance method avoids this problem by wrapping any exception thrown by the constructor in a (checked) InvocationTargetException." Clearly, Class.newInstance should have done the same thing, but it's far too late to correct this deficiency. Doing so would introduce a source-level incompatibility, breaking the many programs that depend on Class.newInstance. It would not be practical to deprecate this method either, because it is so commonly used. Just be aware when you use it that **Class.newInstance can throw checked exceptions that it does not declare.**

Generics, which were added in release 5.0, enable a completely different solution to this puzzle. For maximal compatibility generics are implemented by *type erasure*: **Generic type information is checked at compile time but not at run time** [JLS 4.7]. The following solution exploits this:

```
// Don't do this either - circumvents exception checking!
class TigerThrower<T extends Throwable> {
    public static void sneakyThrow(Throwable t) {
        new TigerThrower<Error>().sneakyThrow2(t);
    }

    private void sneakyThrow2(Throwable t) throws T {
        throw (T) t;
    }
}
```

This program will generate a warning when you compile it:

```
TigerThrower.java:7: warning: [unchecked] unchecked cast
found    : java.lang.Throwable, required: T
        throw (T) t;
                  ^
```

A warning is the compiler's way of telling you that you may be shooting yourself in the foot, and in fact you are. The *unchecked cast* warning tells you that the cast in question will not be checked at run time. **When you get an unchecked cast warning, modify your program to eliminate it, or convince yourself that the cast cannot fail.** If you don't, some other cast may fail at an undetermined time in the future, and you may have a hard time tracing the error to its source. In this case, it's even worse: The exception that is thrown at run time may not conform to the signature of the method. The sneakyThrow2 method exploits this methodically.

There are several lessons for platform designers. When designing libraries that are implemented outside the language, such as the reflection library, preserve all guarantees made by the language. When designing from scratch a platform that supports generic types, consider enforcing their correctness at run time. The designers of Java's generic typing facility did not have this luxury, as they were constrained by the requirement that generified libraries interoperate with existing clients. To eliminate the possibility of an exception that violates a method's signature, consider enforcing exception checking at run time.

In summary, **Java's exception checking is not enforced by the virtual machine**. It is a compile-time facility designed to make it easier to write correct programs, but it can be circumvented at run time. To reduce your exposure, **do not ignore compiler warnings.**

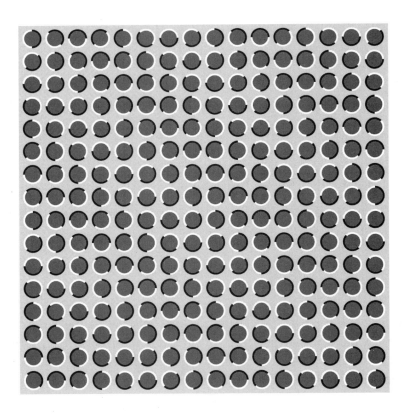

Puzzle 44: Cutting Class

Consider these two classes:

```java
public class Strange1 {
    public static void main(String[] args) {
        try {
            Missing m = new Missing();
        } catch (java.lang.NoClassDefFoundError ex) {
            System.out.println("Got it!");
        }
    }
}

public class Strange2 {
    public static void main(String[] args) {
        Missing m;
        try {
            m = new Missing();
        } catch (java.lang.NoClassDefFoundError ex) {
            System.out.println("Got it!");
        }
    }
}
```

Both Strange1 and Strange2 use this class:

```java
class Missing {
    Missing() { }
}
```

If you were to compile all three classes and then delete the file
Missing.class before running Strange1 and Strange2, you'd find that the two
programs behave differently, assuming you were running a release prior to 6.0.
One throws an uncaught NoClassDefFoundError, whereas the other prints
Got it! Which is which, and how can you explain the difference in behavior?

Solution 44: Cutting Class

The Strange1 program mentions the missing type only within its try block, so you might expect it to catch the NoClassDefFoundError and print Got it! The Strange2 program, on the other hand, declares a variable of the missing type outside the try block, so you might expect the NoClassDefFoundError generated there to be uncaught. If you tried running the programs on a release prior to 6.0, you saw the opposite behavior: Strange1 throws a NoClassDefFoundError, and Strange2 prints Got it! What could explain this strange behavior?

If you look to the Java language specification to find out where the NoClassDefFoundError should be thrown, you don't get much guidance. It says that the error may be thrown "at any point in the program that (directly or indirectly) uses the type" [JLS 12.2.1]. When the VM invokes the main method of Strange1 or Strange2, the program is using class Missing indirectly, so either program would be within its rights to throw the error at this point.

The answer to the puzzle, then, is that either program may exhibit either behavior, depending on the implementation. But that doesn't explain why in practice these programs behave exactly opposite to what you would naturally expect, on all Java implementations we know of. To find out why this is so, we need to study the compiler-generated bytecode for these programs.

If you compare the bytecode for Strange1 and Strange2, you'll find them nearly identical. Aside from the class name, the only difference is the mapping of the catch parameter ex to a VM local variable. Although the details of which program variables are assigned to which VM variables can vary from compiler to compiler, they are unlikely to vary much for programs as simple as these. Here is the code for Strange1.main as displayed by javap -c Strange1:

```
 0: new            #2; // class Missing
 3: dup
 4: invokespecial  #3; // Method Missing."<init>":()V
 7: astore_1
 8: goto 20
11: astore_1
12: getstatic      #5; // Field System.out:Ljava/io/PrintStream;
15: ldc            #6; // String "Got it!"
17: invokevirtual  #7; // Method PrintStream.println:(String;)V
20: return
Exception table:
 from to target type
    0   8    11   Class java/lang/NoClassDefFoundError
```

The corresponding code for `Strange2.main` differs in only one instruction:

```
11: astore_2
```

This is the instruction that stores the caught exception of the `catch` block into the catch parameter `ex`. In `Strange1`, this parameter is stored in VM variable 1; in `Strange2`, it is stored in VM variable 2. That is the *only* difference between these two classes, but what a difference it makes in their behavior!

To run a program, the VM loads *links* and initializes the class containing its `main` method [JLS 12.3]. The first phase of linking is *verification*. Verification ensures that a class is well formed and obeys the semantic requirements of the language. Verification is critical to maintaining the guarantees that distinguish a *safe language* like Java from an *unsafe language* like C or C++.

In classes `Strange1` and `Strange2`, the local variable `m` happens to be stored in VM variable 1. Both versions of `main` also have a *join point*, where the flow of control from two different places converge. The join point is instruction 20, which returns from `main`. Instruction 20 can be reached either by completing the `try` block normally, in which case we `goto 20` at instruction 8, or by completing the `catch` block and falling through from instruction 17 to instruction 20.

The existence of the join point causes an exception during the verification of class `Strange1` but not class `Strange2`. When it performs *flow analysis* [JLS 12.3.1] of `Strange1.main`, the verifier must *merge* the types contained in variable 1 when instruction 20 is reached by the two different paths. Two types are merged by computing their *first common superclass* [JVMS 4.9.2]. The first common superclass of two classes is the most specific superclass they share.

The state of VM variable 1 when instruction 20 is reached from instruction 8 in `Strange1.main` is that it contains an instance of the class `Missing`. When reached from instruction 17, it contains an instance of the class `NoClassDefFoundError`. In order to compute the first common superclass, the verifier must load the class `Missing` to determine its superclass. Because `Missing.class` has been deleted, the verifier can't load it and throws a `NoClassDefFoundError`. Note that this exception is thrown during verification, before class initialization and long before the `main` method begins execution. This explains why there is no stack trace printed for the uncaught exception.

If you tried running the programs in release 6.0 or later, both probably printed `Got it!` In this release, a new verifier finds the least common superclass of `Missing` and `NoClassDefFoundError` without trying to load either class. Instead, it processes a *stack map* in the class file for `Strange1` or `Strange2`. Verification succeeds, and both programs fail only once they invoke the `Missing` constructor.

To write a program that can detect when a class is missing, use reflection to refer to the class rather than using the usual language constructs [EJ Item 35]. Here is how the program looks when rewritten to use this technique:

```java
public class Strange {
    public static void main(String[] args) throws Exception {
        try {
            Object m = Class.forName("Missing").newInstance();
        } catch (ClassNotFoundException ex) {
            System.err.println("Got it!");
        }
    }
}
```

In summary, **do not depend on catching NoClassDefFoundError.** The language specification carefully describes when class initialization occurs [JLS 12.4.1], but class loading is far less predictable. More generally, **it is rarely appropriate to catch Error or its subclasses**. These exceptions are reserved for failures from which recovery is not feasible.

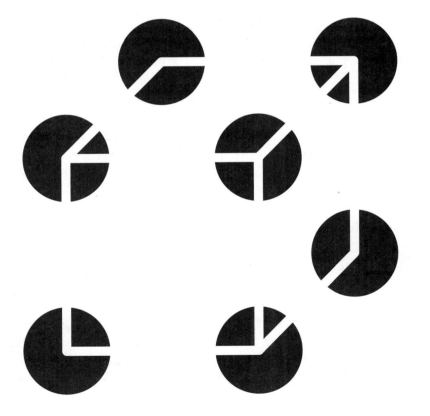

Puzzle 45: Exhausting Workout

This puzzle tests your knowledge of recursion. What does this program do?

```java
public class Workout {
    public static void main(String[] args) {
        workHard();
        System.out.println("It's nap time.");
    }

    private static void workHard() {
        try {
            workHard();
        } finally {
            workHard();
        }
    }
}
```

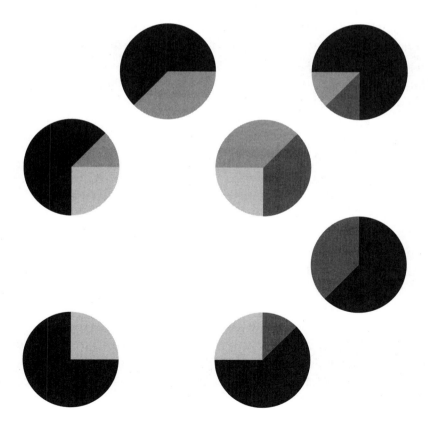

Solution 45: Exhausting Workout

If it weren't for the try-finally statement, it would be obvious what this program does: The workHard method calls itself recursively until the program throws a StackOverflowError, at which point it terminates with an uncaught exception. The try-finally statement complicates matters. When it tries to throw a StackOverflowError, the program ends up in a finally block in the workHard method, where it calls itself recursively. This seems like a prescription for an infinite loop. Does the program loop indefinitely? If you run it, it appears to do exactly that, but the only way to know for sure is to analyze its behavior.

The Java virtual machine limits the stack depth to some preset level. When this level is exceeded, the VM throws a StackOverflowError. In order to make it easier to think about the behavior of the program, let's pretend that the stack depth limit is much smaller than it really is: say, 3. Now let's trace the execution.

The main method calls workHard, which calls itself recursively from its try block. Again it calls itself from its try block. At this point, the stack depth is 3. When the workHard method attempts once more to call itself from its try block, the call fails immediately with a StackOverflowError. This error is caught in the innermost finally block, where the stack depth is already 3. From there the workHard method attempts to call itself recursively, but the call fails with a StackOverflowError. This error is caught in the finally block one level up, where the stack depth is 2. The call from this finally block has the same behavior as the call from the corresponding try block: It results eventually in a StackOverflowError. A pattern appears to be emerging, and indeed it is.

The execution of WorkOut is illustrated in Figure 5.1. In this figure, calls to workHard are represented by arrows, and executions of workHard are represented by circles. All calls are recursive except for first one. Calls that result in an immediate StackOverflowError are represented by arrows leading to gray circles. Calls from try blocks are represented by arrows pointing down and to the left, and calls from finally blocks are represented by arrows pointing down and to the right. The numbers on the arrows describe the sequence of calls.

The figure shows one call from depth 0—the call from main—two calls from depth 1, four calls from depth 2, and eight calls from depth 3, a total of fifteen calls. The eight calls from depth 3 each result in an immediate StackOverflowError. At least on a VM that limits the stack depth to 3, the program is not an infinite loop: It terminates after fifteen calls and eight exceptions.

But what about on a real VM? It still isn't an infinite loop. The call diagram looks just like the one in Figure 5.1 only much, much bigger.

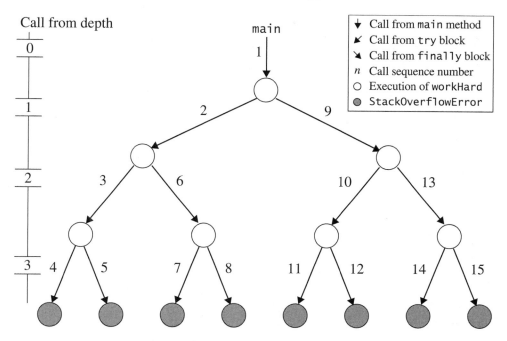

Figure 5.1   The execution of Workout.

How much bigger? A quick experiment shows that many VMs limit stack depth to 1,024. The number of calls is therefore $1 + 2 + 4 + 8 \ldots + 2^{1,024} = 2^{1,025} - 1$. The number of exceptions thrown is $2^{1,024}$. Let's assume that our machine can execute 10^{10} calls per second and generate 10^{10} exceptions per second, which is quite generous by current standards. Under these assumptions, the program will terminate in about 1.7×10^{291} years. To put this in perspective, the lifetime of our sun is estimated at 10^{10} years, so it is a safe bet that none of us will be around to see this program terminate. Although it isn't an infinite loop, it might as well be.

Technically speaking, the call diagram is a complete binary tree whose depth is the stack depth limit of the VM. The execution of the Workout program amounts to a *preorder traversal* of this tree. In a preorder traversal, the program visits a node and then recursively visits its left and right subtrees. One call is made for each edge in the tree, and one exception is thrown for each leaf node.

This puzzle doesn't have much in the way of a lesson. It does demonstrate that exponential algorithms are impractical for all but the smallest inputs, and it shows that you can write an exponential algorithm without even trying.

6

Classy Puzzlers

This chapter contains puzzlers that concern the use of classes and their instances, methods, and fields.

Puzzle 46: The Case of the Confusing Constructor

This puzzle presents you with two Confusing constructors. The main method invokes a constructor, but which one? The program's output depends on the answer. What does the program print, or is it even legal?

```java
public class Confusing {
    private Confusing(Object o) {
        System.out.println("Object");
    }

    private Confusing(double[] dArray) {
        System.out.println("double array");
    }

    public static void main(String[] args) {
        new Confusing(null);
    }
}
```

Solution 46: Case of the Confusing Constructor

The parameter passed to the constructor is the null object reference, so at first glance, it seems that the program should invoke the `Object` overloading and print `Object`. On the other hand, arrays are reference types too, so `null` could just as well apply to the `double[]` overloading. You might therefore conclude that the call is ambiguous, which suggests that the program shouldn't compile. If you tried running the program, you found that neither of these intuitions is correct: The program prints `double array`. This behavior may seem perverse, but there is a good reason for it.

Java's overload resolution process operates in two phases. The first phase selects all the methods or constructors that are accessible and applicable. The second phase selects the *most specific* of the methods or constructors selected in the first phase. One method or constructor is *less specific* than another if it can accept any parameters passed to the other [JLS 15.12.2.5].

In our program, both constructors are accessible and applicable. The constructor `Confusing(Object)` accepts any parameter passed to `Confusing(double[])`, so `Confusing(Object)` is less specific. (Every `double` array is an `Object`, but not every `Object` is a `double` array.) The most specific constructor is therefore `Confusing(double[])`, which explains the program's output.

This behavior makes sense if you pass a value of type `double[]`; it is counterintuitive if you pass `null`. The key to understanding this puzzle is that **the test for which method or constructor is most specific does not use the *actual parameters*:** the parameters appearing in the invocation. They are used only to determine which overloadings are applicable. Once the compiler determines which overloadings are applicable and accessible, it selects the most specific overloading, using only the *formal parameters*: the parameters appearing in the declaration.

To invoke the `Confusing(Object)` constructor with a `null` parameter, write `new Confusing((Object)null)`. This ensures that only `Confusing(Object)` is applicable. More generally, **to force the compiler to select a specific overloading, cast actual parameters to the declared types of the formal parameters.**

Selecting among overloadings in this fashion is unpleasant. In your APIs, ensure that clients aren't forced to go to these extremes. Ideally, you should **avoid overloading:** Use different names for different methods. Sometimes, this is not possible. Constructors don't have names, so they can't be given different names. You can, however, alleviate the problem by making constructors private and providing public static factories [EJ Item 1]. If constructors have many parameters, you can reduce the need for overloading with the Builder pattern [Gamma95].

If you do overload, ensure that all overloadings accept mutually incompatible parameter types, so that no two are applicable at the same time. Failing that, ensure that all applicable overloadings have the same behavior [EJ Item 26].

In summary, overload resolution can be confusing. Avoid overloading where possible. If you must overload, obey the guidelines outlined here to minimize confusion. If a poorly designed API forces you to select among overloadings, cast actual parameters to the types of the formal parameters of the desired overloading.

Puzzle 47: Well, Dog My Cats!

This program uses a Counter class to keep track of how many times each kind of house pet makes a noise. What does the program print?

```java
class Counter {
    private static int count;
    public static void increment() { count++; }
    public static int getCount()   { return count; }
}

class Dog extends Counter {
    public Dog() { }
    public void woof() { increment(); }
}

class Cat extends Counter {
    public Cat() { }
    public void meow() { increment(); }
}

public class Ruckus {
    public static void main(String[] args) {
        Dog[] dogs = { new Dog(), new Dog() };
        for (int i = 0; i < dogs.length; i++)
            dogs[i].woof();
        Cat[] cats = { new Cat(), new Cat(), new Cat() };
        for (int i = 0; i < cats.length; i++)
            cats[i].meow();
        System.out.print(Dog.getCount() + " woofs and ");
        System.out.println(Cat.getCount() + " meows");
    }
}
```

Solution 47: Well, Dog My Cats!

We have two dogs woofing and three cats meowing—a ruckus, to be sure—so the program should print 2 woofs and 3 meows, no? No: It prints 5 woofs and 5 meows. Where is all the extra noise coming from, and what can we do to stop it?

The sum of the number of woofs and meows printed by the program is 10, fully twice what it should be. The problem is that Dog and Cat inherit the count field from a common superclass, and count is a static field. **A single copy of each static field is shared among its declaring class and all subclasses,** so Dog and Cat use the same count field. Each call to woof or meow increments this field, so it is incremented five times. The program reads it twice, by calling Dog.getCount and Cat.getCount. In each case, 5 is returned and printed.

We cannot fix the problem by making count an instance field. That would create one counter per pet rather than one counter per kind of pet. To fix the program, we must correct a fundamental design error.

When designing one class to build on the behavior of another, you have two options: *inheritance*, in which one class extends the other; or *composition*, in which one class contains an instance of the other. Choose based on whether each instance of one class *is* an instance of the other class or *has* an instance of the other. In the first case, use inheritance; in the second, use composition. **When in doubt, favor composition over inheritance** [EJ Item 14].

Neither a dog nor a cat *is* a kind of counter, so it was wrong to use inheritance. Instead of extending Counter, Dog and Cat should each have a counter field. One counter is required for each kind of pet, rather than for each individual pet, so the fields must be static. We needn't bother with a Counter class; an int will do fine. Here is the redesigned program, which prints 2 woofs and 3 meows as expected:

```
class Dog {
    private static int woofCounter;
    public Dog() { }
    public static int woofCount() { return woofCounter; }
    public void woof() { woofCounter++; }
}

class Cat {
    private static int meowCounter;
    public Cat() { }
    public static int meowCount() { return meowCounter; }
    public void meow() { meowCounter++; }
}
```

The Ruckus class is unchanged with the exception of the two print statements, which are modified to use the new method names to access the counts:

```
System.out.print(Dog.woofCount() + " woofs, ");
System.out.println(Cat.meowCount() + " meows");
```

In summary, static fields are shared by their declaring class and any subclasses. If you need a separate copy of a field for each subclass, you must declare a separate static field in each subclass. If you need a separate copy for each instance, declare a nonstatic field in the base class. Also, favor composition over inheritance unless the derived class really is a kind of the base class.

Puzzle 48: All I Get Is Static

The following program models the behavioral difference between Basenjis and other dogs. In case you didn't know, the Basenji is a breed of small, curly-tailed dogs of African origin that do not bark. What does the program print?

```
class Dog {
    public static void bark() {
        System.out.print("woof ");
    }
}

class Basenji extends Dog {
    public static void bark() { }
}

public class Bark {
    public static void main(String args[]) {
        Dog woofer = new Dog();
        Dog nipper = new Basenji();
        woofer.bark();
        nipper.bark();
    }
}
```

Solution 48: All I Get Is Static

On casual inspection, it would appear that this program should just print woof. After all, Basenji extends Dog and defines its bark method to do nothing. The main method invokes the bark method, first on woofer the Dog and again on nipper the Basenji. Basenjis don't bark, but apparently this one does. If you ran the program, you found that it prints woof woof. What is the matter with poor Nipper?

The title of this puzzle gives a big hint. The problem is that bark is a static method, and **there is no dynamic dispatch on static methods** [JLS 15.12.4.4]. When a program calls a static method, the method to be invoked is selected at compile time, based on the compile-time type of the *qualifier*, which is the name we give to the part of the method invocation expression to the left of the dot. In this case, the qualifiers of the two method invocations are the variables woofer and nipper, both of which are declared to be of type Dog. Because they have the same compile-time type, the compiler causes the same method to be invoked: Dog.bark. This explains why the program prints woof woof. It doesn't matter that the runtime type of nipper is Basenji; only its compile-time type is considered.

To fix this program, simply remove the static modifier from the two bark method declarations. Then the bark method in Basenji will *override* rather than *hide* the bark method in Dog, and the program will print woof instead of woof woof. With overriding, you get dynamic dispatch; with hiding, you don't.

When you invoke a static method, you typically qualify it with a class rather than an expression: for example Dog.bark or Basenji.bark. When you read a Java program, you expect classes to be used as the qualifiers for static methods, which are statically dispatched, and expressions to be used as the qualifiers for instance methods, which are dynamically dispatched. Coupled with the different naming conventions for classes and variables, this provides a strong visual cue as to whether a given method invocation is static or dynamic. The program in this puzzle uses an expression as the qualifier for a static method invocation, which is misleading. **Never qualify a static method invocation with an expression.**

The confusion is compounded by the appearance of overriding. The bark method in Basenji has the same signature as the one in Dog. That is the usual formula for overriding, which suggests dynamic dispatch. In this case, however, the methods are declared static. Static methods cannot be overridden; they can only be hidden, and just because you can doesn't mean you should. To avoid confusion, **do not hide static methods**. There is nothing to gain, and much to lose, from reusing the name of a superclass's static method in a subclass.

The lesson for language designers is that invocations of class and instance methods should look different from each other. One way to further this goal is to disallow the use of expressions as qualifiers for static methods. A second way to distinguish static and instance method invocations is to use different operators, as C++ does. A third alternative is to finesse the issue by dispensing with the concept of static methods altogether, as Smalltalk does.

In summary, qualify static methods invocations with a class name, or don't qualify them at all if you're invoking them from within their own class, but never qualify them with an expression. Also, avoid hiding static methods. Together, these guidelines help eliminate the misleading appearance of overriding with dynamic dispatch for static methods.

Puzzle 49: Larger Than Life

Lest you think that this book is going entirely to the dogs, this puzzle concerns royalty. If the tabloids are to be believed, the King of Rock 'n' Roll is still alive. Not one of his many impersonators but the one true Elvis. This program estimates his current belt size by projecting the trend observed during his public performances. The program uses the idiom `Calendar.getInstance().get(Calendar.YEAR)`, which returns the current calendar year. What does the program print?

```java
public class Elvis {
    public static final Elvis INSTANCE = new Elvis();
    private final int beltSize;
    private static final int CURRENT_YEAR =
        Calendar.getInstance().get(Calendar.YEAR);

    private Elvis() {
        beltSize = CURRENT_YEAR - 1930;
    }

    public int beltSize() {
        return beltSize;
    }

    public static void main(String[] args) {
        System.out.println("Elvis wears a size " +
                    INSTANCE.beltSize() + " belt.");
    }
}
```

Solution 49: Larger Than Life

At first glance, this program appears to compute the current year minus 1930. If that were correct, in the year 2006, the program would print Elvis wears a size 76 belt. If you tried running the program, you learned that the tabloids were wrong, proving that you can't believe everything you read in the papers. It prints Elvis wears a size -1930 belt. Perhaps the King has gone on to inhabit an anti-matter universe?

This program suffers a problem caused by a circularity in the order of *class initialization* [JLS 12.4]. Let's follow it in detail. Initialization of the class Elvis is triggered by the VM's call to its main method. First, static fields are set to their default values [JLS 4.12.5]. The field INSTANCE is set to null, and CURRENT_YEAR is set to 0. Next, static field initializers are executed in order of appearance. The first static field is INSTANCE. Its value is computed by invoking the Elvis() constructor.

The constructor initializes beltSize to an expression involving the static field CURRENT_YEAR. Normally, reading a static field is one of the things that causes a class to be initialized, but we are already initializing the class Elvis. Recursive initialization attempts are simply ignored [JLS 12.4.2, step 3]. Consequently, the value of CURRENT_YEAR still has its default value of 0. That is why Elvis's belt size turns out to be -1930.

Finally, returning from the constructor to complete the class initialization of Elvis, we initialize the static field CURRENT_YEAR to 2006, assuming you're running the program in 2006. Unfortunately, it is too late for the now correct value of this field to affect the computation of Elvis.INSTANCE.beltSize, which already has the value -1930. This is the value that will be returned by all subsequent calls to Elvis.INSTANCE.beltSize().

This program shows that **it is possible to observe a final static field before it is initialized,** when it still contains the default value for its type. That is counterintuitive, because we usually think of final fields as constants. Final fields are constants only if the initializing expression is a *constant expression* [JLS 15.28].

Problems arising from cycles in class initialization are difficult to diagnose but once diagnosed are usually easy to fix. **To fix a class initialization cycle, reorder the static field initializers so that each initializer appears before any initializers that depend on it.** In this program, the declaration for CURRENT_YEAR belongs before the declaration for INSTANCE, because the creation of an Elvis instance requires that CURRENT_YEAR be initialized. Once the declaration for CURRENT_YEAR has been moved, Elvis will indeed be larger than life.

Some common design patterns are naturally subject to initialization cycles, notably the Singleton [Gamma95], which is illustrated in this puzzle, and the Service Provider Framework [EJ Item 1]. The Typesafe Enum pattern [EJ Item 21] also causes class initialization cycles. Release 5.0 adds linguistic support for this pattern with enum types. To reduce the likelihood of problems, there are some restrictions on static initializers in enum types [JLS 16.5, 8.9].

In summary, **be careful of class initialization cycles.** The simplest ones involve only a single class, but they can also involve multiple classes. It isn't always wrong to have class initialization cycles, but they may result in constructor invocation before static fields are initialized. Static fields, even final static fields, may be observed with their default value before they are initialized.

Puzzle 50: Not Your Type

This puzzle tests your understanding of Java's two classiest operators: instanceof and cast. What does each of the following three programs do?

```java
public class Type1 {
    public static void main(String[] args) {
        String s = null;
        System.out.println(s instanceof String);
    }
}

public class Type2 {
    public static void main(String[] args) {
        System.out.println(new Type2() instanceof String);
    }
}

public class Type3 {
    public static void main(String args[]) {
        Type3 t3 = (Type3) new Object();
    }
}
```

Solution 50: Not Your Type

The first program, Type1, illustrates the behavior of the instanceof operator when applied to a null object reference. Although null is a subtype of every reference type, **the instanceof operator is defined to return false when its left operand is null**. Therefore, Type1 prints false. This turns out to be the most useful behavior in practice. If instanceof tells you that an object reference is an instance of a particular type, you are assured that you can cast it to that type and invoke methods of the type without fear of a ClassCastException or a NullPointerException.

The second program, Type2, illustrates the behavior of the instanceof operator when testing an instance of one class to see whether it is an instance of an unrelated class. You might expect this program to print false. After all, an instance of Type2 isn't an instance of String, so the test should fail, right? No. The instanceof test fails at compile time with an error message like this:

```
Type2.java: inconvertible types
found: Type2, required: java.lang.String
        System.out.println(new Type2() instanceof String);
                           ^
```

The program fails to compile because **the instanceof operator requires that if both operands are class types, one must be a subtype of the other** [JLS 15.20.2, 15.16, 5.5]. Neither Type2 nor String is a subtype of the other, so the instanceof test results in a compile-time error. This error helps alert you to instanceof tests that probably don't do what you want.

The third program, Type3, illustrates the behavior of the cast operator when the static type of the expression to be cast is a superclass of the cast type. Like the instanceof operation, if both types in a cast operation are class types, one must be a subtype of the other. Although it is obvious to us that this cast will fail, the type system is not powerful enough to know that the run-time type of the expression new Object() cannot be a subtype of Type3. Therefore, the program throws a ClassCastException at run time. This is a bit counterintuitive: The second program makes perfect sense but doesn't compile; this one makes no sense but does.

In summary, the first program illustrates a useful corner case in the run-time behavior of instanceof. The second program illustrates a useful corner case in its compile-time behavior. The third program illustrates a corner case in the behavior of the cast operator where the compiler fails to save you from your folly, and the VM is left to take up the slack at run time.

Puzzle 51: What's the Point?

This program has two immutable *value classes*, which are classes whose instances represent values. One class represents a point on the plane with integer coordinates, and the second class adds a bit of color to the puzzle. The main program creates and prints an instance of the second class. What does the program print?

```java
class Point {
    private final int x, y;
    private final String name; // Cached at construction time

    Point(int x, int y) {
        this.x = x;
        this.y = y;
        name = makeName();
    }

    protected String makeName() {
        return "[" + x + "," + y + "]";
    }

    public final String toString() {
        return name;
    }
}

public class ColorPoint extends Point {
    private final String color;

    ColorPoint(int x, int y, String color) {
        super(x, y);
        this.color = color;
    }

    protected String makeName() {
        return super.makeName() + ":" + color;
    }

    public static void main(String[] args) {
        System.out.println(new ColorPoint(4, 2, "purple"));
    }
}
```

Solution 51: What's the Point?

The main method creates and prints a ColorPoint instance. The println method invokes the toString method of the ColorPoint instance, which is defined in Point. The toString method simply returns the value of the name field, which is initialized in the Point constructor by calling the makeName method. For a Point instance, the makeName method returns a string of the form [x,y]. For a ColorPoint instance, makeName is overridden to return a string of the form [x,y]:color. In this case, x is 4, y is 2, and the color is purple, so the program prints [4,2]:purple, right? No. If you ran the program, you found that it prints [4,2]:null. What is the matter with the program?

The program suffers from a problem with the order of instance initialization. To understand the problem, we will trace the program execution in detail. Here is an annotated program listing to guide us:

```
class Point {
    protected final int x, y;
    private final String name;

    Point(int x, int y) {
        this.x = x;
        this.y = y;
        name = makeName(); // 3. Invoke subclass method
    }

    protected String makeName() {
        return "[" + x + "," + y + "]";
    }

    public final String toString() {
        return name;
    }
}

public class ColorPoint extends Point {
    private final String color;

    ColorPoint(int x, int y, String color) {
        super(x, y);        // 2. Chain to Point constructor
        this.color = color; // 5. Initialize blank final-Too late
    }
```

```
    protected String makeName() {
        // 4. Executes before subclass constructor body!
        return super.makeName() + ":" + color;
    }

    public static void main(String[] args) {
        // 1. Invoke subclass constructor
        System.out.println(new ColorPoint(4, 2, "purple"));
    }
}
```

In the explanation that follows, the numbers in parentheses refer to the numbers in the comments in the annotated listing. First, the program creates a ColorPoint instance by invoking the ColorPoint constructor (1). This constructor starts by chaining to the superclass constructor, as all constructors do (2). The superclass constructor assigns 4 to the x field of the object under construction and 2 to its y field. Then the constructor invokes makeName, which is overridden by the subclass (3).

The makeName method in ColorPoint (4) executes before the body of the ColorPoint constructor, and therein lies the heart of the problem. The makeName method first invokes super.makeName, which returns [4,2] as expected. Then the method appends the string ":" and the value of the color field, converted to a string. But what is the value of the color field at this point? It has yet to be initialized, so it still contains its default value of null. Therefore, the makeName method returns the string "[4,2]:null". The superclass constructor assigns this value to the name field (3) and returns control to the subclass constructor.

The subclass constructor then assigns the value "purple" to the color field (5), but it is too late. The color field has already been used to initialize the name field in the superclass to an incorrect value. The subclass constructor returns, and the newly created ColorPoint instance is passed to the println method, which duly invokes its toString method. This method returns the contents of its name field, "[4,2]:null", so that is what the program prints.

This puzzle illustrates that **it is possible to observe the value of a final instance field before its value has been assigned,** when it still contains the default value for its type. In a sense, this puzzle is the instance analog of Puzzle 49, which observed the value of a final static field before its value had been assigned. In both cases, the puzzle resulted from a circularity in initialization. In Puzzle 49, it was class initialization; in this puzzle, it is instance initialization. Both cases have the potential for enormous confusion. There is one point where the analogy breaks down: Circular class initialization is a necessary evil, but **circular instance initialization can and should always be avoided.**

The problem arises whenever a constructor calls a method that has been over-ridden in its subclass. A method invoked in this way always runs before the instance has been initialized, when its declared fields still have their default values. To avoid this problem, **never call overridable methods from constructors,** either directly or indirectly [EJ Item 15]. This prohibition extends to instance initializers and the bodies of the *pseudoconstructors* readObject and clone. (These methods are called pseudoconstructors because they create objects without invoking a constructor.)

You can fix the problem by initializing the field name lazily, when it is first used, rather than eagerly, when the Point instance is created. With this change, the program prints [4,2]:purple as expected:

```java
class Point {
    protected final int x, y;
    private String name; // Lazily initialized

    Point(int x, int y) {
        this.x = x;
        this.y = y;
        // name initialization removed
    }

    protected String makeName() {
        return "[" + x + "," + y + "]";
    }

    // Lazily computes and caches name on first use
    public final synchronized String toString() {
        if (name == null)
            name = makeName();
        return name;
    }
}
```

Although lazy initialization fixes the problem, it is a bad idea to have one value class extend another, adding a field that affects equals comparisons. You can't provide value-based equals methods on both the superclass and subclass without violating the general contract for Object.equals or eliminating the possibility of meaningful comparisons between superclass and subclass instances [EJ Item 7].

The circular instance initialization problem is a can of worms for language designers. C++ addresses the problem by treating the type of the object as the superclass type instead of the subclass type during execution of the superclass constructor. In effect, the type of the object changes from the superclass type to the subclass once the superclass constructor finishes executing. With this solution, the original program in this puzzle would print [4,2]. We're not aware of any popular language that addresses this issue satisfactorily. Perhaps it is worth considering making circular instance initialization illegal by throwing an unchecked exception when a superclass constructor calls a subclass method.

To summarize, you must never call an overridable method from a constructor under any circumstances. The resulting circularities in instance initialization can be fatal. The solution to this problem is lazy initialization [EJ Items 13, 48].

Puzzle 52: Sum Fun

This program computes and caches a sum in one class and prints it from another. What does the program print? Here's a hint: As you may recall from algebra, the sum of the integers from 1 to n is $n(n + 1) / 2$.

```
class Cache {
    static {
        initializeIfNecessary();
    }

    private static int sum;
    public static int getSum() {
        initializeIfNecessary();
        return sum;
    }

    private static boolean initialized = false;
    private static synchronized void initializeIfNecessary() {
        if (!initialized) {
            for (int i = 0; i < 100; i++)
                sum += i;
            initialized = true;
        }
    }
}

public class Client {
    public static void main(String[] args) {
        System.out.println(Cache.getSum());
    }
}
```

Solution 52: Sum Fun

On cursory inspection, you might think that this program adds the numbers from 1 to 100, but it doesn't. Take a closer look at the loop. It is the typical half-open loop, so it goes from 0 to 99. With that in mind, you might think that the program prints the sum of the numbers from 0 to 99. Using the formula from the hint, this sum is 99 × 100 / 2, or 4,950. The program, however, thinks otherwise. It prints 9900, fully twice this value. What accounts for its enthusiasm?

The author of the program obviously went to a lot of trouble to make sure that sum was initialized before use. The program combines lazy and eager initialization and even uses synchronization to make sure that the cache works in the presence of multiple threads. It seems that this program has all the bases covered, yet it doesn't work. What's the matter with it?

Like the program in Puzzle 49, this program suffers from a class initialization ordering problem. To understand its behavior, let's trace its execution. Before it can invoke Client.main, the VM must initialize the class Client. This initialization is so simple that it isn't worth talking about. The Client.main method invokes Cache.getSum. Before the getSum method can be executed, the VM must initialize the class Cache.

Recall that class initialization executes static initializers in the order they appear in the source. The Cache class has two static initializers: the static block at the top of the class and the initialization of the static field initialized. The block appears first. It invokes the method initializeIfNecessary, which tests the field initialized. Because no value has been assigned to this field, it has the default boolean value of false. Similarly, sum has the default int value of 0. Therefore, the initializeIfNecessary method does what you'd expect, adding 4,950 to sum and setting initialized to true.

After the static block executes, the static initializer for the initialized field sets it back to false, completing the class initialization of Cache. Unfortunately, sum now contains the correct cached value, but initialized contains false: The Cache class's two pieces of critical state are out of sync.

The main method in the Client class then invokes Cache.getSum, which in turn invokes initializeIfNecessary. Because the initialized flag is false, the initializeIfNecessary method enters its loop, which adds another 4,950 to the value of sum, increasing its value to 9,900. The getSum method returns this value, and the program prints it.

Clearly, the author of this program didn't think about the order in which the initialization of the Cache class would take place. Unable to decide between eager and lazy initialization, the author tried to do both, resulting in a big mess. **Use either eager initialization or lazy initialization, never both.**

If the time and space cost to initialize a field is low or the field is required in every execution of the program, eager initialization is appropriate. If the cost is high and the field might not be required in some executions, lazy initialization may be preferable [EJ Item 48]. Also, lazy initialization may be necessary to break a cycle in class or instance initialization (Puzzle 51).

The Cache class could be repaired either by reordering the static initializations so the initialized field was not reset to false after sum was initialized or by removing the explicit static initialization of the initialized field. Although the resulting programs would work, they would still be confusing and ill-structured. The Cache class should be rewritten to use eager initialization. The resulting version is obviously correct and much simpler than the original. With this version of the Cache class, the program prints 4950 as expected:

```
class Cache {
    private static final int SUM = computeSum();

    private static int computeSum() {
        int result = 0;
        for (int i = 0; i < 100; i++)
            result += i;
        return result;
    }

    public static int getSum() {
        return SUM;
    }
}
```

Note that we use a helper method to initialize sum. A helper method is generally preferable to a static block, as it lets you name the computation. In the rare cases when you must use a static block to initialize a static field, put the block immediately after the field declaration. This enhances clarity and eliminates the possibility of static initialization competing with a static block, as in the original program.

In summary, **think about class initialization order, especially when it is nontrivial.** Do your best to keep the class initialization sequence simple. Use eager initialization unless you have some good reason to use lazy initialization, such as performance or the need to break a cycle in initialization.

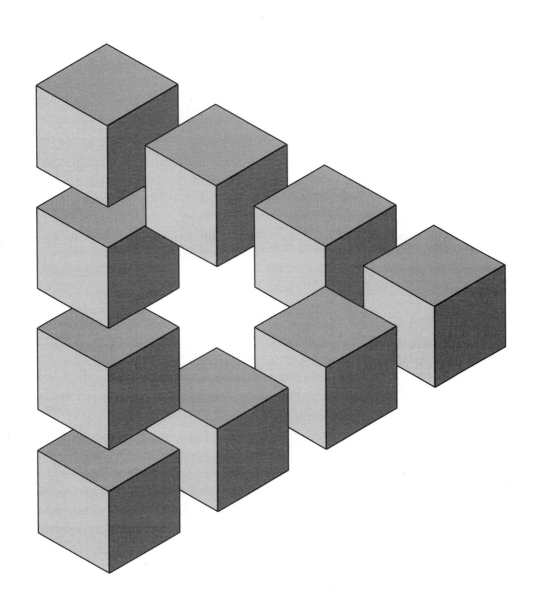

Puzzle 53: Do Your Thing

Now it's your turn to write some code. Suppose that you have a library class called `Thing` whose sole constructor takes an `int` parameter:

```
public class Thing {
    public Thing(int i) { ... }
    ...
}
```

A `Thing` instance provides no way to get the value of its constructor parameter. Because `Thing` is a library class, you have no access to its internals, and you can't modify it.

Suppose that you want to write a subclass called `MyThing`, with a constructor that computes the parameter to the superclass constructor by invoking the method `SomeOtherClass.func()`. The value returned by this method changes unpredictably from call to call. Finally, suppose that you want to store the value that was passed to the superclass constructor in a final instance field of the subclass for future use. This is the code that you'd naturally write:

```
public class MyThing extends Thing {
    private final int arg;

    public MyThing() {
        super(arg = SomeOtherClass.func());
        ...
    }
    ...
}
```

Unfortunately, it isn't legal. If you try to compile it, you'll get an error message that looks something like this:

```
MyThing.java:
  can't reference arg before supertype constructor has been called
        super(arg = SomeOtherClass.func());
              ^
```

How can you rewrite `MyThing` to achieve the desired effect? The `MyThing()` constructor must be thread-safe: Multiple threads may invoke it concurrently.

Solution 53: Do Your Thing

You could try to stash the result of the invocation SomeOtherClass.func() in a static field prior to invoking the Thing constructor. This solution is workable but awkward. In order to achieve thread-safety, you must synchronize access to the stashed value, which requires unimaginable contortions. Some of these contortions can be avoided by using a thread-local static field (java.util.ThreadLocal), but a much better solution exists.

The preferred solution is inherently thread-safe as well as elegant. It involves the use of second, private constructor in MyThing:

```
public class MyThing extends Thing {
    private final int arg;

    public MyThing() {
        this(SomeOtherClass.func());
    }

    private MyThing(int i) {
        super(i);
        arg = i;
    }
}
```

This solution uses an *alternate constructor invocation* [JLS 8.8.7.1]. This feature allows one constructor in a class to chain to another constructor in the same class. In this case, MyThing() chains to the private constructor MyThing(int), which performs the required instance initialization. Within the private constructor, the value of the expression SomeOtherClass.func() has been captured in the parameter i and can be stored in the final field arg after the superclass constructor returns.

The *Private Constructor Capture* idiom illustrated by the solution to this puzzle is a useful pattern to add to your bag of tricks. We've seen some genuinely ugly code that could have been avoided with this pattern.

Puzzle 54: Null and Void

Here is yet another variant on the classic Hello World program. What does this one do?

```
public class Null {
    public static void greet() {
        System.out.println("Hello world!");
    }

    public static void main(String[] args) {
        ((Null) null).greet();
    }
}
```

Solution 54: Null and Void

This program looks as though it ought to throw a `NullPointerException`. The `main` method invokes the `greet` method on the constant `null`, and you can't invoke a method on `null`, can you? Well, sometimes you can. If you ran the program, you found that it prints "`Hello world!`"

The key to understanding this puzzle is that `Null.greet` is a static method. As you saw in Puzzle 48, it is a bad idea to use an expression as the qualifier in a static method invocation, but that is exactly what this program does. Not only does the run-time type of the object referenced by the expression's value play no role in determining which method gets invoked, but also the identity of the object, if any, plays no role. In this case, there is no object, but that makes no difference. **A qualifying expression for a static method invocation is evaluated, but its value is ignored.** There is no requirement that the value be non-null.

To eliminate the confusion in this program, you could invoke the `greet` method by using its class as a qualifier:

```
public static void main(String[] args) {
    Null.greet();
}
```

Better yet, you could eliminate the qualifier entirely:

```
public static void main(String[] args) {
    greet();
}
```

In summary, the lesson of this puzzle is exactly the same as that of Puzzle 48: Qualify static method invocations with a type, or don't qualify them at all. For language designers, it should not be possible to pollute the invocation of a static method with an expression, which serves only to confuse.

Puzzle 55: Creationism

Sometimes, it is useful for a class to keep track of how many instances have been created. This is typically done by having its constructors increment a private static field. In the program that follows, the Creature class demonstrates this technique, and the Creator class exercises it, printing the number of Creature instances it has created. What does the program print?

```java
public class Creator {
    public static void main(String[] args) {
        for (int i = 0; i < 100; i++)
            Creature creature = new Creature();
        System.out.println(Creature.numCreated());
    }
}

class Creature {
    private static long numCreated = 0;

    public Creature() {
        numCreated++;
    }

    public static long numCreated() {
        return numCreated;
    }
}
```

Solution 55: Creationism

This is a trick question. The program looks as though it ought to print 100, but it doesn't print anything, because it doesn't compile. If you tried to compile it, you may have found the compiler diagnostics to be less than helpful. This is what javac prints:

```
Creator.java:4: not a statement
        Creature creature = new Creature();
        ^

Creator.java:4: ';' expected
        Creature creature = new Creature();
              ^
```

A local variable declaration looks like a statement but technically speaking is not; it is a *local variable declaration statement* [JLS 14.4]. The syntax of the language does not allow a local variable declaration statement as the statement repeated by a for, while, or do loop [JLS 14.12-14]. **A local variable declaration can appear only as a statement directly within a block.** (A block is a pair of curly braces and the statements and declarations contained within it.)

There are two ways to fix the problem. The obvious way is to place the declaration in a block:

```
for (int i = 0; i < 100; i++) {
    Creature creature = new Creature();
}
```

Note, however, that the program is not using the local variable creature. Therefore, it makes more sense to replace the declaration with a naked constructor invocation, emphasizing that the reference to the newly created object is being discarded:

```
for (int i = 0; i < 100; i++)
    new Creature();
```

If either of these changes is made, the program will print 100 as expected.

Note that the variable used to keep track of the number of Creature instances (numCreated) is a long rather than an int. It is quite conceivable that a program might create more instances of some class than the maximum int value but not the maximum long value. The maximum int value is $2^{31} - 1$, or about 2.1×10^9;

the maximum long value is $2^{63} - 1$, or about 9.2×10^{18}. Today, it is possible to create about 10^8 objects per second, which means that a program would have to run about three thousand years before a long object counter would overflow. Even in the face of increasing hardware speeds, long object counters should be adequate for the foreseeable future.

Also note that the creation counting strategy in this puzzle is not thread-safe. If multiple threads can create objects in parallel, the code to increment the counter and the code to read it must be synchronized:

```java
// Thread-safe creation counter
class Creature {
    private static long numCreated;

    public Creature() {
        synchronized (Creature.class) {
            numCreated++;
        }
    }

    public static synchronized long numCreated() {
        return numCreated;
    }
}
```

Alternatively, if you are using release 5.0 or a later release, you can use an AtomicLong instance, which obviates the need for synchronization in the face of concurrency.

```java
// Thread-safe creation counter using AtomicLong;
import java.util.concurrent.atomic.AtomicLong;

class Creature {
    private static AtomicLong numCreated = new AtomicLong();

    public Creature() {
        numCreated.incrementAndGet();
    }

    public static long numCreated() {
        return numCreated.get();
    }
}
```

Note that it is *not* sufficient to declare numCreated to be volatile. The volatile modifier guarantees that other threads will see the most recent value assigned to a field, but it does not make the increment operation atomic.

In summary, a local variable declaration cannot be used as the repeated statement in a for, while, or do loop but can appear only as a statement directly within a block. Also, **when using a variable to count instance creations, use a long rather than an int, to prevent overflow.** Finally, if you are going to create instances in multiple threads, either synchronize access to the instance counter or use an AtomicLong.

7

Library Puzzlers

The puzzles in this chapter concern basic library-related topics, such as Object methods, collections, Date, and Calendar.

Puzzle 56: Big Problem

As a warm-up, test your knowledge of BigInteger. What does this program print?

```java
import java.math.BigInteger;
public class BigProblem {
    public static void main(String[] args) {
        BigInteger fiveThousand    = new BigInteger("5000");
        BigInteger fiftyThousand   = new BigInteger("50000");
        BigInteger fiveHundredThousand
                                   = new BigInteger("500000");
        BigInteger total = BigInteger.ZERO;
        total.add(fiveThousand);
        total.add(fiftyThousand);
        total.add(fiveHundredThousand);
        System.out.println(total);
    }
}
```

Solution 56: Big Problem

You might think that this program prints 555000. After all, it sets total to the BigInteger representation for 0 and then adds 5,000, 50,000, and 500,000. If you ran the program, you found that it doesn't print 555000 but 0. Apparently all that addition has no effect on total.

There is a good reason for this: **BigInteger instances are immutable.** So are instances of String, BigDecimal, and the wrapper types: Integer, Long, Short, Byte, Character, Boolean, Float, and Double. You can't change their values. Instead of modifying existing instances, operations on these types return new instances. At first, immutable types might seem unnatural, but they have many advantages over their mutable counterparts. Immutable types are easier to design, implement, and use; they are less error prone and more secure [EJ Item 13].

To perform a computation on a variable containing a reference to an immutable object, assign the result of the computation to the variable. Doing this yields the following program, which prints the expected result of 555000:

```
import java.math.BigInteger;

public class BigProblem {
    public static void main(String [] args) {
        BigInteger fiveThousand  = new BigInteger("5000");
        BigInteger fiftyThousand = new BigInteger("50000");
        BigInteger fiveHundredThousand
                                 = new BigInteger("500000");

        BigInteger total = BigInteger.ZERO;
        total = total.add(fiveThousand);
        total = total.add(fiftyThousand);
        total = total.add(fiveHundredThousand);
        System.out.println(total);
    }
}
```

The lesson of this puzzle is: **Do not be misled into thinking that immutable types are mutable.** This is a common error among beginning Java programmers. In fairness, the names of some methods in Java's immutable types help to lead them astray. Names like add, subtract, and negate suggest that these methods mutate the instance on which they're invoked. Better names would be plus, minus, and negation.

A lesson for API designers, then, is: When naming methods for immutable types, prefer prepositions and nouns to verbs. Prepositions are appropriate for methods with parameters and nouns for parameterless methods. A lesson for language designers is, as in Puzzle 2, that it might be worth offering limited support for operator overloading so that arithmetic operators can be made to work with numerical reference types, such as BigInteger. Not even a beginner would think that evaluating the expression total + fiveThousand would have any effect on the value of total.

Puzzle 57: What's in a Name?

This program consists of a simple immutable class that represents a name, with a main method that puts a name into a set and checks whether the set contains the name. What does the program print?

```java
import java.util.*;

public class Name {
    private final String first, last;

    public Name(String first, String last) {
        this.first = first;
        this.last = last;
    }

    public boolean equals(Object o) {
        if (!(o instanceof Name))
            return false;
        Name n = (Name)o;
        return n.first.equals(first) && n.last.equals(last);
    }

    public static void main(String[] args) {
        Set<Name> s = new HashSet<Name>();
        s.add(new Name("Mickey", "Mouse"));
        System.out.println(
            s.contains(new Name("Mickey", "Mouse")));
    }
}
```

Solution 57: What's in a Name?

A Name instance consists of a first name and a last name. Two Name instances are equal, as computed by the equals method, if their first names are equal and their last names are equal. First names and last names are compared using the equals method defined in String. Two strings are equal if they consist of the same characters in the same order. Therefore, two Name instances are equal if they represent the same name. For example, the following method invocation returns true:

```
new Name("Mickey", "Mouse").equals(new Name("Mickey", "Mouse"))
```

The main method of the program creates two Name instances, both representing Mickey Mouse. The program puts the first instance into a hash set and then checks whether the set contains the second. The two Name instances are equal, so it might seem that the program should print true. If you ran it, it almost certainly printed false. What is wrong with the program?

The bug is that Name violates the hashCode contract. This might seem strange, as Name doesn't even have a hashCode method, but that is precisely the problem. The Name class overrides the equals method, and the hashCode contract demands that equal objects have equal hash codes. To fulfill this contract, **you must override hashCode whenever you override equals** [EJ Item 8].

Because it fails to override hashCode, the Name class inherits its hashCode implementation from Object. This implementation returns an *identity-based* hash code. In other words, distinct objects are likely to have unequal hash values, even if they are equal. Name does not fulfill the hashCode contract, so the behavior of a hash set containing Name elements is unspecified.

When the program puts the first Name instance into the hash set, the set puts an entry for this instance into a hash bucket. The set chooses the hash bucket based on the hash value of the instance, as computed by its hashCode method. When it checks whether the second Name instance is contained in the hash set, the program chooses which bucket to search based on the hash value of the second instance. Because the second instance is distinct from the first, it is likely to have a different hash value. If the two hash values map to different buckets, the contains method will return false: The beloved rodent is in the hash set, but the set can't find him.

Suppose that the two Name instances map to the same bucket. Then what? All HashSet implementations that we know of have an optimization in which each entry stores the hash value of its element in addition to the element itself. When searching for an element, the implementation selects the appropriate hash bucket and traverses its entries, comparing the hash value stored in each entry with the hash value of the desired element. Only if the two hash values are equal does the implementation check the elements for equality. This optimization makes sense because it is usually much cheaper to compare hash codes than elements.

Because of this optimization, it is not enough for the hash set to search in the right bucket; the two Name instances must have equal hash values in order for the hash set to recognize them as equal. The odds that the program prints true are therefore the odds that two consecutively created objects have the same identity hash code. A quick experiment showed these odds to be about one in 25,000,000. Results may vary depending on which Java implementation is used, but you are highly unlikely to see the program print true on any JRE we know of.

To fix the problem, simply add an appropriate hashCode method to the Name class. Although any method whose return value is determined solely by the first and last name will satisfy the contract, a high-quality hash function should attempt to return different hash values for different names. The following method will do nicely [EJ Item 8]. Once this method is added, the program will print true as expected:

```
public int hashCode() {
    return 37 * first.hashCode() + last.hashCode();
}
```

In summary, always override hashCode when you override equals. More generally, obey the general contract when you override a method that has one. This is an issue for most of the non-final methods declared in Object [EJ Chapter 3]. Failure to follow this advice can result in arbitrary, unspecified behavior.

Puzzle 58: Making a Hash of It

This puzzle attempts to learn from the mistakes of the previous one. Again the program consists of a Name class and a main method that puts a name into a hash set and checks whether the set contains the name. This time, however, the Name class does override the hashCode method. What does this program print?

```java
import java.util.*;

public class Name {
    private final String first, last;

    public Name(String first, String last) {
        this.first = first; this.last = last;
    }

    public boolean equals(Name n) {
        return n.first.equals(first) && n.last.equals(last);
    }

    public int hashCode() {
        return 31 * first.hashCode() + last.hashCode();
    }

    public static void main(String[] args) {
        Set<Name> s = new HashSet<Name>();
        s.add(new Name("Donald", "Duck"));
        System.out.println(
            s.contains(new Name("Donald", "Duck")));
    }
}
```

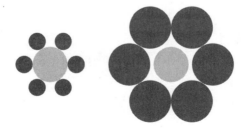

Solution 58: Making a Hash of It

As in Puzzle 57, the `main` method of this program creates two `Name` instances, both representing the same name. This time it, happens to be Donald Duck rather than Mickey Mouse, but that shouldn't make much difference. Again, the `main` method puts the first instance into a hash set and then checks whether the set contains the second. This time, the `hashCode` method is clearly correct, so it looks as though the program ought to print `true`. Once again, appearances are deceiving: It always prints `false`. What's wrong this time?

The flaw in this program is similar to the one in Puzzle 57. In that puzzle, `Name` overrides the `equals` method but fails to override `hashCode`; in this puzzle, `Name` overrides the `hashCode` method but fails to override `equals`. That is not to say that `Name` doesn't declare an `equals` method; it does, but it's the wrong one. The `Name` class declares an `equals` method whose argument is of type `Name` rather than `Object`. The author of this class probably intended to override the `equals` method but mistakenly *overloaded* it [JLS 8.4.8.1, 8.4.9].

The `HashSet` class uses the `equals(Object)` method to test elements for equality; it is of no consequence to `HashSet` that `Name` declares an `equals(Name)` method. So where does `Name` get its `equals(Object)` method? It is inherited from `Object`. This method returns `true` only if its argument and the object on which it is invoked are one and the same. The `main` method of our program inserts one `Name` instance into the hash set and tests for the presence of another, so the test is guaranteed to return `false`. To us, both instances may represent the wonderful waterfowl, but to the hash map, they're just two unequal objects.

Fixing the program is as simple as replacing the overloaded `equals` method with the overriding one found in Puzzle 57. With this `equals` method, the program prints `true` as expected:

```
public boolean equals(Object o) {
    if (!(o instanceof Name))
        return false;
    Name n = (Name)o;
    return n.first.equals(first) && n.last.equals(last);
}
```

To make the program work, you merely have to add the overriding `equals` method. You don't have to eliminate the overloaded one, but you are better off without it. **Overloadings represent opportunities for error and confusion** [EJ Item 26]. If compatibility dictates that you must retain a "self-typed" `equals` method, implement the Object overloading in terms of the self-typed overloading to ensure identical behavior:

```
public boolean equals(Object o) {
    return o instanceof Name && equals((Name) o);
}
```

The lesson of this puzzle is: Don't overload a method when you want to override. **To avoid unintentional overloading, mechanically copy the declaration of each superclass method that you want to override,** or better yet, let your IDE do it for you. Besides protecting you against unintentional overloading, this protects you against misspelling method names. If you are using release 5.0 or a later release, apply the @Override annotation to each method declaration that is intended to override a superclass method:

```
@Override public boolean equals(Object o) { ... }
```

With this annotation, the program will not compile unless the annotated method overrides a superclass method. For language designers, it is worth considering a mandatory modifier on each method declaration that overrides a superclass method.

Puzzle 59: What's the Difference?

This program computes the differences between pairs of elements in an int array, puts these differences into a set, and prints the size of the set. What does the program print?

```
import java.util.*;

public class Differences {
    public static void main(String[] args) {
        int[] vals = { 789, 678, 567, 456,
                        345, 234, 123, 012 };
        Set<Integer> diffs = new HashSet<Integer>();

        for (int i = 0; i < vals.length; i++)
            for (int j = i; j < vals.length; j++)
                diffs.add(vals[i] - vals[j]);
        System.out.println(diffs.size());
    }
}
```

Solution 59: What's the Difference?

The outer loop iterates over every element in the array. The inner loop iterates over every element from the current element in the outer-loop iteration to the last element in the array. Therefore, the nested loop iterates over every possible pair of elements from the array exactly once. (Elements may be paired with themselves.) Each iteration of the nested loop computes the (positive) difference between the pair of elements and stores that difference in the set, which eliminates duplicates. Therefore, this puzzle amounts to the question, How many unique positive differences are there between pairs of elements from the vals array?

When you look at the array, a pattern becomes evident: The difference between consecutive elements is 111. Therefore, the difference between two elements is a function of how far apart they are in the array. If two elements are identical, the difference is 0; if they're adjacent, it's 111; if they're separated by one element, it's 222; and so on. It would appear that the number of differences is the same as the number of distances, which is the size of the array, or 8. If you ran the program, however, you found that it prints 14. What's going on?

This analysis contains one small flaw. To investigate the flaw, we can print out the contents of the set by removing the characters .size() from the println statement. Doing this produces the following output:

```
[111, 222, 446, 557, 668, 113, 335, 444, 779, 224, 0, 333, 555, 666]
```

Not all these numbers are multiples of 111. There must be two adjacent elements in the vals array whose difference is 113. If you look at the array declaration, it may not be clear why this is so:

```
int vals[] = { 789, 678, 567, 456,
               345, 234, 123, 012 };
```

But if you print the contents of the array, here is what you will see:

```
[789, 678, 567, 456, 345, 234, 123, 10]
```

Why is the final element of the array 10 instead of 12? Because **integer literals beginning with a 0 are interpreted as octal values** [JLS 3.10.1]. This obscure construct is a holdover from the C programming language. C dates from the 1970s, when octal was much more commonly used than it is today.

Once you know that 012 == 10, it is obvious why the program prints 14: There are 6 unique nonzero differences not involving the final array element, 7 unique nonzero differences involving the final array element, and there is zero, for a total of 14 unique differences. It is even more obvious how to fix the program: Replace the octal integer literal 012 with the decimal integer literal 12. If you do this, the program will print 8 as expected.

The lesson of this puzzle is simple: **Never pad an integer literal with zeros;** this turns it into an octal literal. The intentional use of octal integer literals is so rare that you should probably comment every use. The lesson for language designers is to exercise restraint when deciding what features to include. When in doubt, leave it out.

Puzzle 60: One-Liners

Now it's your turn to write some code. Each of the following puzzles can be solved with a method whose body contains but a single line. On your mark, get set, code!

A. Write a method that takes a List of elements and returns a new List containing the same elements in the same order with the second and subsequent occurrences of any duplicate elements removed. For example, if you pass in a list containing "spam", "sausage", "spam", "spam", "bacon", "spam", "tomato", and "spam", you'll get back a new list containing "spam", "sausage", "bacon", and "tomato".

B. Write a method that takes a string containing zero or more tokens separated by commas and returns an array of strings representing the tokens in the order they occur in the input string. Each comma may be followed by zero or more white space characters, which must be ignored by the method. For example, if you pass the string "fear, surprise, ruthless efficiency, an almost fanatical devotion to the Pope, nice red uniforms", you'll get back a five-element string array containing "fear", "surprise", "ruthless efficiency", "an almost fanatical devotion to the Pope", and "nice red uniforms".

C. Suppose that you have a multidimensional array that you want to print for debugging purposes. You don't know how many levels the array has or what type of objects are stored at each level in the array. Write a method that shows you all the elements at each level.

D. Write a method that takes two int values and returns true if the first value has more bits set than the second in its two's-complement binary representation.

Solution 60: One-Liners

A. It is well known that you can eliminate all the duplicate elements in a collection by putting its contents into a Set. In this puzzle, you were also asked to preserve the order of the original collection. Luckily, there is a Set implementation that maintains its elements in insertion order, and it offers near-HashMap performance to boot. It's called LinkedHashSet, and it was added to the platform in release 1.4. Internally, it is implemented as a hash table with a linked list running through it. There is also a map version that you can use to make custom caches. Once you know about LinkedHashSet, it's easy to solve this puzzle. The only other wrinkle is that you were asked to return a List, so you have to initialize a List with the contents of the LinkedHashSet. Putting it all together, here is the solution:

```
static <E> List<E> withoutDuplicates(List<E> original) {
    return new ArrayList<E>(new LinkedHashSet<E>(original));
}
```

B. When it comes to parsing a string into tokens, many programmers' thoughts turn immediately to StringTokenizer. This is most unfortunate, as StringTokenizer became obsolete as of release 1.4, when regular expressions were added to the platform (java.util.regex). If you tried to solve this puzzle with StringTokenizer, you quickly realized that it isn't a very good fit. With regular expressions, it's a snap. To solve this puzzle in one line, use the convenience method String.split, which takes a regular expression describing the token delimiter. If you haven't used regular expressions before, they may look a bit cryptic, but they're amazingly powerful and well worth learning:

```
static String[] parse(String string) {
    return string.split(",\\s*");
}
```

C. This is a trick question. You don't even have to write a method. The method is provided for you in release 5.0 and later releases, and is called Arrays.deepToString. If you pass it an array of object references, it returns a nice string representation. It can deal with nested arrays and even circular references, where an array element refers to the enclosing array, directly or indirectly. In fact, the Arrays class in release 5.0 provides a whole family of toString, equals, and hashCode methods that allow you to print, compare, or hash the contents of any array of primitives or object references.

D. In order to solve this puzzle in one line, you need to know that a whole family of *bit-twiddling* methods were added to the platform in release 5.0. The wrapper classes for the integral types (`Integer`, `Long`, `Short`, `Byte`, and `Char`) now support common bit-manipulation operations, including `highestOneBit`, `lowestOneBit`, `numberOfLeadingZeros`, `numberOfTrailingZeros`, `bitCount`, `rotateLeft`, `rotateRight`, `reverse`, `signum`, and `reverseBytes`. In this case, what you need is `Integer.bitCount`, which returns the number of set bits in an `int` value:

```
static boolean hasMoreBitsSet(int i, int j) {
    return (Integer.bitCount(i) > Integer.bitCount(j));
}
```

In summary, each major release of the Java platform has a few new "hidden treasures" in the libraries. All four parts of this puzzle relied on such treasures. Each time a new release of the platform comes out, you should study the *new features and enhancements* page so you don't miss out on any of the goodies that the release has to offer [Features-1.4, Features-5.0]. **Knowing what's in the libraries can save you lots of time and effort and can enhance the speed and quality of your programs.**

Puzzle 61: The Dating Game

The following program exercises some basic features of the `Date` and `Calendar` classes. What does it print?

```
import java.util.*;

public class DatingGame {
    public static void main(String[] args) {
        Calendar cal = Calendar.getInstance();
        cal.set(1999, 12, 31); // Year, Month, Day
        System.out.print(cal.get(Calendar.YEAR) + " ");

        Date d = cal.getTime();
        System.out.println(d.getDay());
    }
}
```

Solution 61: The Dating Game

This program creates a `Calendar` instance that appears to represent New Year's Eve, 1999, and prints the year followed by the day. It seems that the program should print 1999 31, but it doesn't; it prints 2000 1. Could this be the dreaded Y2K problem?

No, it's something much worse: It is the dreaded `Date`/`Calendar` problem. When the Java platform was first released, its only support for calendar calculations was the `Date` class. This class was limited in power, especially when it came to support for internationalization, and it had a basic design flaw: `Date` instances were mutable. In release 1.1, the `Calendar` class was added to the platform to rectify the shortcomings of `Date`; most `Date` methods were deprecated. Unfortunately, this only made a bad situation worse. Our program illustrates a few of the problems with the `Date` and `Calendar` APIs.

The program's first bug is in the method invocation `cal.set(1999, 12, 31)`. When months are represented numerically, convention dictates that the first month be assigned the number 1. Unfortunately, **Date represents January as 0, and Calendar perpetuates this mistake.** Therefore, this method invocation sets the calendar to the thirty-first day of the thirteenth month of 1999. But the standard (Gregorian) calendar has only 12 months; surely this method invocation should cause an `IllegalArgumentException`? It should, but it doesn't. The `Calendar` class silently substitutes the first month of the next year, in this case, 2000. This explains the first number printed by our program (2000).

There are two ways to fix this problem. You could change the second parameter of the `cal.set` invocation from 12 to 11, but that would be confusing. The number 11 would suggest November to readers. It would be better to use the constant that `Calendar` declares for this purpose, which is `Calendar.DECEMBER`.

What about the second number printed by the program? The `cal.set` invocation clearly indicates that the calendar is set to the thirty-first day of the month. The `Date` instance d represents the same point in time as the `Calendar`, so its getDay method should return 31, but the program prints 1. What is going on?

To find out, you have to read the documentation, which says that **Date.getDay returns the day of the *week* represented by the Date instance, not the day of the month.** The returned value is 0-based, starting at Sunday, so the 1 printed by the program indicates that January 31, 2000, fell on a Monday. Note that the corresponding `Calendar` method, `get(Calendar.DAY_OF_WEEK)`, inexplicably returns a day-of-the-week value that is 1-based, not 0-based like the value returned by its `Date` counterpart.

There are also two ways to fix this problem. You could call the confusingly named `Date.date` method, which returns the day of the month. Like most `Date` methods, however, it is deprecated, so you would be better off dispensing with `Date` entirely and calling the `Calendar` method `get(Calendar.DAY_OF_MONTH)`. With both problems fixed, the program prints 1999 31 as expected:

```java
public class DatingGame {
    public static void main(String[] args) {
        Calendar cal = Calendar.getInstance();
        cal.set(1999, Calendar.DECEMBER, 31);
        System.out.print(cal.get(Calendar.YEAR) + " ");
        System.out.println(cal.get(Calendar.DAY_OF_MONTH));
    }
}
```

This puzzle only scratches the surface of the defects in `Calendar` and `Date`. These APIs are minefields. Other serious problems with `Calendar` include weak typing (nearly everything is an `int`), an overly complex state-space, poor structure, inconsistent naming, and inconsistent semantics. **Be careful when using `Calendar` or `Date`; always consult the API documentation.**

The lesson for API designers is: If you can't get it right the first time, at least get it right the second; there may not be a third. If your first attempt at an API has serious problems, your customers may be forgiving and give you another chance. If your second attempt has problems, you may be stuck with them for good.

Puzzle 62: The Name Game

This program puts two mappings into a map and prints its size. What does it print?

```java
import java.util.*;

public class NameGame {
    public static void main(String args[]) {
        Map<String, String> m =
            new IdentityHashMap<String, String>();
        m.put("Mickey", "Mouse");
        m.put("Mickey", "Mantle");
        System.out.println(m.size());
    }
}
```

Solution 62: The Name Game

A naive analysis of this program suggests that it should print 1. The program puts two mappings into the map, but both have the same key (Mickey). It's a map, not a multimap, so the baseball legend (Mickey Mantle) should overwrite the animated rodent (Mickey Mouse), leaving a single mapping in the map.

A more thorough analysis casts doubt on this prediction. The documentation for IdentityHashMap says, "this class implements the Map interface with a hash table, using reference-equality in place of [value]-equality when comparing keys" [Java-API]. In other words, the program will print 2 rather than 1 if the second occurrence of the string literal "Mickey" evaluates to a different String instance from the first. So does the program print 1, does it print 2, or might its behavior vary from implementation to implementation?

If you tried running the program, you found that it prints 1, as suggested by our naive analysis, even though the analysis is flawed. Why? The language specification guarantees that string constants are *interned*. In other words, string constants that are equal will also be identical [JLS 15.28]. This ensures that the second occurrence of the string literal "Mickey" in our program refers to the same String instance as the first, so our use of an IdentityHashMap in place of a general-purpose Map implementation, such as HashMap, does not affect the program's behavior. Our naive analysis neglects two details, but these details effectively cancel each other out.

The important lesson of this puzzle is: **Don't use IdentityHashMap unless you need its identity-based semantics; it is not a general-purpose Map implementation.** These semantics are useful for implementing *topology-preserving object graph transformations*, such as serialization or deep-copying. A secondary lesson is that string constants are interned. As mentioned in Puzzle 13, programs should rarely, if ever, depend on this behavior for their correct operation.

Puzzle 63: More of the Same

This program is similar to the previous one, except this one is object-oriented. Learning from our previous mistake, this version uses a general-purpose Map implementation, a HashMap, in place of the previous program's IdentityHashMap. What does this program print?

```java
import java.util.*;

public class MoreNames {
    private Map<String,String> m = new HashMap<String,String>();

    public void MoreNames() {
        m.put("Mickey", "Mouse");
        m.put("Mickey", "Mantle");
    }

    public int size() {
        return m.size();
    }

    public static void main(String args[]) {
        MoreNames moreNames = new MoreNames();
        System.out.println(moreNames.size());
    }
}
```

Solution 63: More of the Same

This program looks straightforward. The main method creates a MoreNames instance by invoking the parameterless constructor. The MoreNames instance contains a private Map field (m), which is initialized to an empty HashMap. The parameterless constructor appears to put two mappings into the map m, both with the same key (Mickey). As we know from the previous puzzle, the ballplayer (Mickey Mantle) should overwrite the rodent (Mickey Mouse), leaving a single mapping. The main method then invokes the size method on the MoreNames instance, which in turn invokes size on the map m and returns the result, presumably 1. There's only one problem with this analysis: The program prints 0, not 1. What's wrong with the analysis?

The problem is that MoreNames has no programmer-declared constructor. What it does have is a void-returning instance method called MoreNames, which the author probably intended as a constructor. Unfortunately, the presence of a return type (void) turned the intended constructor declaration into a method declaration, and the method never gets invoked. Because the MoreNames has no programmer-declared constructor, the compiler helpfully (?) generates a public parameterless constructor that does nothing beyond initializing the fields of the instance that it creates. As previously mentioned, m is initialized to an empty HashMap. When the size method is invoked on this HashMap, it returns 0, and that is what the program prints.

Fixing the program is as simple as removing the void return type from the MoreNames declaration, which turns it from an instance method declaration into a constructor declaration. With this change, the program prints 1 as expected.

The lesson of this puzzle is: **Don't accidentally turn a constructor declaration into a method declaration by adding a return type.** Although it is legal for a method to have the same name as the class in which it's declared, you should never do this. More generally, **obey the standard naming conventions,** which dictate that method names begin with lowercase letters, whereas class names begin with uppercase letters.

For language designers, perhaps it was not such a good idea to generate a default constructor automatically if no programmer-declared constructor is provided. If such constructors are generated, perhaps they should be private. There are several other approaches to eliminating this trap. One is to prohibit method names that are the same as their class name, as does C#. Another is to dispense with constructors altogether, as does Smalltalk.

Puzzle 64: The Mod Squad

This program generates a histogram of the numbers mod 3. What does it print?

```java
public class Mod {
    public static void main(String[] args) {
        final int MODULUS = 3;
        int[] histogram = new int[MODULUS];

        // Iterate over all ints (Idiom from Puzzle 26)
        int i = Integer.MIN_VALUE;
        do {
            histogram[Math.abs(i) % MODULUS]++;
        } while (i++ != Integer.MAX_VALUE);

        for (int j = 0; j < MODULUS; j++)
            System.out.print(histogram[j] + " ");
    }
}
```

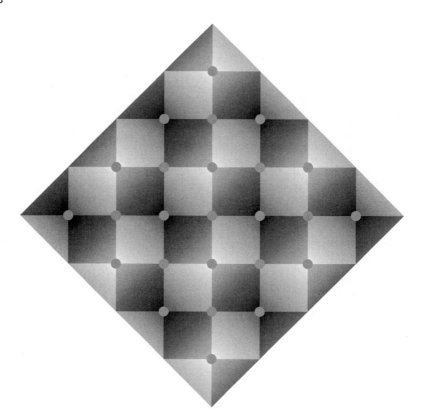

Solution 64: The Mod Squad

The program initializes the int array histogram with one location for each of the mod 3 values (0, 1, and 2). All three locations are initially 0. Then the program loops the variable i over all 2^{32} int values, using the idiom introduced in Puzzle 26. Because the integer remainder operator (%) can return a negative value if its first operand is negative, as discussed in Puzzle 1, the program takes the absolute value of i before computing its remainder when divided by 3. Then it increments the array location indexed by this remainder. After the loop finishes, the program prints the contents of the histogram array, whose elements represent the number of int values whose mod 3 values are 0, 1, and 2.

The three numbers printed by the program should be roughly equal to one another, and they should add up to 2^{32}. If you want to know how to figure out their exact values and you're in the mood for a bit of math, read the next two paragraphs. Otherwise, feel free to skip them.

The three numbers printed by the program can't be exactly equal, because they have to add up to 2^{32}, which is not divisible by 3. If you look at the mod 3 values of successive powers of 2, you'll see that they alternate between 1 and 2: 2^0 mod 3 is 1, 2^1 mod 3 is 2, 2^2 mod 3 is 1, 2^3 mod 3 is 2, and so forth. The mod 3 value of every even power of 2 is 1, and the mod 3 value of every odd power of 2 is 2. Because 2^{32} mod 3 is 1, one of the three numbers printed by the program will be one greater than the other two, but which one?

The loop takes turns incrementing each of the three array values, so the last value incremented by the loop must be the high one. This is the value representing the mod 3 value of Integer.MAX_VALUE or $(2^{31} - 1)$. Because 2^{31} is an odd power of 2, its mod 3 value is 2, so $(2^{31} - 1)$ mod 3 is 1. The second of the three numbers printed by the program represents the number of int values whose mod 3 value is 1, so we expect this value to be one more than the first and the last.

The program should therefore print floor(2^{32} / 3) ceil(2^{32} / 3) floor(2^{32} / 3), or 1431655765 1431655766 1431655765—after running for a fair amount of time. But does it? No, it throws this exception almost immediately:

```
Exception in thread "main" ArrayIndexOutOfBoundsException: -2
        at Mod.main(Mod.java:9)
```

What is going on here?

The problem lies in the program's use of the Math.abs method, which results in erroneous mod 3 values. Consider what happens when i is −2. The program computes the value Math.abs(-2) % 3, which is 2, but the mod 3 value of −2 is 1. This would explain incorrect numerical results, but it leaves us in the dark as to why the program throws an ArrayIndexOutOfBoundsException. This exception indicates that the program is using a negative array index, but surely that is impossible: The array index is calculated by taking the absolute value of i and computing the remainder when this value is divided by 3. Computing the remainder when a nonnegative int is divided by a positive int is guaranteed to produce a nonnegative result [JLS 15.17.3]. Again we ask, What is going on here?

To answer that question, we must go to the documentation for Math.abs. This method is named a bit deceptively. It nearly always returns the absolute value of its argument, but in one case, it does not. The documentation says, "If the argument is equal to the value of Integer.MIN_VALUE, the result is that same value, which is negative." Armed with this knowledge, it is obvious why the program throws an immediate ArrayIndexOutOfBoundsException. The initial value of the loop index i is Integer.MIN_VALUE, which generates an array index of Math.abs(Integer.MIN_VALUE) % 3, which is Integer.MIN_VALUE % 3, or -2.

To fix the program, we must replace the bogus mod calculation (Math.abs(i) % MODULUS) with one that actually works. If we replace this expression with an invocation of the following method, the program produces the expected output of 1431655765 1431655766 1431655765:

```
private static int mod(int i, int modulus) {
    int result = i % modulus;
    return result < 0 ? result + modulus : result;
}
```

The lesson of this puzzle is that **Math.abs is not guaranteed to return a nonnegative result.** If its argument is Integer.MIN_VALUE—or Long.MIN_VALUE for the long version of the method—it returns its argument. The method is not doing this just to be ornery; this behavior stems from the asymmetry of two's-complement arithmetic, which is discussed in more detail in Puzzle 33. Briefly, there is no int value that represents the negation of Integer.MIN_VALUE and no long value that represents the negation of Long.MIN_VALUE. For library designers, it might have been preferable if Math.abs threw IllegalArgumentException when it was passed Integer.MIN_VALUE or Long.MIN_VALUE. One could, however, argue that the actual behavior is more consistent with Java's built-in integer arithmetic operations, all of which overflow silently.

Puzzle 65: A Strange Saga of a Suspicious Sort

This program sorts an array of randomly chosen `Integer` instances, using a custom comparator, and then prints a word describing the order of the array. Recall that the `Comparator` interface has a single method, `compare`, which returns a negative value if its first argument is less than its second, zero if its two arguments are equal, and a positive value if its first argument is greater than its second. This program is a showcase for release 5.0 features. It uses autoboxing and unboxing, generics, and enum types. What does it print?

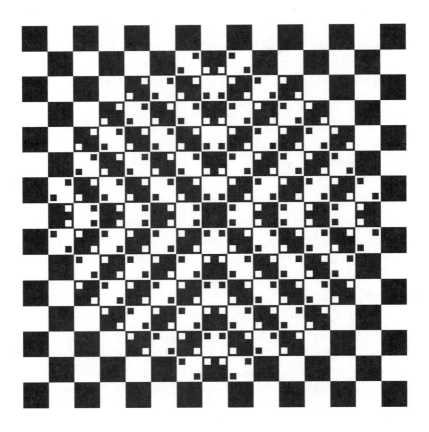

```java
import java.util.*;

public class SuspiciousSort {
    public static void main(String[] args) {
        Random rnd = new Random();
        Integer[] arr = new Integer[100];

        for (int i = 0; i < arr.length; i++)
            arr[i] = rnd.nextInt();

        Comparator<Integer> cmp = new Comparator<Integer>() {
            public int compare(Integer i1, Integer i2) {
                return i2 - i1;
            }
        };
        Arrays.sort(arr, cmp);
        System.out.println(order(arr));
    }

    enum Order { ASCENDING, DESCENDING, CONSTANT, UNORDERED };

    static Order order(Integer[] a) {
        boolean ascending  = false;
        boolean descending = false;

        for (int i = 1; i < a.length; i++) {
            ascending  |= (a[i] > a[i-1]);
            descending |= (a[i] < a[i-1]);
        }

        if (ascending  && !descending)
            return Order.ASCENDING;
        if (descending && !ascending)
            return Order.DESCENDING;
        if (!ascending)
            return Order.CONSTANT;    // All elements equal
        return Order.UNORDERED;       // Array is not sorted
    }
}
```

Solution 65: A Strange Saga of a Suspicious Sort

The main method creates an array of Integer instances, initializes it with random values, and sorts the array using the comparator cmp. This comparator's compare method returns its second argument minus its first, which is positive if its second argument represents a larger value than its first, zero if they're equal, and negative if its second argument represents a smaller value than its first. This is the opposite of what is normally done by the compare method, so this comparator should impose a descending order.

After sorting the array, the main method passes it to the static method order and prints the result returned by this method. This method returns CONSTANT if all the elements in the array represent equal values, ASCENDING if the second element in every adjacent pair is greater than or equal to the first, DESCENDING if the second element in every adjacent pair is less than or equal to the first, and UNORDERED if none of these conditions holds. Although it is theoretically possible that all 100 random numbers in the array are equal to one another, the odds of this happening are infinitesimal: 1 in $2^{32 \times 99}$, which is approximately 1 in 5×10^{953}. Therefore, it seems likely that the program should print DESCENDING. If you ran it, you almost certainly saw it print UNORDERED. Why would it do such a thing?

The order method is straightforward, and it does not lie. The Arrays.sort method has been around for years, and it works fine. This leaves only one place to look for bugs: the comparator. At first glance, it may seem unlikely that the comparator is broken. After all, it uses a standard idiom: If you have two numbers and you want a value whose sign indicates their order, compute their difference. This idiom has been around at least since the early 1970s. It was commonly used in the early days of UNIX. Unfortunately, this idiom never worked properly. Perhaps this puzzle should have been called "The Case of the Idiotic Idiom?" The problem with this idiom is that a fixed-width integer is not big enough to hold the difference of two arbitrary integers of the same width. When you subtract two int or

long values, the result can overflow, in which case it will have the wrong sign. For example, consider this program:

```
public class Overflow {
    public static void main(String[] args) {
        int x = -2000000000;
        int z = 2000000000;
        System.out.println(x - z);
    }
}
```

Clearly, x is less than z, yet the program prints 294967296, which is positive. Given that this comparison idiom is broken, why is it used so commonly? Because it works most of the time. It breaks only if the numbers to which it is applied differ by more than Integer.MAX_VALUE. This means that for many applications, failures won't be observed in practice. Worse, they may be observed infrequently enough that the bug will never get found and fixed.

So what does this mean for the behavior of our program? If you look at the Comparator documentation, you will see that the relation it implements must be *transitive*. In other words, (compare(x, y) > 0) && (compare(y, z) > 0) implies that compare(x, z) > 0. Consider the case in which x and z have the values in the Overflow example and y has the value 0. Our comparator violates transitivity for these values. In fact, it returns the wrong value for one quarter of all int pairs chosen at random. Performing a search or sort with such a comparator or using it to order a sorted collection can cause unspecified behavior, which is what we observed when we ran the program. For the mathematically inclined, the general contract of the Comparator.compare method requires that comparators impose a *total order*, but this one fails to do so on several counts.

We can fix our program by substituting a Comparator implementation that obeys the general contract. Because we want to reverse the natural order, we don't even have to write our own comparator. The Collections class provides one that's made to order. If you replace the original Arrays.sort invocation by Arrays.sort(arr, Collections.reverseOrder()), the program will print DESCENDING as expected.

Alternatively, you can write your own comparator. The following code is not "clever," but it works, causing the program to print DESCENDING as expected:

```
public int compare(Integer i1, Integer i2) {
    return (i2 < i1 ? -1 : (i2 > i1 ? 1: 0));
}
```

This puzzle has several lessons. The most specific is: **Do not use a subtraction-based comparator unless you are sure that the difference between values will never be greater than Integer.MAX_VALUE** [EJ Item 11]. More generally, beware of `int` overflow, as discussed in Puzzles 3, 26, and 33. Another lesson is that you should avoid "clever" code. Strive to write clear, correct code, and do not optimize it unless it proves necessary [EJ Item 37].

For language designers, the lesson is the same as for Puzzles 3, 26, and 33: It is perhaps worth considering support for some form of integer arithmetic that does not overflow silently. Also, it might be worth providing a three-valued comparator operator in the language, as Perl does (the <=> operator).

Classier Puzzlers

The puzzles in this chapter concern inheritance, overriding, and other forms of name reuse.

Puzzle 66: A Private Matter

In this program, a subclass field has the same name as a superclass field. What does the program print?

```java
class Base {
    public String className = "Base";
}

class Derived extends Base {
    private String className = "Derived";
}

public class PrivateMatter {
    public static void main(String[] args) {
        System.out.println(new Derived().className);
    }
}
```

Solution 66: A Private Matter

A superficial analysis of the program might suggest that it should print Derived, because that is what is stored in the className field of each Derived instance. A deeper analysis suggests that class Derived won't compile, because the variable className in Derived has more restrictive access than it does in Base: It is declared private in Derived and public in Base. If you tried compiling the program, you found that neither analysis is correct. The program doesn't compile, but the error is in the class PrivateMatter.

Had className been an instance method instead of an instance field, Derived.className() would have *overridden* Base.className(), and the program would have been illegal. The access modifier of an overriding method must provide at least as much access as that of the overridden method [JLS 8.4.8.3]. Because className is a field, Derived.className *hides* Base.className rather than overriding it [JLS 8.3]. It is legal, though inadvisable, for one field to hide another when the hiding field has an access modifier that provides less access than the hidden field. In fact, it is legal for a hiding field to have a type that is completely unrelated to that of the field it hides: The Derived class would be legal even if Derived.className were of type GregorianCalendar.

The compilation error in our program occurs when class PrivateMatter tries to access Derived.className. Although Base has a public field className, this field is not inherited into Derived because it is hidden by Derived.className. Within the class Derived, the field name className refers to the private field Derived.className. Because this field is declared private, it is not accessible to the class PrivateMatter. Therefore, the compiler generates an error message something like this:

```
PrivateMatter.java:11: className has private access in Derived
        System.out.println(new Derived().className);
                           ^
```

Note that it is possible to access the public field `Base.className` in a `Derived` instance even though it is hidden, by casting the `Derived` instance to `Base`. The following version of `PrivateMatter` prints `Base`:

```
public class PrivateMatter {
    public static void main(String[] args) {
        System.out.println(((Base)new Derived()).className);
    }
}
```

This demonstrates a big difference between overriding and hiding. Once a method is overridden in a subclass, you can't invoke it on an instance of the subclass (except from within the subclass, by using the `super` keyword). You can, however, access a hidden field by casting the subclass instance to a superclass in which the field is not hidden.

If you want the program to print `Derived`—that is, you want it to exhibit overriding behavior—use public methods in place of public fields. This is, in any case, a good idea because it provides better encapsulation [EJ Item 19]. The following version of the program uses this technique and prints `Derived` as expected:

```
class Base {
    public String getClassName() {
        return "Base";
    }
}

class Derived extends Base {
    public String getClassName() {
        return "Derived";
    }
}

public class PublicMatter {
    public static void main(String[] args) {
        System.out.println(new Derived().getClassName());
    }
}
```

Note that we declared the method `getClassName` to be public in class `Derived` even though the corresponding field was private in the original program. As mentioned previously, an overriding method must have an access modifier that is no less restrictive than the method it overrides.

The lesson of this puzzle is that hiding is generally a bad idea. The language allows you to hide variables, nested types, and even static methods (as in Puzzle

48), but just because you can doesn't mean that you should. The problem with hiding is that it leads to confusion in the mind of the reader. Are you using the hidden entity or the entity that is doing the hiding? To avoid this confusion, simply **avoid hiding**.

A class that hides a field with one whose accessibility is more restrictive than that of the hidden field, as in our original program, violates the principle of *subsumption,* also known as the *Liskov Substitution Principle* [Liskov87]. This principle says that everything you can do with a base class, you can also do with a derived class. Subsumption is an integral part of the natural mental model of object-oriented programming. Whenever it is violated, a program becomes more difficult to understand. There are other ways that hiding one field with another can violate subsumption: if the two fields are of different types, if one field is static and the other isn't, if one field is final and the other isn't, if one field is constant and the other isn't, or if both are constant and have different values.

For language designers, consider eliminating the possibility of hiding: for example, by making all fields implicitly private. If this seems too draconian, at least consider restricting hiding so that it preserves subsumption.

In summary, hiding occurs when you declare a field, a static method, or a nested type whose name is identical to an accessible field, method, or type, respectively, in a superclass. Hiding is confusing; avoid it. Hiding fields in a manner that violates subsumption is especially harmful. More generally, avoid name reuse other than overriding.

Puzzle 67: All Strung Out

One name can be used to refer to multiple classes in different packages. This program explores what happens when you reuse a platform class name. What do you think it does? Although this is the kind of program you'd normally be embarrassed to be seen with, go ahead and lock the doors, close the shades, and give it a try:

```java
public class StrungOut {
    public static void main(String[] args) {
        String s = new String("Hello world");
        System.out.println(s);
    }
}

class String {
    private final java.lang.String s;

    public String(java.lang.String s) {
        this.s = s;
    }

    public java.lang.String toString() {
        return s;
    }
}
```

Solution 67: All Strung Out

This program looks simple enough, if a bit repulsive. The class `String` in the unnamed package is simply a wrapper for a `java.lang.String` instance. It seems the program should print `Hello world`. If you tried to run the program, though, you found that you could not. The VM emits an error message something like this:

```
Exception in thread "main" java.lang.NoSuchMethodError: main
```

But surely there *is* a `main` method: It's right there in black and white. Why can't the VM find it?

The VM can't find the `main` method because it isn't there. Although `StrungOut` has a method *named* `main`, it has the wrong signature. A `main` method must accept a single argument that is an array of strings [JVMS 5.2]. What the VM is struggling to tell us is that `StrungOut.main` accepts an array of *our* `String` class, which has nothing whatsoever to do with `java.lang.String`.

If you really must write your own string class, for heaven's sake, don't call it `String`. **Avoid reusing the names of platform classes, and *never* reuse class names from java.lang,** because these names are automatically imported everywhere. Programmers are used to seeing these names in their unqualified form and naturally assume that these names refer to the familiar classes from `java.lang`. If you reuse one of these names, the unqualified name will refer to the new definition any time it is used inside its own package.

To fix the program, simply pick a reasonable name for the nonstandard string class. If you compiled the original code for this puzzle, delete `String.class` *now* to prevent confusing behavior in the future! The following version of the program is clearly correct and much easier to understand than the original. It prints `Hello world` just as you'd expect:

```java
public class StrungOut {
    public static void main(String[] args) {
        MyString s = new MyString("Hello world");
        System.out.println(s);
    }
}
class MyString {
    private final String s;
    public MyString(String s) { this.s = s; }
    public String toString()  { return s; }
}
```

Broadly speaking, the lesson of this puzzle is to avoid the reuse of class names, especially Java platform class names. Never reuse class names from the package `java.lang`. The same lesson applies to library designers. The Java platform designers slipped up a few times. Notable examples include `java.sql.Date`, which conflicts with `java.util.Date`, and `org.omg.CORBA.Object`. As in many other puzzles in this chapter, the lesson is a specific case of the principle that you should avoid name reuse, with the exception of overriding. For platform implementers, the lesson is that diagnostics should make clear the reason for a failure. The VM could easily have distinguished the case where there is no `main` method with the correct signature from the case where there is no `main` method at all.

Puzzle 68: Shades of Gray

This program has two declarations of the same name in the same scope and no obvious way to choose between them. Does the program print `Black`? Does it print `White`? Is it even legal?

```java
public class ShadesOfGray {
    public static void main(String[] args){
        System.out.println(X.Y.Z);
    }
}

class X {
    static class Y {
        static String Z = "Black";
    }
    static C Y = new C();
}

class C {
    String Z = "White";
}
```

Solution 68: Shades of Gray

There is no obvious way to decide whether this program should print Black or White. The compiler generally rejects ambiguous programs, and this one certainly appears ambiguous. Therefore, it seems only natural that it should be illegal. If you tried it, you found that it is legal and prints White. How could you possibly have known?

It turns out that there is a rule that governs program behavior under these circumstances. **When a variable and a type have the same name and both are in scope, the variable name takes precedence** [JLS 6.5.2]. The variable name is said to *obscure* the type name [JLS 6.3.2]. **Similarly, variable and type names can obscure package names.** This rule is indeed obscure, and any program that depends on it is likely to confuse its readers.

Fortunately, programs that obey the standard Java naming conventions almost never encounter this issue. Classes begin with a capital letter and are written in MixedCase, variables begin with a lowercase letter and are written in mixedCase, and constants begin with a capital letter and are written in ALL_CAPS. Single capital letters are used only for type parameters, as in the generic interface Map<K, V>. Package names are written in lower.case [JLS 6.8].

To avoid conflict between constant names and class names, treat acronyms as ordinary words in class names [EJ Item 38]. For example, a class representing a universally unique identifier should be named Uuid rather than UUID, even though the acronym is typically written UUID. (The Java platform libraries violate this advice with such class names as UUID, URL, and URI.) To avoid conflicts between variable names and package names, don't use a top-level package or domain name as a variable name. Specifically, don't name a variable com, org, net, edu, java, or javax.

To remove all ambiguity from the ShadesOfGray program, simply rewrite it to obey the naming conventions. It is clear that the following program prints Black. As an added bonus, it sounds the same as the original program when read aloud.

```
public class ShadesOfGray {
    public static void main(String[] args){
        System.out.println(Ex.Why.z);
    }
}

class Ex {
    static class Why {
        static String z = "Black";
    }
    static See y = new See();
}

class See {
    String z = "White";
}
```

In summary, obey the standard naming conventions to avoid conflicts between different namespaces (and because your program will be illegible if you violate these conventions). Also, avoid variable names that conflict with common top-level package names, and use MixedCase for class names even if they are acronyms. By following these rules, you'll ensure that your programs never obscure class or package names. Yet again, this is a case of the general rule that you should avoid name reuse except for overriding. For language designers, consider eliminating the possibility of obscuring. C# does this by putting fields and nested classes into the same name space.

Puzzle 69: Fade to Black

Suppose that you can't modify classes X and C in the previous puzzle (Puzzle 68). Can you write a class whose main method reads the value of the field Z in class X.Y and prints it? Do not use reflection.

Solution 69: Fade to Black

At first, this puzzle may appear impossible. After all, the class X.Y is obscured by a field of the same name, so an attempt to name it will refer to the field instead.

In fact, **it is possible to refer to an obscured type name. The trick is to use the name in a syntactic context where a type is allowed but a variable is not.** One such context is the region between the parentheses in a cast expression. The following program solves the puzzle by using this technique and prints Black as expected:

```
public class FadeToBlack {
    public static void main(String[] args) {
        System.out.println(((X.Y)null).Z);
    }
}
```

Note that we are accessing the Z field of class X.Y by using an expression of type X.Y. As we saw in Puzzles 48 and 54, accessing a static member using an expression in place of a type name is a legal but questionable practice.

You can also solve this puzzle without resorting to questionable practices, by using the obscured class in the extends clause of a class declaration. Because a base class is always a type, names appearing in extends clauses are never resolved as variable names. The following program demonstrates this technique. It too prints Black:

```
public class FadeToBlack {
    static class Xy extends X.Y { }

    public static void main(String[] args) {
        System.out.println(Xy.Z);
    }
}
```

If you are using release 5.0 or a later release you can also solve the puzzle by using X.Y in the extends clause of a type variable declaration:

```
public class FadeToBlack {
    public static <T extends X.Y> void main(String[] args) {
        System.out.println(T.Z);
    }
}
```

In summary, to solve a problem caused by the obscuring of a type by a variable, rename the type and variable in accordance with standard naming conventions, as discussed in Puzzle 68. If this is not possible, use the obscured type name in a context where only type names are allowed. With any luck, you will never have to resort to such contortions, as most library authors are sane enough to avoid the questionable practices that make them necessary. If, however, you do find yourself in this situation, it's nice to know that there is a workaround.

Puzzle 70: Package Deal

This program involves the interaction of two classes in different packages. The main method is in class hack.TypeIt. What does the program print?

```
package click;
public class CodeTalk {
    public void doIt() {
        printMessage();
    }

    void printMessage() {
        System.out.println("Click");
    }
}
```

```
package hack;
import click.CodeTalk;

public class TypeIt {
    private static class ClickIt extends CodeTalk {
        void printMessage() {
            System.out.println("Hack");
        }
    }

    public static void main(String[] args) {
        ClickIt clickit = new ClickIt();
        clickit.doIt();
    }
}
```

Solution 70: Package Deal

This puzzle appears straightforward. The main method in hack.TypeIt instantiates the class TypeIt.ClickIt and invokes its doIt method, which is inherited from CodeTalk. This method, in turn, calls printMessage, which is declared in TypeIt.ClickIt to print Hack. And yet, if you run the program, it prints Click. How can this be?

This analysis incorrectly assumes that hack.TypeIt.ClickIt.printMessage overrides click.CodeTalk.printMessage. **A package-private method cannot be directly overridden by a method in a different package** [JLS 8.4.8.1]. The two printMessage methods in this program are unrelated; they merely have the same name. When the program calls printMessage from within the package click, the package-private method click.CodeTalk.printMessage is run. This method prints Click, which explains the observed behavior.

If you want the printMessage method in hack.TypeIt.ClickIt to override the method in click.CodeTalk, you must add the protected or public modifier to the method declaration in click.CodeTalk. To make the program compile, you must also add a modifier to the overriding declaration in hack.TypeIt.ClickIt. This modifier must be no more restrictive than the one you placed on the declaration for printMessage in click.CodeTalk [JLS 8.4.8.3]. In other words, both printMessage methods may be declared public, both may be declared protected, or the superclass method may be declared protected and the subclass method public. If any of these three changes is made, the program will print Hack, indicating that overriding is taking place.

In summary, package-private methods cannot be directly overridden outside the package in which they're declared. Although the combination of package-private access and overriding can lead to some confusion, Java's current behavior enables packages to support encapsulation of abstractions larger than a single class. Package-private methods are implementation details of their package, and reuse of their names outside the package should have no effect inside the package.

Puzzle 71: Import Duty

In release 5.0, the Java platform introduced a number of facilities that make it eas-ier to work with arrays. This program uses varargs, autoboxing, static import (see http://java.sun.com/j2se/5.0/docs/guide/language [Java-5.0]) and the convenience method `Arrays.toString` (see Puzzle 60). What does the program print?

```java
import static java.util.Arrays.toString;

class ImportDuty {
    public static void main(String[] args) {
        printArgs(1, 2, 3, 4, 5);
    }

    static void printArgs(Object... args) {
        System.out.println(toString(args));
    }
}
```

Solution 71: Import Duty

You might expect the program to print [1, 2, 3, 4, 5], and indeed it would, if only it compiled. Sadly, the compiler just can't seem to find the right `toString` method:

```
ImportDuty.java:9:Object.toString can't be applied to (Object[])
System.out.println(toString(args));
                   ^
```

Is the compiler just being dense? Why would it try to apply `Object.toString()`, which doesn't match the call's parameter list, when `Arrays.toString(Object[])` matches perfectly?

The first thing the compiler does when selecting a method to be invoked at run time is to choose the scope in which the method must be found [JLS 15.12.1]. The compiler chooses the smallest enclosing scope that has a method with the right name. In our program, this scope is the class `ImportDuty`, which contains the `toString` method inherited from `Object`. This scope has no applicable method for the invocation `toString(args)`, so the compiler must reject the program.

In other words, the desired `toString` method isn't in scope at the point of the invocation. The imported `toString` method is *shadowed* by a method with the same name inherited into `ImportDuty` from `Object` [JLS 6.3.1]. Shadowing is a lot like obscuring (Puzzle 68). The key distinction is that a declaration can shadow another declaration only of the same kind: One type declaration can shadow another, one variable declaration can shadow another, and one method declaration can shadow another. By contrast, variable declarations can obscure type and package declarations, and type declarations can obscure package declarations.

When one declaration shadows another, the simple name refers to the entity in the shadowing declaration. In this case, `toString` refers to the `toString` method from `Object`. Simply put, **members that are naturally in scope take precedence over static imports.** One consequence is that static methods with the same name as `Object` methods cannot be used with the static import facility.

Since you can't use static import with `Arrays.toString`, use a normal import declaration instead. This is the way `Arrays.toString` was meant to be used:

```java
import java.util.Arrays;
class ImportDuty {
    static void printArgs(Object... args) {
        System.out.println(Arrays.toString(args));
    }
}
```

If you are desperate to avoid qualifying `Arrays.toString` invocations explicitly, you can write your own private static forwarding method:

```
private static String toString(Object[] a) {
    return Arrays.toString(a);
}
```

The static import facility was intended for situations in which static members of another class are used repeatedly, and qualifying each use would seriously clutter a program. In such situations, the static import facility can significantly enhance readability. It is far safer than implementing interfaces to inherit their constants, which you should never do [EJ Item 17]. Overuse of the static import facility can, however, harm readability by making the class of a static member unclear at the point of use. **Use the static import facility sparingly and only when there is a compelling need.**

For API designers, be aware that the static import facility cannot be used effectively on a method if its name is already in scope. This means that static import can seldom be used on static methods that share names with methods in common interfaces, and it can never be used on static methods that share names with methods found in `Object`. Once again, this puzzle demonstrates that name reuse other than overriding is generally confusing. We have seen this with overloading, hiding, and obscuring, and now we see it with shadowing.

Puzzle 72: Final Jeopardy

This puzzle examines what happens when you attempt to hide a final field. What does this program do?

```
class Jeopardy {
    public static final String PRIZE = "$64,000";
}

public class DoubleJeopardy extends Jeopardy {
    public static final String PRIZE = "2 cents";

    public static void main(String[] args) {
        System.out.println(DoubleJeopardy.PRIZE);
    }
}
```

Solution 72: Final Jeopardy

Because the PRIZE field in Jeopardy is declared public and final, you might think that the language would prevent you from reusing this field name in a subclass. After all, final methods cannot be overridden or hidden. If you tried the program, you found that it compiles without a hitch and prints 2 cents. What went wrong?

It turns out that **the final modifier means something completely different on methods and fields**. On a method, final means that the method may not be overridden (for instance methods) or hidden (for static methods) [JLS 8.4.3.3]. On a field, final means the field may not be assigned more than once [JLS 8.3.1.2]. The keyword is the same, but the behavior is unrelated.

In the program, the final field DoubleJeopardy.PRIZE hides final field Jeopardy.PRIZE, for a net loss of $63,999.98. Although it is possible to hide fields, it is generally a bad idea. As we discussed in Puzzle 66, hiding fields can violate subsumption and confound our intuition about the relationship between types and their members.

If you want to guarantee the prize in the Jeopardy class even while preserving the ability to subclass it, use a final method instead of a final field:

```
class Jeopardy {
    private static final String PRIZE = "$64,000";

    public static final String prize() {
        return PRIZE;
    }
}
```

For language designers, the lesson is to avoid reusing the same keyword for unrelated concepts. A keyword should be reused only for closely related concepts, where it helps programmers build an intuition about the relationship among the language features in question. In the case of the Java's final keyword, reuse leads to confusion. It should be noted that as a language ages, there is a natural tendency to reuse keywords for unrelated concepts. This avoids the need to introduce new keywords, which is enormously destabilizing. When language designers do this, they are generally choosing the lesser of two evils.

In summary, avoid reusing names for unrelated variables or unrelated concepts. Using distinct names for unrelated concepts helps readers and programmers to keep the concepts separate.

Puzzle 73: Your Privates Are Showing

The idea behind private members—methods, fields, and types—is that they're simply implementation details: The implementer of a class can feel free to add new ones and change or remove old ones without fear of harming clients of the class. In other words, private members are fully encapsulated by the class that contains them.

Unfortunately, there are a few chinks in the armor. For example, serialization can break this encapsulation. Making a class serializable and accepting the default serialized form causes the class's private instance fields to become part of its exported API [EJ Items 54, 55]. Changes in the private representation can then lead to exceptions or erratic behavior when clients use existing serialized objects.

But what about compile-time errors? Can you write a final "library" class and a "client" class, both of which compile without error, and then add a private member to the library class so that it still compiles but the client class no longer does?

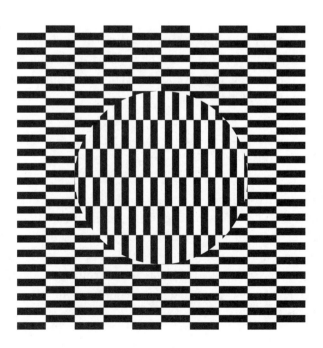

Solution 73: Your Privates Are Showing

If your solution involves adding a private constructor to the library class to suppress the creation of a default public constructor, give yourself half a point. The puzzle required you to add a private member and, strictly speaking, constructors aren't members [JLS 6.4.3].

This puzzle has several solutions. One solution uses shadowing:

```
package library;
public final class Api {
    // private static class String {}
    public static String newString() {
        return new String();
    }
}

package client;
import library.Api;
public class Client {
    String s = Api.newString();
}
```

As written, the program compiles without error. If we uncomment the private declaration of the local class `String` in `library.Api`, the method `Api.newString` no longer has the return type `java.lang.String`, so the initialization of the variable `Client.s` fails to compile:

```
client/Client.java:4: incompatible types
found: library.Api.String, required: java.lang.String
    String s = Api.newString();
                          ^
```

Although the only textual change we made was to add a private class declaration, we indirectly changed the return type of an existing public method, which is an incompatible API change. We changed the meaning of a name used in our exported API.

Many variations on this solution are possible. The shadowed type could come from an enclosing class instead of `java.lang`. You could shadow a variable instead of a type. The shadowed variable could come from a `static import` declaration or an enclosing class.

It is possible to solve this puzzle without changing the type of an exported member of the library class. Here is such a solution, which uses hiding in place of shadowing:

```
package library;
class ApiBase {
    public static final int ANSWER = 42;
}
public final class Api extends ApiBase {
    // private static final int ANSWER = 6 * 9;
}

package client;
import library.Api;
public class Client {
    int answer = Api.ANSWER;
}
```

As written, this program compiles without error. If we uncomment the private declaration in `library.Api`, the client fails to compile:

```
client/Client.java:4: ANSWER has private access in library.Api
int answer = Api.ANSWER;
                ^
```

The new private field `Api.ANSWER` hides the public field `ApiBase.ANSWER`, which would otherwise be inherited into `Api`. Because the new field is declared `private`, it can't be accessed from `Client`. Many variations on this solution are possible. You can hide an instance field instead of a static field, or a type instead of a field.

You can also solve this puzzle with obscuring. All the solutions involve reusing a name to break the client. **Reusing names is dangerous; avoid hiding, shadowing, and obscuring.** Is this starting to sound familiar? Good!

Puzzle 74: Identity Crisis

This program is incomplete. It lacks a declaration for `Enigma`, a class that extends `java.lang.Object`. Provide a declaration for `Enigma` that makes the program print `false`:

```
public class Conundrum {
    public static void main(String[] args) {
        Enigma e = new Enigma();
        System.out.println(e.equals(e));
    }
}
```

Oh, and one more thing: You must not override `equals`.

Solution 74: Identity Crisis

At first glance, this may seem impossible. The `Object.equals` method tests for object identity, and the object passed to `equals` by `Enigma` is certainly the same as itself. If you can't override `Object.equals`, the `main` method must print `true`, right?

Not so fast, cowboy. Although the puzzle forbids you to *override* `Object.equals`, you are permitted to *overload* it, which leads to the following solution:

```
final class Enigma {
    // Don't do this!
    public boolean equals(Enigma other) {
        return false;
    }
}
```

Although this solves the puzzle, it is a very bad thing to do. It violates the advice of Puzzle 58: **If two overloadings of the same method can be applied to some parameters, they should have identical behavior.** In this case, `e.equals(e)` and `e.equals((Object)e)` return different results. The potential for confusion is obvious.

There is, however, a solution that doesn't violate this advice:

```
final class Enigma {
    public Enigma() {
        System.out.println(false);
        System.exit(0);
    }
}
```

Arguably, this solution violates the spirit of the puzzle: The `println` invocation that produces the desired output appears in the `Enigma` constructor, not the main `method`. Still, it does solve the puzzle, and you have to admit it's cute.

As for the lesson, see the previous eight puzzles and Puzzle 58. If you do overload a method, make sure that all overloadings behave identically.

Puzzle 75: Heads or Tails?

The behavior of this program changed between release 1.4 of the Java platform
and release 5.0. What does the program do under each of these releases? (If you
have access only to release 5.0, you can emulate the 1.4 behavior by compiling
with the -source 1.4 flag.)

```java
import java.util.Random;

public class CoinSide {
    private static Random rnd = new Random();

    public static CoinSide flip() {
        return rnd.nextBoolean() ?
            Heads.INSTANCE : Tails.INSTANCE;
    }

    public static void main(String[] args) {
        System.out.println(flip());
    }
}

class Heads extends CoinSide {
    private Heads() { }
    public static final Heads INSTANCE = new Heads();

    public String toString() {
        return "heads";
    }
}

class Tails extends CoinSide {
    private Tails() { }
    public static final Tails INSTANCE = new Tails();

    public String toString() {
        return "tails";
    }
}
```

Solution 75: Heads or Tails?

This program doesn't appear to use any release 5.0 features at all, so it is difficult to see why there should be any difference in behavior. In fact, the program fails to compile in release 1.4 or any earlier release:

```
CoinSide.java:7:
  incompatible types for ?: neither is a subtype of the other
    second operand: Heads
    third operand : Tails
      return rnd.nextBoolean() ?
                               ^
```

The behavior of the conditional (? :) operator was more restrictive before release 5.0 [JLS2 15.25]. When both the second and third operands were of a reference type, the conditional operator required that one of them be a subtype of the other. As neither class Heads nor Tails is a subtype of the other, there is an error. To get this code to compile, you could cast one of the operands to the common supertype:

```
return rnd.nextBoolean() ?
    (CoinSide)Heads.INSTANCE : Tails.INSTANCE;
```

In release 5.0 and later releases, the language is much more forgiving. The conditional operator is always legal when its second and third operands have reference types. The result type is the *least common supertype* of these two types. A common supertype always exists, because Object is the supertype of every object type. As a practical matter, the main consequence of this change is that the conditional operator just does the right thing more often and gives compile-time errors less often. For the language nerds among us, the compile-time type of the result of the conditional operator for reference types is the same as the result of invoking the following method on the second and third operands [JLS 15.25]:

```
<T> T choose(T a, T b) { }
```

The problem illustrated by this puzzle did come up fairly often under release 1.4 and earlier releases, forcing you to insert casts that served merely to obscure the purpose of your code. That said, the puzzle itself is artificial. Before release

5.0, it would have been more natural to write `CoinSide` using the Typesafe Enum pattern [EJ Item 21]:

```
import java.util.Random;
public class CoinSide {
    public static final CoinSide HEADS = new CoinSide("heads");
    public static final CoinSide TAILS = new CoinSide("tails");

    private final String name;
    private CoinSide(String name) {
        this.name = name;
    }

    public String toString() {
        return name;
    }

    private static Random rnd = new Random();
    public static CoinSide flip() {
        return rnd.nextBoolean() ? HEADS : TAILS;
    }

    public static void main(String[] args) {
        System.out.println(flip());
    }
}
```

In release 5.0 and later releases, it is natural to write `CoinSide` as an enum type:

```
public enum CoinSide {
    HEADS, TAILS;

    public String toString() {
        return name().toLowerCase();
    }

    // flip and main same as in 1.4 implementation above
}
```

The lesson of this puzzle is: **Upgrade to the latest release of the Java platform.** Newer releases include many improvements that make life easier for programmers. You don't have to go out of your way to take advantage of all the new features; some of them benefit you with no effort on your part. For language and library designers, the lesson is: Do not make programmers do things that the language or library could do for them.

A Glossary of Name Reuse

Most of the puzzles in this chapter were based on name reuse. This section summarizes the various forms of name reuse.

Overriding

An instance method *overrides* all accessible instance methods with the same signature in superclasses [JLS 8.4.8.1], enabling *dynamic dispatch;* in other words, the VM chooses which overriding to invoke based on an instance's run-time type [JLS 15.12.4.4]. Overriding is fundamental to object-oriented programming and is the only form of name reuse that is not generally discouraged:

```
class Base {
    public void f() { }
}

class Derived extends Base {
    public void f() { } // overrrides Base.f()
}
```

Hiding

A field, static method, or member type *hides* all accessible fields, static methods, or member types, respectively, with the same name (or, for methods, signature) in supertypes. Hiding a member prevents it from being inherited [JLS 8.3, 8.4.8.2, 8.5]:

```
class Base {
    public static void f() { }
}

class Derived extends Base {
    public static void f() { } // hides Base.f()
}
```

Overloading

Methods in a class *overload* one another if they have the same name and different signatures. The overloaded method designated by an invocation is selected at compile time [JLS 8.4.9, 15.12.2]:

```
class CircuitBreaker {
    public void f(int i)   { }  // int overloading
    public void f(String s) { }  // String overloading
}
```

Shadowing

A variable, method, or type *shadows* all variables, methods, or types, respectively, with the same name in a textually enclosing scope. If an entity is shadowed, you cannot refer to it by its simple name; depending on the entity, you cannot refer to it at all [JLS 6.3.1]:

```
class WhoKnows {
    static String sentence = "I don't know.";

    public static void main(String[] args) {
        String sentence = "I know!";   // shadows static field
        System.out.println(sentence);  // prints local variable
    }
}
```

Although shadowing is generally discouraged, one common idiom does involve shadowing. Constructors often reuse a field name from their class as a parameter name to pass the value of the named field. This idiom is not without risk, but most Java programmers have decided that the stylistic benefits outweigh the risks:

```
class Belt {
    private final int size;
    public Belt(int size) { // Parameter shadows Belt.size
        this.size = size;
    }
}
```

Obscuring

A variable *obscures* a type with the same name if both are in scope: If the name is used where variables and types are permitted, it refers to the variable. Similarly, a variable or a type can obscure a package. Obscuring is the only kind of name reuse where the two names are in different namespaces: variables, packages, methods, or types. If a type or a package is obscured, you cannot refer to it by its simple name except in a context where the syntax allows only a name from its namespace. Adhering to the naming conventions largely eliminates obscuring [JLS 6.3.2, 6.5]:

```
public class Obscure {
    static String System; // Obscures type java.lang.System

    public static void main(String[] args) {
        // Next line won't compile: System refers to static field
        System.out.println("hello, obscure world!");
    }
}
```

More Library Puzzlers

The puzzles in this chapter feature more advanced library topics, such as threading, reflection, and I/O.

Puzzle 76: Ping Pong

This program consists entirely of synchronized static methods. What does it print? Is it guaranteed to print the same thing every time you run it?

```java
public class PingPong {
    public static synchronized void main(String[] a) {
        Thread t = new Thread() {
            public void run() { pong(); }
        };
        t.run();
        System.out.print("Ping");
    }

    static synchronized void pong() {
        System.out.print("Pong");
    }
}
```

Solution 76: Ping Pong

In a multithreaded program, it is generally a good bet that the behavior can vary from run to run, but this program always prints the same thing. Before a synchronized static method executes, it obtains the monitor lock associated with its Class object [JLS 8.4.3.6]. Therefore, the main thread acquires the lock on PingPong.class before creating the second thread. As long as the main thread holds on to this lock, the second thread can't execute a synchronized static method. In particular, the second thread can't execute the pong method until the main method prints Ping and completes execution. Only then does the main thread relinquish the lock, allowing the second thread to acquire it and print Pong. This analysis leaves little doubt that the program should always print PingPong. There is one small problem: If you tried the program, you found that it always prints PongPing. What on earth is going on?

Strange as it may seem, this is not a multithreaded program. Not a multithreaded program? How can that be? Surely it creates a second thread. Well, yes, it does *create* a second thread, but it never *starts* that thread. Instead, the main thread simply invokes the run method of the new Thread instance, and the run method executes synchronously in the main thread. Because a thread is allowed to acquire the same lock repeatedly [JLS 17.1], the main thread is permitted to reacquire the lock on PingPong.class when the run method invokes the pong method. The pong method prints Pong and returns to the run method, which returns to the main method. Finally, the main method prints Ping, which explains the program's output.

Fixing the program is as simple as changing t.run to t.start. Once this is done, the program reliably prints PingPong as expected.

The lesson is simple: **Be careful not to invoke a thread's run method when you mean to invoke its start method.** Unfortunately, this mistake is all too common, and it can be very difficult to spot. Perhaps the main lesson of this puzzle is for API designers: If Thread didn't have a public run method, it would be impossible for programmers to invoke it accidentally. The Thread class has a public run method because it implements Runnable, but it didn't have to be that way. An alternative design would be for each Thread instance to encapsulate a Runnable, giving rise to composition in place of interface inheritance. As discussed in Puzzle 47, composition is generally preferable to inheritance. This puzzle demonstrates that the principle holds even for interface inheritance.

Puzzle 77: The Lock Mess Monster

This program runs a little workplace simulation. It starts a worker thread that works—or at least pretends to work—until quitting time. Then the program schedules a timer task representing an evil boss who tries to make sure that it's never quitting time. Finally, the main thread, representing a good boss, tells the worker when it's quitting time and waits for the worker to finish. What does the program print?

```java
import java.util.*;
public class Worker extends Thread {
    private volatile boolean quittingTime = false;
    public void run() {
        while (!quittingTime)
            pretendToWork();
        System.out.println("Beer is good");
    }
    private void pretendToWork() {
        try {
            Thread.sleep(300); // Sleeping on the job?
        } catch (InterruptedException ex) { }
    }
    // It's quitting time, wait for worker - Called by good boss
    synchronized void quit() throws InterruptedException {
        quittingTime = true;
        join();
    }
    // Rescind quitting time - Called by evil boss
    synchronized void keepWorking() {
        quittingTime = false;
    }

    public static void main(String[] args)
            throws InterruptedException {
        final Worker worker = new Worker();
        worker.start();

        Timer t = new Timer(true); // Daemon thread
        t.schedule(new TimerTask() {
            public void run() { worker.keepWorking(); }
        }, 500);

        Thread.sleep(400);
        worker.quit();
    }
}
```

Solution 77: The Lock Mess Monster

The best way to figure out what this program does is to simulate its execution by hand. Here's an approximate time line; the times are relative to the time the program starts running:

- **300 ms:** The worker thread checks the volatile `quittingTime` field to see whether it's quitting time; it isn't, so the thread goes back to "work."

- **400 ms:** The main thread, representing the good boss, invokes the `quit` method on the worker thread. The main thread acquires the lock on the worker `Thread` instance (because `quit` is a synchronized method), sets `quittingTime` to `true`, and invokes `join` on the worker thread. The `join` invocation does not return immediately but waits for the worker thread to complete.

- **500 ms:** The timer task, representing the evil boss, executes. It tries to invoke the `keepWorking` method on the worker thread, but the invocation blocks because `keepWorking` is a synchronized method and the main thread is currently executing a synchronized method on the worker thread (the `quit` method).

- **600 ms:** The worker thread again checks whether it's quitting time. Because the `quittingTime` field is volatile, the worker thread is guaranteed to see the new value of `true`, so it prints `Beer is good` and completes execution. This causes the main thread's `join` invocation to return, and the main thread completes execution. The timer thread is a daemon, so it too completes execution, and the program terminates.

Therefore, we expect the program to run for a bit under a second, print `Beer is good`, and terminate normally. If you tried running the program, though, you found that it prints nothing; it just hangs. What is wrong with our analysis?

There is no guarantee that the events will interleave as indicated in the time line. Neither the `Timer` class nor the `Thread.sleep` method offers real-time guarantees. That said, it's very likely that these events *will* interleave as indicated by the time line, as the time granularity is so coarse. A hundred milliseconds is an eternity to a computer. Moreover, the program hangs repeatedly; it looks as if there is something else at work here, and indeed there is.

Our analysis contains a fundamental flaw. At 500 ms, when the timer task, representing the evil boss executes, the time line indicates that its `keepWorking` invocation will block because `keepWorking` is a synchronized method and the main thread is currently executing the synchronized `quit` method on the same object (waiting in `Thread.join`). It is true that `keepWorking` is a synchronized method and that the main thread is currently executing the synchronized `quit` method on the same object. Even so, the timer thread is able to obtain the lock on this object and execute the `keepWorking` method. How can this be?

The answer concerns the implementation of `Thread.join`. It can't be found in the documentation for this method, at least in releases up to and including release 5.0. **Internally, `Thread.join` calls `Object.wait` on the `Thread` instance representing the thread being joined. This releases the lock for the duration of the wait.** In the case of our program, this allows the timer thread, representing the evil boss, to waltz in and set `quittingTime` back to `false`, even though the main thread is currently executing the synchronized `quit` method. As a consequence, the worker thread never sees that it's quitting time and keeps running forever. The main thread, representing the good boss, never returns from the `join` method.

The fundamental cause of the misbehavior of the program is that the author of the `WorkerThread` class used the instance lock to ensure mutual exclusion between the `quit` and `keepWorking` methods, but this use conflicts with the internal use of this lock by the superclass (`Thread`). The lesson is: **Don't assume anything about what a library class will or won't do with locks** on its instances or on the class, beyond what is guaranteed by the class's specification. Any call to a library could result in a call to `wait`, `notify`, `notifyAll`, or a synchronized method. All these things can have an effect on application-level code.

If you need full control over a lock, make sure that no one else can gain access to it. If your class extends a library class that might use its locks or if untrusted parties might gain access to instances of your class, don't use the locks that are automatically associated with the class or its instances. Instead, create a separate lock object in a private field. Prior to release 5.0, the correct type to use for this lock object was simply `Object` or a trivial subclass. As of release 5.0, `java.util.concurrent.locks` provides two alternatives: `ReentrantLock` and `ReentrantReadWriteLock`. These classes provide more flexibility than `Object` but are a bit more cumbersome to use. They cannot be used with a `synchronized` block, but must be acquired and released explicitly with the aid of a `try-finally` statement.

The most straightforward way to fix the program is to add a private `lock` field of type `Object` and to synchronize on this object in the `quit` and `keepWorking` methods. With these changes, the program prints `Beer is good` as expected. The correct behavior of the program is not dependent on its obeying the time line shown in our previous analysis:

```
private final Object lock = new Object();

// It's quitting time, wait for worker - Called by good boss
void quit() throws InterruptedException {
    synchronized (lock) {
        quittingTime = true;
        join();
    }
}

// Rescind quitting time - Called by evil boss
void keepWorking() {
    synchronized (lock) {
        quittingTime = false;
    }
}
```

It is also possible to fix the program by having the Worker class implement Runnable rather than extending Thread, and creating each worker thread using the Thread(Runnable) constructor. This decouples the lock on each Worker instance from the lock on its Thread instance. It is a larger refactoring and is left as an exercise to the reader.

Just as a library class's use of a lock can interfere with an application, an application's use of a lock can interfere with a library class. For example, in all releases up to and including release 5.0, the system requires the class lock on Thread in order to create a new Thread instance. Executing the following code would prevent the creation of any new threads:

```
synchronized (Thread.class) {
    Thread.sleep(Long.MAX_VALUE);
}
```

In summary, never make assumptions about what a library class will or won't do with its locks. To isolate yourself from the use of locks by a library class, avoid inheriting from library classes except those specifically designed for inheritance [EJ Item 15]. To guarantee that your locks are immune to external interference, prevent others from gaining access to your locks by keeping them private.

For language designers, consider whether it is appropriate to associate a lock with every object. If you elect to do so, consider restricting access to these locks. In Java, locks are effectively public attributes of objects; perhaps it would make more sense if they were private. Also note that in Java, an object effectively *is* a lock: You synchronize on the object itself. Perhaps it would make more sense if an object *had* a lock that you could obtain by calling an accessor method.

Puzzle 78: Reflection Infection

This puzzle illustrates a simple application of reflection. What does this program print?

```java
import java.util.*;
import java.lang.reflect.*;

public class Reflector {
    public static void main(String[] args) throws Exception {
        Set<String> s = new HashSet<String>();
        s.add("foo");
        Iterator it = s.iterator();
        Method m = it.getClass().getMethod("hasNext");
        System.out.println(m.invoke(it));
    }
}
```

Solution 78: Reflection Infection

The program creates a set with a single element in it, gets an iterator over the set, invokes the iterator's hasNext method reflectively, and prints the result of the method invocation. As the iterator hasn't yet returned the set's sole element, hasNext should return true. Running the program, however, tells a different story:

```
Exception in thread "main" IllegalAccessException:
  Class Reflector can not access a member of class HashMap
  $HashIterator with modifiers "public"
    at Reflection.ensureMemberAccess(Reflection.java:65)
    at Method.invoke(Method.java:578)
    at Reflector.main(Reflector.java:11)
```

How can this be? Of course the hasNext method is public, just as the exception tells us, and so can be accessed from anywhere. So why should the reflective method invocation be illegal?

The problem isn't the access level of the method; it's the access level of the type from which the method is selected. This type plays the same role as the *qualifying type* in an ordinary method invocation [JLS 13.1]. In this program, the method is selected from the class represented by the Class object that is returned by it.getClass. This is the dynamic type of the iterator, which happens to be the private nested class java.util.HashMap.KeyIterator. The reason for the IllegalAccessException is that this class is not public and comes from another package: **You cannot legally access a member of a nonpublic type from another package** [JLS 6.6.1].

This prohibition applies whether the access is normal or reflective. Here is a program that runs afoul of this rule without resorting to reflection:

```
package library;
public class Api {
    static class PackagePrivate {}
    public static PackagePrivate member = new PackagePrivate();
}

package client;
import library.Api;
class Client {
    public static void main(String[] args) {
        System.out.println(Api.member.hashCode());
    }
}
```

Attempting to compile the program results in this error:

```
Client.java:5: Object.hashCode() isn't defined in a public
class or interface; can't be accessed from outside package
        System.out.println(Api.member.hashCode());
                                      ^
```

This diagnostic makes about as much sense as the runtime error generated by the original reflective program. The class Object and the method hashCode are both public. The problem is that the hashCode method is invoked with a qualifying type that is inaccessible to the client. The qualifying type of the method invocation is library.Api.PackagePrivate, which is a nonpublic class in a different package.

This does not imply that Client can't invoke hashCode on Api.member. To do this, it has merely to use an accessible qualifying type, which it can do by casting Api.member to Object. With this change, Client compiles and runs successfully:

```
System.out.println(((Object)Api.member).hashCode());
```

As a practical matter, this problem doesn't arise in ordinary nonreflective access, because API writers use only public types in their public APIs. Even if the problem were to occur, it would manifest itself as a compile-time error, so it would be fixed quickly and easily. Reflective access is another matter. **Although common, the idiom object.getClass().getMethod("methodName") is broken and should not be used.** It can easily result in an IllegalAccessException at run time, as we saw in the original program.

When accessing a type reflectively, use a Class object that represents an accessible type. Going back to our original program, the hasNext method is declared in the public type java.util.Iterator, so its class object should be used for reflective access. With this change, the Reflector program prints true as expected:

```
Method m = Iterator.class.getMethod("hasNext");
```

You can avoid this whole category of problem if you use reflection only for instantiation and use interfaces to invoke methods [EJ Item 35]. This use of reflection isolates the class that invokes methods from the class that implements them and provides a high degree of type-safety. It is commonly used in Service Provider Frameworks. This pattern does not solve every problem that demands reflective access, but if it solves your problem, by all means use it.

In summary, it is illegal to access a member of a nonpublic type in a different package, even if the member is also declared `public` in a public type. This is true whether the member is accessed normally or reflectively. The problem is likely to manifest itself only in reflective access. For platform designers, the lesson, as in Puzzle 67, is to make diagnostics as clear as possible. Both the runtime exception and the compiler diagnostic leave something to be desired.

Puzzle 79: It's a Dog's Life

This class models the life of a house pet. The `main` method creates a `Pet` instance representing a dog named Fido and lets it run. Although most dogs run in the backyard, this one runs in the background. What does the program print?

```java
public class Pet {
    public final String name;
    public final String food;
    public final String sound;

    public Pet(String name, String food, String sound) {
        this.name = name;
        this.food = food;
        this.sound = sound;
    }

    public void eat() {
        System.out.println(name + ": Mmmmm, " + food);
    }
    public void play() {
        System.out.println(name + ": " + sound + " " + sound);
    }
    public void sleep() {
        System.out.println(name + ": Zzzzzzz...");
    }

    public void live() {
        new Thread() {
            public void run() {
                while (true) {
                    eat();
                    play();
                    sleep();
                }
            }
        }.start();
    }

    public static void main(String[] args) {
        new Pet("Fido", "beef", "Woof").live();
    }
}
```

Solution 79: It's a Dog's Life

The main method creates a Pet instance representing Fido and invokes its live method. The live method, in turn, creates and starts a Thread that repeatedly executes the eat, play, and sleep methods from the enclosing Pet instance. Forever. Each of those methods prints a single line, so one would expect the program to print these three lines repeatedly:

```
Fido: Mmmmm, beef
Fido: Woof Woof
Fido: Zzzzzzz...
```

If you tried the program, you found that it won't even compile. The compiler error is less than helpful:

```
Pet.java:28: cannot find symbol
symbol: method sleep()
                  sleep();
                  ^
```

Why can't the compiler find the symbol? It's right there in black and white. As in Puzzle 74, the problem stems from the details of the overload resolution process. The compiler searches for the method in the innermost enclosing scope containing a method with the correct name [JLS 15.12.1]. For the sleep invocation in our program, that scope is the anonymous class containing the invocation, which inherits the methods Thread.sleep(long) and Thread.sleep(long,int). These are the only methods named sleep in that scope, and neither is applicable to this invocation because both require parameters. As neither candidate for the invocation is applicable, the compiler prints an error message.

The sleep methods inherited into the anonymous class from Thread *shadow* [JLS 6.3.1] the desired sleep method. As you saw in Puzzles 71 and 73, you should **avoid shadowing.** The shadowing in this puzzle is indirect and unintentional, which makes it even more insidious than usual.

The obvious way to fix the program is to change the name of the sleep method in Pet to snooze, doze, or nap. Another way to fix the problem is to name the class explicitly in the method invocation, using the *qualified* this construct [JLS 15.8.4]. The resulting invocation is Pet.this.sleep().

The third and arguably best way to fix the problem is to take the advice of Puzzle 77 and **use the Thread(Runnable) constructor instead of extending**

Thread. If you do this, the problem goes away because the anonymous class does not inherit `Thread.sleep`. This simple modification to the program produces the expected, if tiresome, output:

```
public void live() {
    new Thread(new Runnable() {
        public void run() {
            while (true) {
                eat();
                play();
                sleep();
            }
        }
    }).start();
}
```

In summary, beware of unintentional shadowing, and learn to recognize compiler errors that indicate its presence. For compiler writers, do your best to generate error messages that are meaningful to the programmer. In this case, for example, the compiler could alert the programmer to the existence of a shadowed method declaration that is applicable to the invocation.

Puzzle 80: Further Reflection

This program produces its output by printing an object that is created reflectively. What does the program print?

```
public class Outer {
    public static void main(String[] args) throws Exception {
        new Outer().greetWorld();
    }

    private void greetWorld() throws Exception {
        System.out.println(Inner.class.newInstance());
    }

    public class Inner {
        public String toString() {
            return "Hello world";
        }
    }
}
```

Solution 80: Further Reflection

This program looks like yet another unusual variant on the usual Hello world program. The main method in Outer creates an Outer instance and calls its greetWorld method, which prints the string form of a new Inner instance that it creates reflectively. The toString method of Inner always returns the standard greeting, so the output of the program should, as usual, be Hello world. If you try running it, you'll find the actual output to be longer and more confusing:

```
Exception in thread "main" InstantiationException: Outer$Inner
    at java.lang.Class.newInstance0(Class.java:335)
    at java.lang.Class.newInstance(Class.java:303)
    at Outer.greetWorld(Outer.java:7)
    at Outer.main(Outer.java:3)
```

Why would this exception be thrown? As of release 5.0, the documentation for Class.newInstance says that it throws InstantiationException if the Class object "represents an abstract class, an interface, an array class, a primitive type, or void; or if the class has no nullary [in other words, parameterless] constructor; or if the instantiation fails for some other reason" [Java-API]. Which of these conditions apply? Unfortunately, the exception message fails to provide even a hint.

Only the last two of these reasons could possibly apply: Either Outer.Inner has no nullary constructor or the instantiation failed "for some other reason." When a class has no explicit constructor, as is the case for Outer.Inner, Java automatically provides a default public constructor that takes no parameters [JLS 8.8.9], so there should be a nullary constructor. Nevertheless, the newInstance invocation fails because Outer.Inner has no nullary constructor!

The constructor of a non-static nested class is compiled such that it has as its first parameter an additional implicit parameter representing the *immediately enclosing instance* [JLS 13.1]. This parameter is passed implicitly when you invoke the constructor from any point in the code where the compiler can find an appropriate enclosing instance. But this applies only when you invoke the constructor normally: nonreflectively. When you invoke the constructor reflectively, this implicit parameter must be passed explicitly, which is impossible with Class.newInstance. The only way to pass this implicit parameter is to use java.lang.reflect.Constructor. When this change is made to the program, it prints Hello world as expected:

```
private void greetWorld() throws Exception {
    Constructor c = Inner.class.getConstructor(Outer.class);
    System.out.println(c.newInstance(Outer.this));
}
```

Alternatively, you might observe that `Inner` instances have no need for an enclosing `Outer` instance and so declare the class `Inner` to be `static`. **Unless you have a compelling need for an enclosing instance, prefer static member classes over nonstatic** [EJ Item 18]. This simple change will fix the program:

```
public static class Inner { ... }
```

The reflective model of Java programs is not the same as the language model. Reflection operates at the level of the virtual machine, exposing many details of the translation of Java programs into class files. Some of these details are mandated by the language specification, but others differ from implementation to implementation. The mapping from Java programs into class files was straightforward in early versions of the language, but it became more complex with the addition of advanced language features that are not directly supported in the VM, such as nested classes, covariant return types, generics, and enums.

Because of the complexity of the mapping from Java programs to class files, **avoid using reflection to instantiate inner classes.** More generally, be aware that when using reflection on program elements defined with advanced language features, the reflective view of the program may differ from the source view. Avoid depending on details of the translation that are not mandated by the language specification. The lesson for platform implementers is, once again, to provide clear and precise diagnostics.

Puzzle 81: Charred Beyond Recognition

This program appears to do the usual thing in an unusual way. What does it print?

```
public class Greeter {
    public static void main (String[] args) {
        String greeting = "Hello world";
        for (int i = 0; i < greeting.length(); i++)
            System.out.write(greeting.charAt(i));
    }
}
```

Solution 81: Charred Beyond Recognition

Although it's a bit strange, there is little reason to suspect that this program should misbehave. It writes "Hello world" to System.out, one character at a time. You may be aware that the write method uses only the low-order byte of its input parameter. This would cause trouble if "Hello world" contained any exotic characters, but it doesn't: It consists entirely of ASCII characters. Whether you print it one character at a time or all at once, the result should be the same: The program should print Hello world. Yet, if you ran it, it almost certainly printed nothing. Where did the greeting go? Perhaps the program just wasn't feeling all that cheerful?

The problem is that System.out is buffered. The characters in Hello world were written to the buffer for System.out, but the buffer was never flushed. Most programmers believe that System.out and System.err flush themselves automatically whenever output is performed. This is almost true but not quite. They are of type PrintStream, whose documentation says, as of release 5.0 [Java-API]:

> A PrintStream can be created so as to flush automatically; this means that the flush method is automatically invoked after a byte array is written, one of the println methods is invoked, or a newline character or byte ('\n') is written.

The streams referenced by System.out and System.err are indeed instances of the automatically flushing variant of PrintStream, but no mention is made of the write(int) method in the above documentation. The documentation for write(int) says: "Write the specified byte to this stream. If the byte is a newline *and* automatic flushing is enabled then the flush method will be invoked" [Java-API]. In practice, **write(int) is the *only* output method that does not flush a PrintStream on which automatic flushing is enabled.**

Curiously, if the program is modified to use print(char) instead of write(int), it flushes System.out and prints Hello world. This behavior contradicts the documentation for print(char), which says [Java-API]:

> Print a character. The character is translated into one or more bytes according to the platform's default character encoding, and these bytes are written in exactly the manner of the write(int) method.

Similarly, if the program is modified to use print(String), it flushes the stream even though the documentation prohibits it. The documentation should almost certainly be changed to describe the actual behavior; it would be too destabilizing to change the behavior.

The simplest change that fixes the program is to add a `System.out.flush` invocation after the loop. If this change is made, the program prints `Hello world` as expected. It would, however, be far better to rewrite the program to use the more familiar `System.out.println` idiom for producing output on the console.

The lesson of this program is, as in Puzzle 23: **Use familiar idioms whenever possible; if you must stray from familiar APIs, be sure to consult the documentation.** There are three lessons for API designers: Make the behavior of your methods clear from their names, document this behavior clearly, and correctly implement the documented behavior.

Puzzle 82: Beer Blast

Several puzzles in this chapter involved multiple threads, but this one involves multiple processes. What does this program print if you run it with the single command line argument `slave`? What does it print if you run it with no command line arguments?

```java
public class BeerBlast {
    static final String COMMAND = "java BeerBlast slave";
    public static void main(String[] args) throws Exception {
        if (args.length == 1 && args[0].equals("slave")) {
            for (int i = 99; i > 0; i--) {
                System.out.println(i +
                    " bottles of beer on the wall");
                System.out.println(i + " bottles of beer");
                System.out.println(
                    "You take one down, pass it around,");
                System.out.println((i-1) +
                    " bottles of beer on the wall");
                System.out.println();
            }
        } else {
            // Master
            Process process = Runtime.getRuntime().exec(COMMAND);
            int exitValue = process.waitFor();
            System.out.println("exit value = " + exitValue);
        }
    }
}
```

Solution 82: Beer Blast

If you run the program with the command line argument `slave`, it prints a stirring rendition of that classic childhood ditty, "99 Bottles of Beer on the Wall"—there's no mystery there. If you run it with no command line argument, it starts a slave process that prints the ditty, but you won't see the output of the slave process. The main process waits for the slave process to finish and then prints the exit value of the slave. By convention, the value 0 indicates normal termination, so that is what you might expect the program to print. If you ran it, you probably found that it just hung there, printing nothing at all. It's as if the slave process were taking forever. Although it might *feel* like it takes forever to listen to "99 Bottles of Beer on the Wall," especially if it is sung out of tune, the song has "only" 99 verses. Besides, computers are fast, so what's wrong with the program?

The clue to this mystery is in the documentation for the `Process` class, which says: "Because some native platforms only provide limited buffer size, failure to promptly read the output stream of the subprocess may cause the subprocess to block, and even deadlock" [Java-API]. That is exactly what's happening here: There is insufficient space in the buffer to hold the interminable ditty. To ensure that the slave process terminates, the parent must drain its output stream, which is an input stream from the perspective of the master. The following utility method performs this task in a background thread:

```java
static void drainInBackground(final InputStream is) {
    new Thread(new Runnable() {
        public void run() {
            try {
                while(is.read() >= 0) ;
            } catch (IOException e) {
                // return on IOException
            }
        }
    }).start();
}
```

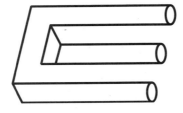

If we modify the program to invoke this method prior to waiting for the slave process, the program prints 0 as expected:

```
    } else {
        // Master
        Process process = Runtime.getRuntime().exec(COMMAND);
        drainInBackground(process.getInputStream());
        int exitValue = process.waitFor();
        System.out.println(exitValue);
    }
```

The lesson is that **you must drain the output stream of a child process in order to ensure its termination; the same goes for the error stream,** which can be even more troublesome because you can't predict when a process will dump lots of output to it. In release 5.0, a class named ProcessBuilder was added to help you drain these streams. Its redirectErrorStream method merges the streams so you have to drain only one. **If you elect not to merge the output and error streams, you must drain them concurrently.** Attempting to drain them sequentially can cause the child process to hang.

Many programmers have been bitten by this bug over the years. The lesson for API designers is that the Process class should have prevented this problem, perhaps by draining the output and error streams automatically unless the client expressed intent to read them. More generally, **APIs should make it easy to do the right thing and difficult or impossible to do the wrong thing.**

Puzzle 83: Dyslexic Monotheism

Once upon a time, there was a man who thought there was only one exceptional dog, so he wrote the following class, which he took to be a *singleton* [Gamma95]:

```
public class Dog extends Exception {
    public static final Dog INSTANCE = new Dog();
    private Dog() { }
    public String toString() {
        return "Woof";
    }
}
```

It turns out that this man was wrong. Can you create a second Dog instance from outside this class without using reflection?

Solution 83: Dyslexic Monotheism

This class may look like a singleton, but it isn't. The problem is that Dog extends Exception and Exception implements java.io.Serializable. This means that Dog is serializable, and deserialization constitutes a hidden constructor. If you serialize Dog.INSTANCE and deserialize the resulting byte sequence, you will end up with another Dog, as demonstrated by the following program. It prints false, indicating that the new Dog instance is distinct from the original, and Woof, indicating that the new Dog instance is functional:

```
import java.io.*;

public class CopyDog { // Not to be confused with copycat
    public static void main(String[] args) {
        Dog newDog = (Dog) deepCopy(Dog.INSTANCE);
        System.out.println(newDog == Dog.INSTANCE);
        System.out.println(newDog);
    }

    // This method is very slow and generally a bad idea!
    public static Object deepCopy(Object obj) {
        try {
            ByteArrayOutputStream bos =
                new ByteArrayOutputStream();
            new ObjectOutputStream(bos).writeObject(obj);
            ByteArrayInputStream bin =
                new ByteArrayInputStream(bos.toByteArray());
            return new ObjectInputStream(bin).readObject();
        } catch (Exception e) {
            throw new IllegalArgumentException(e);
        }
    }
}
```

To fix the problem, add a readResolve method to Dog, which turns the hidden constructor into a hidden static factory that returns the one true Dog [EJ Items 2, 57]. With the addition of this method to Dog, CopyDog will print true instead of false, indicating that the "copy" is in fact the original:

```
private Object readResolve() {
    // Accept no substitutes!
    return INSTANCE;
}
```

The main lesson of this puzzle is that **a singleton class that implements Serializable must have a readResolve method that returns its sole instance.** A secondary lesson is that it is possible to implement Serializable unintentionally, by extending a class that implements Serializable or by implementing an interface that extends Serializable. A lesson for platform designers is that hidden constructors, such as the one provided by serialization, can harm the reader's intuition about program behavior.

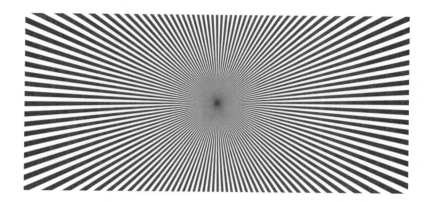

Puzzle 84: Rudely Interrupted

In this program, a thread tries to interrupt itself and then checks whether it succeeded. What does the program print?

```java
public class SelfInterruption {
    public static void main(String[] args) {
        Thread.currentThread().interrupt();

        if (Thread.interrupted()) {
            System.out.println("Interrupted: " +
                Thread.interrupted());
        } else {
            System.out.println("Not interrupted: " +
                Thread.interrupted());
        }
    }
}
```

Solution 84: Rudely Interrupted

Although it is not common for a thread to interrupt itself, it isn't unheard of, either. When a method catches an InterruptedException and is not prepared to deal with it, the method usually rethrows the exception. Because it is a checked exception, a method can rethrow it only if the method declaration permits. If not, the method can "reraise" the exception without rethrowing it, by interrupting the current thread. This works fine, so our program should have no trouble interrupting itself. Therefore, the program should take the first branch of the if statement and print Interrupted: true. If you ran the program, you found that it doesn't. It doesn't print Not interrupted: false, either; it prints Interrupted: false.

It looks as if the program can't make up its mind about whether the thread was interrupted. Of course, this makes no sense. What really happened was that the first invocation of Thread.interrupted returned true and cleared the interrupted status of the thread, so the second invocation—in the then branch of the if-then-else statement—returned false. **Calling Thread.interrupted always clears the interrupted status of the current thread.** The method name gives no hint of this behavior and, as of release 5.0, the one-sentence summary in the documentation is equally misleading: "Tests whether the current thread has been interrupted" [Java-API]. Therefore, it is understandable that many programmers are unaware that Thread.interrupted has any effect on the interrupted status of the thread.

The Thread class has two methods to query the interrupted status of a thread. The other one is an instance method named isInterrupted, and it does *not* clear the interrupted status of the thread. If rewritten to use this method, the program produces the expected output of Interrupted: true:

```java
public class SelfInterruption {
    public static void main(String[] args) {
        Thread.currentThread().interrupt();

        if (Thread.currentThread().isInterrupted()) {
            System.out.println("Interrupted: " +
                Thread.currentThread().isInterrupted());
        } else {
            System.out.println("Not interrupted: " +
                Thread.currentThread().isInterrupted());
        }
    }
}
```

The lesson of this puzzle is: **Don't use `Thread.interrupted` unless you want to clear the interrupted status of the current thread.** If you just want to query it, use `isInterrupted` instead. The lesson for API designers is that methods should have names that describe their primary functions. Given the behavior of `Thread.interrupted`, it should have been named `clearInterruptStatus`. Its return value is secondary to the state change it effects. Especially when a method has a name that is less than perfect, it is important that its documentation clearly describe its behavior.

Puzzle 85: Lazy Initialization

This poor little class is too lazy to initialize itself in the usual way, so it calls on the help of background thread. What does the program print? Is it guaranteed to print the same thing every time you run it?

```
public class Lazy {
    private static boolean initialized = false;

    static {
        Thread t = new Thread(new Runnable() {
            public void run() {
                initialized = true;
            }
        });
        t.start();
        try {
            t.join();
        } catch (InterruptedException e) {
            throw new AssertionError(e);
        }
    }

    public static void main(String[] args) {
        System.out.println(initialized);
    }
}
```

Solution 85: Lazy Initialization

This program looks straightforward, if a bit strange. The static field `initialized` is initially set to `false`. Then the main thread creates a background thread whose run method sets `initialized` to `true`. The main thread starts the background thread and waits for it to complete by calling `join`. Once the background thread has completed, there can be no doubt that `initialized` has been set to `true`. Then and only then does the main thread invoke `main`, which prints the value of `initialized`. Surely the program must print `true`? If only it were so. If you ran the program, you found that it prints nothing; it just hangs.

In order to understand the behavior of this program, we have to simulate its initialization in detail. When a thread is about to access a member of a class, the thread checks to see if the class has been initialized. Ignoring serious errors, there are four possible cases [JLS 12.4.2]:

1. The class is not yet initialized.

2. The class is being initialized by the current thread: a recursive request for initialization.

3. The class is being initialized by some thread other than the current thread.

4. The class is already initialized.

When the main thread invokes `Lazy.main`, it checks whether the class `Lazy` has been initialized. It hasn't (case 1), so the thread records that initialization is now in progress and begins to initialize the class. As per our previous analysis, the main thread now sets `initialized` to `false`, creates and starts a background thread whose run method sets `initialized` to `true`, and waits for the background thread to complete. Then the fun begins.

The background thread invokes its `run` method. Before the thread sets `Lazy.initialized` to `true`, it too checks whether the class `Lazy` has been initialized. This time, the class is currently being initialized by another thread (case 3). Under these circumstances, the current thread, which is the background thread, waits on the `Class` object until initialization is complete. Unfortunately, the thread that is doing the initialization, the main thread, is waiting for the background thread to complete. Because the two threads are now waiting for each other, the program is deadlocked. That's all there is to it, and what a pity it is.

There are two ways to fix the problem. By far the best way is not to start any background threads during class initialization: Sometimes, two threads aren't better than one. More generally, **keep class initialization as simple as possible.** A second way to fix the problem is to allow the main thread to finish initializing the class before waiting for the background thread:

```java
// Bad way to eliminate the deadlock. Complex and error prone.
public class Lazy {
    private static boolean initialized = false;
    private static Thread t = new Thread(new Runnable() {
        public void run() {
            initialized = true;
        }
    });

    static {
        t.start();
    }

    public static void main(String[] args) {
        try {
            t.join();
        } catch (InterruptedException e) {
            throw new AssertionError(e);
        }
        System.out.println(initialized);
    }
}
```

Although this does eliminate the deadlock, it is a very bad idea. The main thread waits for the background thread to finish its work, but other threads don't have to. They can use the class Lazy as soon as the main thread has finished initializing it, allowing them to observe initialized when its value is still false.

In summary, **waiting for a background thread during class initialization is likely to result in deadlock.** Keep class initialization sequences as simple as possible. Automatic class initialization is known to be a very difficult language design problem, and Java's designers did a fine job in this area. Still, there are many ways to shoot yourself in the foot if you write complex class initialization code.

10

Advanced Puzzlers

The puzzles in this chapter concern advanced topics, such as nested classes, generics, serialization, and binary compatibility.

Puzzle 86: Poison-Paren Litter

Can you come up with a legal Java expression that can be made illegal by parenthesizing a subexpression, where the added parentheses serve only to document the order of evaluation that would take place in their absence?

Solution 86: Poison-Paren Litter

It seems that inserting a pair of parentheses serving only to document the existing order of evaluation should have no effect on the legality of a program. Indeed, this is true in nearly all cases. In two cases, however, inserting a seemingly innocuous pair of parentheses can make a legal Java program illegal. This strange state of affairs stems from the asymmetry of the two's-complement binary numbers, discussed in Puzzle 33 and Puzzle 64.

You may recall that the most negative int value has a magnitude that is one greater than the most positive: Integer.MIN_VALUE is -2^{31}, or $-2{,}147{,}483{,}648$, whereas Integer.MAX_VALUE is $2^{31} - 1$, or $2{,}147{,}483{,}647$. Java does not support negative decimal literals; negative int and long constants are constructed by prefixing positive decimal literals with the unary minus operator (-). A special language rule governs this construction: The largest decimal literal of type int is 2147483648. Decimal literals from 0 to 2147483647 may appear anywhere an int literal may appear, but the literal 2147483648 may appear *only* as the operand of the unary negation operator [JLS 3.10.1].

Once you know this rule, the puzzle is easy. The characters -2147483648 form a legal Java expression consisting of the unary minus operator followed by the int literal 2147483648. Adding a pair of parentheses to document the (trivial) order of evaluation gives -(2147483648), which violates the rule. Believe it or not, this program really does generate a compile-time error, and the error goes away if you remove the parentheses:

```java
public class PoisonParen {
    int i = -(2147483648);
}
```

The situation for long literals is analogous. This program too generates a compile-time error that goes away if you remove the parentheses:

```java
public class PoisonParen {
    long j = -(9223372036854775808L);
}
```

As for a lesson, this puzzle has none. It's a corner case, pure and simple. But you must admit, it's amusing.

Puzzle 87: Strained Relations

In mathematics, the equals sign (=) defines an *equivalence relation* on the real numbers. An equivalence relation partitions a set into *equivalence classes*, each consisting of all the values that are equivalent to one another. Other equivalence relations include "is congruent to" on the set of all triangles and "has the same number of pages as" on the set of all books. Formally, a relation ~ is an equivalence relation if and only if it is *reflexive*, *transitive*, and *symmetric*. These properties are defined as follows:

- Reflexive: *x* ~ *x* for all *x*. In other words, every value is related to itself.

- Transitive: if *x* ~ *y* and *y* ~ *z*, then *x* ~ *z*. In other words, if one value is related to a second and the second is related to a third, the first value is related to the third.

- Symmetric: if *x* ~ *y*, then *y* ~ *x*. In other words, if one value is related to a second, the second value is related to the first.

But this isn't a book about set theory; it's a book about Java. In Java, does the == operator define an equivalence relation over the primitive values? If not, which of the three properties does it violate? Provide code snippets to demonstrate any violations.

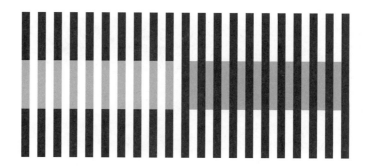

Solution 87: Strained Relations

If you did Puzzle 29, you know that the == operator is not reflexive, because the expression (Double.NaN == Double.NaN) evaluates to false, as does the expression (Float.NaN == Float.NaN). But does the == operator violate symmetry or transitivity? It turns out that it does not violate symmetry: (x == y) implies that (y == x) for all values x and y. Transitivity is another matter entirely.

Puzzle 35 provides a clue as to why the == operator is not transitive over the primitive values. When comparing two numeric primitive values, the == operator first performs *binary numeric promotion* [JLS 5.6.2]. This may result in a *widening primitive conversion* on one of the two values [JLS 5.1.2]. Most widening primitive conversions are harmless, with three notable exceptions: **Converting an int or a long value to float, or a long value to double can result in loss of precision.** This loss of precision can manifest itself as nontransitivity of the == operator.

The trick to achieving this nontransitivity is to lose precision in two of the three value comparisons, resulting in false positives. This can be accomplished, for example, by choosing large but distinct long values for x and z, and a double value that is close to both long values for y. The following program does exactly that. It prints true true false, clearly demonstrating the nontransitivity of the == operator over primitives:

```java
public class Transitive {
    public static void main(String[] args) throws Exception {
        long x = Long.MAX_VALUE;
        double y = (double) Long.MAX_VALUE;
        long z = Long.MAX_VALUE - 1;

        System.out.print ((x == y) + " "); // Imprecise!
        System.out.print ((y == z) + " "); // Imprecise!
        System.out.println(x == z);        // Precise
    }
}
```

The lesson is: **Beware of lossy widening primitive conversions to float and double.** They are silent but deadly. They can violate your intuition and cause subtle bugs (Puzzle 34). More generally, beware of mixed-type operations (Puzzles 5, 8, 24, and 31). The lesson for language designers is the same as for Puzzle 34: Silent loss of precision confuses programmers.

Puzzle 88: Raw Deal

This program consists of a single class representing a pair of like-typed objects. It makes heavy use of release 5.0 features, including generics, autoboxing, varargs, and the for-each loop. See http://java.sun.com/j2se/5.0/docs/guide/language for an introduction to these features [Java-5.0]. The main method of this program gently exercises the class. What does it print?

```java
import java.util.*;

public class Pair<T> {
    private final T first;
    private final T second;

    public Pair(T first, T second) {
        this.first = first;
        this.second = second;
    }

    public T first() {
        return first;
    }
    public T second() {
        return second;
    }
    public List<String> stringList() {
        return Arrays.asList(String.valueOf(first),
                             String.valueOf(second));
    }

    public static void main(String[] args) {
        Pair p = new Pair<Object>(23, "skidoo");
        System.out.println(p.first() + " " + p.second());
        for (String s : p.stringList())
            System.out.print(s + " ");
    }
}
```

Solution 88: Raw Deal

This program appears reasonably straightforward. It creates a pair whose first element is the Integer representing 23 and whose second element is the string "skidoo". Then the program prints the first and second elements of the pair, separated by a space. Finally, it iterates over the string representations of these elements and prints them again, so it ought to print 23 skidoo twice. Sadly, it doesn't even compile. Worse, the compiler's error message is terribly confusing:

```
Pair.java:26: incompatible types;
found: Object, required: String
        for (String s : p.stringList())
                         ^
```

This message would make sense if Pair.stringList were declared to return List<Object>, but it returns List<String>. What on earth is going on?

This rather surprising behavior is caused by the program's use of *raw* types. A raw type is simply the name of a generic class or interface without any type parameters. For example, List<E> is a generic interface, List<String> is a parameterized type, and List is a raw type. In our program, the sole use of raw types is the declaration of the local variable p in main:

```
Pair p = new Pair<Object>(23, "skidoo");
```

A raw type is like its parameterized counterpart, but all its instance members are replaced by their *erased* counterparts. In particular, each parameterized type appearing in an instance method declaration is replaced with its raw counterpart [JLS 4.8]. The variable p in our program is of the raw type Pair, so its instance methods are erased. This includes the stringList method, which is declared to return List<String>. The compiler interprets the program as if this method returned the raw type List.

While List<String> implements the parameterized type Iterable<String>, List implements the raw type Iterable. Where Iterable<String> has an iterator method that returns the parameterized type Iterator<String>, Iterable has an iterator method that returns the raw type Iterator. Where the next method of Iterator<String> returns String, the next method of Iterator returns Object. Therefore, iterating over p.stringList() requires a loop variable of type Object, which explains the compiler's bizarre error message. The reason this behavior is so counterintuitive is that the parameterized type

List<String>, which is the return type of the stringList method, has nothing to do with the type parameter of Pair, but it gets erased anyway.

You could attempt to fix the problem by changing the type of the loop variable from String to Object:

```
// Don't do this; it doesn't really fix the problem!
for (Object s : p.stringList())
    System.out.print(s + " ");
```

This does cause the program to generate the expected output, but it doesn't really fix the problem. You lose all the benefits of generics, and the program wouldn't even compile if the loop invoked any String methods on s. The right way to fix the program is to provide a proper parameterized declaration for the local variable p:

```
Pair<Object> p = new Pair<Object>(23, "skidoo");
```

This underscores a key point: **The raw type List is not the same as the parameterized type List<Object>.** If the raw type is used, the compiler has no idea whether there are any restrictions on the type of elements permitted by the list, but it lets you insert elements of any type. This is not typesafe: If you insert an object of the wrong type, you may get a ClassCastException at any point in the future execution of the program. If the parameterized type List<Object> is used, the compiler knows that the list is allowed to contain elements of all types, so it is safe to let you insert any object.

There is a third type that is closely related to these two: List<?> is a special kind of parameterized type known as a *wildcard* type. Like the raw type List, the compiler does not know what type of element is permitted, but because List<?> is a parameterized type, the language requires stronger type-checking. To avoid the possibility of a ClassCastException, the compiler won't let you insert any element except null into a list of type List<?>.

Raw types are a concession to existing code, which could not use generics prior to release 5.0. Many core library classes, such as collections, have been modified to take advantage of generics, but existing clients of those classes continue to behave as in previous releases. The behavior of raw types and their members was designed to mirror the pre-5 language, so as to retain compatibility.

The real problem with the Pair program is that the author did not decide what version of Java to use. Although most of the program uses generics, the variable p is declared with a raw type. To avoid bewildering compile-time errors, **avoid writing raw types in code intended for release 5.0 or later.** If an existing library method returns a raw type, store its result in a variable of an appropriate parameterized type. Better yet, upgrade to a version of the library that use generics, if possible. Although Java provides graceful interoperability between raw and parameterized types, limitations of raw types can interfere with the utility of generics.

This issue can arise in practice when reading `Class` annotations at run time with the `getAnnotation` method, which was added to class `Class` in release 5.0. Two `Class` objects are involved in each invocation of `getAnnotation`: the object on which the invocation is made and the object that is passed to indicate which annotation is desired. In a typical invocation, the former is obtained reflectively; the latter is a class literal, as in the following example:

```
Author a = Class.forName(name).getAnnotation(Author.class);
```

You do not have to cast the return value from `getAnnotation` to `Author`. Two things conspire to make this work: (1) The `getAnnotation` method is generic. It infers its return type from its parameter type. Specifically, it takes a parameter of type `Class<T>` and returns a value of type `T`. (2) Class literals provide generic type information. For example, the type of `Author.class` is `Class<Author>`. The class literal conveys both run-time and compile-time type information. Class literals used in this fashion are known as *type tokens* [Bracha04].

In contrast to class literals, `Class` objects obtained through reflection do not provide full generic type information: The return type of `Class.forName` is the wildcard type `Class<?>`. It is critical that you use this wildcard type rather than the raw type `Class` for the expression on which you invoke the `getAnnotation` method. If you use the raw type, the returned annotation will have the compile-time type of `Annotation` instead of the type indicated by the class literal. The following program fragment, which violates this advice, won't compile for the same reason that the original program in this puzzle did not:

```
Class c = Class.forName(name);              // Raw type!
Author a = c.getAnnotation(Author.class);   // Type mismatch
```

In summary, the members of a raw type are erased to simulate the behavior of the type before generics were added to the language. If you mix raw and parameterized types, you will not get the full benefit of generics, and you may get some very confusing compile-time errors. Also, a raw type is not the same as a parameterized type whose type parameter is `Object`. Finally, if you are migrating an existing code base to take advantage of generics, the best approach is to migrate one API at a time and to avoid entirely the use of raw types in new code.

Puzzle 89: Generic Drugs

Like the previous puzzle, this one makes heavy use of generics. Learning from our previous mistakes, we refrain from using raw types. This program implements a simple linked list data structure. The main program builds a list with two elements and dumps its contents. What does the program print?

```java
public class LinkedList<E> {
    private Node<E> head = null;

    private class Node<E> {
        E value;
        Node<E> next;

        // Node constructor links the node as a new head
        Node(E value) {
            this.value = value;
            this.next = head;
            head = this;
        }
    }

    public void add(E e) {
        new Node<E>(e);
        // Link node as new head
    }

    public void dump() {
        for (Node<E> n = head; n != null; n = n.next)
            System.out.print(n.value + " ");
    }

    public static void main(String[] args) {
        LinkedList<String> list = new LinkedList<String>();
        list.add("world");
        list.add("Hello");
        list.dump();
    }
}
```

Solution 89: Generic Drugs

Again, this program appears reasonably straightforward. New elements are added to the head of the list and the dump method prints the list starting with the head. Therefore, elements are printed in the opposite order they are added. In this case, the program first adds "world" and then "Hello", so it looks as if it is just a convoluted Hello world program. Sadly, if you tried to compile it, you found that it doesn't compile. The error messages from the compiler are downright baffling:

```
LinkedList.java:11: incompatible types
found  : LinkedList<E>.Node<E>
required: LinkedList<E>.Node<E>
            this.next = head;
                        ^

LinkedList.java:12: incompatible types
found  : LinkedList<E>.Node<E>
required: LinkedList<E>.Node<E>
            head = this;
                   ^
```

It appears that the compiler is complaining that a type isn't compatible with itself! Appearances, as usual, are deceiving. The "found" and "required" types are unrelated to each other. They appear identical because the program uses the same name to refer to different types. Specifically, the program contains two different declarations for type parameters named E. The first is the type parameter for LinkedList, and the second is the type parameter for the inner class LinkedList.Node. The latter shadows the former within the inner class. The lesson that we learned in Puzzles 71, 73, and 79 applies here as well: **Avoid shadowing type parameter names.**

There is no way to refer to a type parameter except by its simple name, so the error message has no way to tell you that these two uses of the name E refer to different types. The error message would be clearer if we systematically renamed the type parameter for Node from E to, say, T. It wouldn't fix the problem, but it would shed some light on it. This approach yields the following error messages:

```
LinkedList.java:11: incompatible types
found  : LinkedList<E>.Node<E>
required: LinkedList<E>.Node<T>
            this.next = head;
                        ^
```

```
LinkedList.java:12: incompatible types
found : LinkedList<E>.Node<T>
required: LinkedList<E>.Node<E>
            head = this;
              ^
```

What the compiler is trying to tell us is that the program is way too complicated. **An inner class of a generic class has access to the type parameters of its outer class.** It was the clear intent of the program's author that the type parameter for a Node would always be the same as for the enclosing LinkedList, so there is no reason for Node to have a type parameter of its own. To fix the program, simply eliminate the type parameter in the inner class:

```
// Fixed but could be MUCH better
public class LinkedList<E> {
    private Node head = null;

    private class Node {
        E value;
        Node next;

        // Node constructor links the node as a new head
        Node(E value) {
            this.value = value;
            this.next = head;
            head = this;
        }
    }

    public void add(E e) {
        new Node(e);
        // Link node as new head
    }

    public void dump() {
        for (Node n = head; n != null; n = n.next)
            System.out.print(n.value + " ");
    }
}
```

This is the simplest change that fixes the program, but it is not the best. The original program used an inner class unnecessarily. As mentioned in Puzzle 80, you should **prefer static member classes over nonstatic** [EJ Item 18]. An instance of LinkedList.Node contains not only the value and next fields but also a hidden field containing a reference to the enclosing LinkedList instance.

Although the enclosing instance is used during construction to read and then modify head, it is dead weight once construction has completed. Worse, placing the side effect of changing head into the constructor makes the program confusing to the reader. **Change instance fields of a class only in its own instance methods.**

A better fix, then, is to modify the original program to move the manipulation of head into LinkedList.add, making Node a static nested class rather than a true inner class. Static nested classes do not have access to the type parameters of enclosing classes, so now Node really does need a type parameter of its own. The resulting program is simple, clear, and correct:

```
class LinkedList<E> {
    private Node<E> head = null;

    private static class Node<T> {
        T value; Node<T> next;

        Node(T value, Node<T> next) {
            this.value = value;
            this.next = next;
        }
    }

    public void add(E e) {
        head = new Node<E>(e, head);
    }

    public void dump() {
        for (Node<E> n = head; n != null; n = n.next)
            System.out.print(n.value + " ");
    }
}
```

In summary, inner classes of generic classes have access to the enclosing class's type parameters, which can be confusing. The misunderstanding illustrated in this puzzle is common among programmers first learning generics. It isn't necessarily wrong to have an inner class in a generic class, but the need for this is rare, and you should consider refactoring your code to avoid it. When you have one generic class nested inside another, give their type parameters different names, even if the nested class is static. For language designers, perhaps it makes sense to forbid shadowing of type parameters, in the same way that shadowing of local variables is forbidden. Such a rule would have caught the bug in this puzzle.

Puzzle 90: It's Absurd, It's a Pain, It's Superclass!

The following program doesn't actually do anything. Worse, it won't compile. Why not? How can you fix it?

```
public class Outer {
    class Inner1 extends Outer {}
    class Inner2 extends Inner1 {}
}
```

Solution 90: It's Absurd, It's a Pain, It's Superclass

This program looks too simple to have anything wrong with it, but if you try to compile it, you get this helpful error message:

```
Outer.java:3: cannot reference this before
               supertype constructor has been called
    class Inner2 extends Inner1 {}
    ^
```

OK, maybe it's not so helpful, but we'll work on that. The problem is that the compiler-generated default constructor for `Inner2` cannot find an appropriate enclosing instance for its `super` invocation. Let's look at the program with the default constructors included explicitly:

```java
public class Outer {
    public Outer() {}

    class Inner1 extends Outer {
        Inner1() {
            super();  // invokes Outer() constructor
        }
    }

    class Inner2 extends Inner1 {
        Inner2() {
            super();  // invokes Inner1() constructor
        }
    }
}
```

Now the error message gives a bit more information:

```
Outer.java:12: cannot reference this before
               supertype constructor has been called
        super(); // invokes Inner1() constructor
        ^
```

Because the superclass of `Inner2` is itself an inner class, an obscure language rule comes into play. As you know, the instantiation of an inner class, such as `Inner1`, requires an enclosing instance to be supplied to the constructor. Normally, it is supplied implicitly, but it can also be supplied explicitly with a *superclass constructor invocation* of the form `expression.super(args)` [JLS 8.8.7].

If the enclosing instance is supplied implicitly, the compiler generates the expression: It uses the `this` reference for the innermost enclosing class of which the superclass is a member. This is, admittedly, quite a mouthful, but it is what the compiler does. In this case, the superclass is `Inner1`. Because the current class, `Inner2`, extends `Outer` indirectly, it has `Inner1` as an inherited member. Therefore, the qualifying expression for the superclass constructor is simply `this`. The compiler supplies an enclosing instance, rewriting `super` to `this.super`. Had we done this ourselves, the compilation error would have made even more sense:

```
Outer.java:12: cannot reference this before
               supertype constructor has been called
      this.super();
      ^
```

Now the problem is clear: The default `Inner2` constructor attempts to reference `this` before the superclass constructor has been called, which is illegal [JLS 8.8.7.1]. The brute-force way to fix this problem is to provide the reasonable enclosing instance explicitly:

```java
public class Outer {
    class Inner1 extends Outer { }

    class Inner2 extends Inner1 {
        Inner2() {
            Outer.this.super();
        }
    }
}
```

This compiles, but it is mind-numbingly complex. There is a better solution: **Whenever you write a member class, ask yourself, Does this class really need an enclosing instance? If the answer is no, make it static.** Inner classes are sometimes useful, but they can easily introduce complications that make a program difficult to understand. They have complex interactions with generics (Puzzle 89), reflection (Puzzle 80), and inheritance (this puzzle). If you declare `Inner1` to be `static`, the problem goes away. If you also declare `Inner2` to be `static`, you can actually understand what the program does: a nice bonus indeed.

In summary, it is rarely appropriate for one class to be both an inner class and a subclass of another. More generally, **it is rarely appropriate to extend an inner class; if you must, think long and hard about the enclosing instance.** Also, prefer static nested classes to nonstatic [EJ Item 18]. Most member classes can and should be declared `static`.

Puzzle 91: Serial Killer

This program creates an object and checks that it obeys a class invariant. Then the program serializes the object, deserializes it, and checks that the deserialized copy also obeys the invariant. Does it? If not, why not?

```java
import java.util.*;
import java.io.*;

public class SerialKiller {
    public static void main(String[] args) {
        Sub sub = new Sub(666);
        sub.checkInvariant();

        Sub copy = (Sub) deepCopy(sub);
        copy.checkInvariant();
    }

    // Copies its argument via serialization (See Puzzle 83)
    static public Object deepCopy(Object obj) {
        try {
            ByteArrayOutputStream bos =
                new ByteArrayOutputStream();
            new ObjectOutputStream(bos).writeObject(obj);
            ByteArrayInputStream bin =
                new ByteArrayInputStream(bos.toByteArray());
            return new ObjectInputStream(bin).readObject();
        } catch (Exception e) {
            throw new IllegalArgumentException(e);
        }
    }
}
```

```java
class Super implements Serializable {
    final Set<Super> set = new HashSet<Super>();
}

final class Sub extends Super {
    private int id;
    public Sub(int id) {
        this.id = id;
        set.add(this); // Establish invariant
    }

    public void checkInvariant() {
        if (!set.contains(this))
            throw new AssertionError("invariant violated");
    }

    public int hashCode() {
        return id;
    }

    public boolean equals(Object o) {
        return (o instanceof Sub) && (id == ((Sub)o).id);
    }
}
```

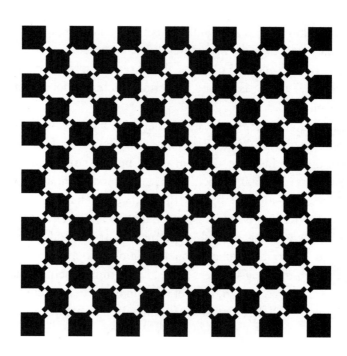

Solution 91: Serial Killer

Save for the fact that the program uses serialization, it looks simple. The subclass Sub overrides hashCode and equals. The overriding methods satisfy the relevant general contracts [EJ Items 7, 8]. The Sub constructor establishes the class invariant, and does so without invoking an overridable method (Puzzle 51). The Super class has a single field, of type Set<Super>, and the Sub class adds another field, of type int. Neither Super nor Sub requires a custom serialized form. What could possibly go wrong?

Plenty. As of release 5.0, running the program produces this stack trace:

```
Exception in thread "main" AssertionError
    at Sub.checkInvariant(SerialKiller.java:41)
    at SerialKiller.main(SerialKiller.java:10)
```

Serializing and deserializing a Sub instance produces a corrupt copy. Why? Looking at the program will not tell you, because the real source of the problem lies elsewhere. It is caused by the readObject method of the class HashSet. Under certain circumstances, this method can indirectly invoke an overridden method on an uninitialized object. In order to populate the hash set that is being deserialized, HashSet.readObject calls HashMap.put, which in turn calls hashCode on each key. Because a whole object graph is being deserialized at once, there is no guarantee that each key has been completely initialized when its hashCode method is invoked. In practice, this is rarely an issue, but occasionally it causes utter chaos. The bug is tickled by certain cycles in the object graph that is being deserialized.

To make this more concrete, let us look at what happens when we deserialize the Sub instance in the program. First, the serialization system deserializes the Super fields of the Sub instance. The only such field is set, which contains a reference to a HashSet. Internally, each HashSet instance contains a reference to a HashMap, whose keys are the hash set's elements. The HashSet class has a readObject method that creates an empty HashMap and inserts a key-value mapping for each element in the set, using the map's put method. This method calls hashCode on the key to determine its bucket. In our program, the sole key in the hash map is the Sub instance whose set field is currently being deserialized. The subclass field of this instance, id, has yet to be initialized, so it contains 0, the initial value assigned to all int fields. Unfortunately, the hashCode method in Sub returns this value instead of 666, which will eventually be stored in this field.

Because hashCode returns the wrong value, the entry for the key-value mapping is placed in the wrong bucket. By the time the id field is initialized to 666, it is too late. Changing the value of this field once the Sub instance is in the HashMap corrupts it, which corrupts the HashSet, which corrupts the Sub instance. The program detects this corruption and throws an appropriate error.

This program illustrates that the serialization system as a whole, which includes the readObject method of HashMap, violates the rule that you must not invoke an overridable method of a class from its constructor or pseudoconstructor [EJ Item 15]. The (default) readObject method of the class Super invokes the (explicit) readObject method of the class HashSet, which invokes the put method on its internal HashMap, which invokes the hashCode method on the Sub instance that is currently in the process of creation. Now we are in big trouble: The hashCode method that Super inherits from Object is overridden in Sub, and this overridden method executes before the initialization of the Sub field, on which it depends.

This failure is nearly identical in nature to the one in Puzzle 51. The only real difference is that in this puzzle, the readObject pseudoconstructor is at fault instead of the constructor. The readObject methods of HashMap and Hashtable are similarly affected.

For platform implementers, it may be possible to fix this problem in HashSet, HashMap, and Hashtable at a slight performance penalty. The strategy, as it applies to HashSet, is to rewrite the readObject method to store the set's elements in an array instead of putting them in the hash set at deserialization time. Then, on the first invocation of a public method on the deserialized hash set, the elements in the array would be inserted into the set before executing the method.

The cost of this approach is that it requires checking whether to populate the hash set on entry to each of its public methods. Because HashSet, HashMap, and Hashtable are all performance-critical, this approach seems undesirable. It is unfortunate that all users would have to pay the cost, even if they did not serialize the collections. This violates the tenet that you should never have to pay for functionality that you don't use.

Another possible approach would be for HashSet.readObject to call ObjectInputStream.registerValidation and to delay population of the hash set until the validateObject callback. This approach seems more attractive in that it adds cost only to deserialization, but it would break any code that tried to use a deserialized HashSet instance while deserialization of the containing stream was still in progress.

Whether either of these approaches is practical remains to be seen. In the meantime, we must live with the current behavior. Luckily, there is a workaround: **If a HashSet, Hashtable, or HashMap will be serialized, ensure that its contents do not refer back to it, directly or indirectly.** By *contents*, we mean elements, keys, and values.

There is also a lesson for developers of serializable classes: **In readObject or readResolve methods, avoid invoking methods directly or indirectly on objects currently being deserialized.** If you must violate this advice in the readObject or readResolve method for some class *C*, ensure that no instance of *C* appears in a cycle in the graph of objects being deserialized. Unfortunately, this is not a local property: In general, you must consider the whole system in order to verify it.

In summary, the Java serialization system is fragile. In order to serialize many classes correctly and efficiently, you must write readObject or readResolve methods [EJ Items 55–57]. This puzzle demonstrates that you must write these methods carefully in order to avoid corruption of deserialized instances. The readObject methods of HashSet, HashMap, and Hashtable are susceptible to corruption. For platform designers, if you choose to provide a serialization system, try to design one that is not so fragile. Robust serialization systems are notoriously difficult to design.

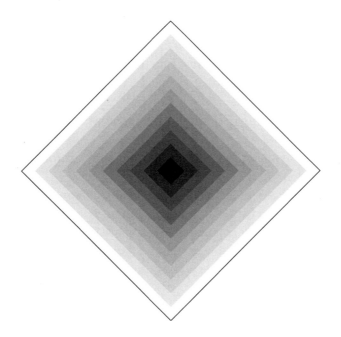

Puzzle 92: Twisted Pair

This program performs an unnatural act with an anonymous class. What does the program print?

```java
public class Twisted {
    private final String name;
    Twisted(String name) {
        this.name = name;
    }
    private String name() {
        return name;
    }
    private void reproduce() {
        new Twisted("reproduce") {
            void printName() {
                System.out.println(name());
            }
        }.printName();
    }
    public static void main(String[] args) {
        new Twisted("main").reproduce();
    }
}
```

Solution 92: Twisted Pair

A superficial analysis suggests that the program shouldn't compile. The anonymous class inside `reproduce` tries to invoke the private method `name` from the class `Twisted`. One class can't invoke a private method of another, can it? If you tried to compile the program, you found that it compiles without a hitch. Within a top-level type—in this case, `Twisted`—all the local, inner, nested, and anonymous classes can access one another's members without any restrictions [JLS 6.6.1]. It's all one big happy family.

With that understanding, you might expect the program to print `reproduce`, because it invokes `printName` on the instance `new Twisted("reproduce")`, which passes the string `"reproduce"` to its superclass constructor to be stored in its `name` field. The `printName` method invokes the `name` method, which returns the contents of this field. But if you ran the program, you found that it prints `main`. Now why would it do a thing like that?

The intuition behind this behavior is that **private members are never inherited** [JLS 8.2]. In this case, the `name` method is not inherited into the anonymous class in `reproduce`. Therefore, the `printName` invocation in the anonymous class must refer to the method in the enclosing (`"main"`) instance rather than the current (`"reproduce"`) instance. This is the smallest enclosing scope that contains a method of the correct name (Puzzles 71 and 79).

This program violates the advice of Puzzle 90: The anonymous class inside `"reproduce"` is both an inner class of `Twisted` and extends it. This alone is sufficient to make the program unreadable. Throw in the complexity of invoking a private superclass method, and the program becomes pure gobbledygook. This puzzle serves to reinforce the lesson of Puzzle 6: **If you can't tell what a program does by looking at it, it probably doesn't do what you want.** Strive for clarity.

Puzzle 93: Class Warfare

This puzzle tests your knowledge of *binary compatibility*: What happens to the behavior of one class when you change another class on which the first class depends? More specifically, suppose that you compile the following two classes. The first is meant to represent a client; the second, a library class:

```
public class PrintWords {
    public static void main(String[] args) {
        System.out.println(Words.FIRST  + " " +
                           Words.SECOND + " " +
                           Words.THIRD);
    }
}

public class Words {
    private Words() { };   // Uninstantiable

    public static final String FIRST  = "the";
    public static final String SECOND = null;
    public static final String THIRD  = "set";
}
```

Now suppose that you modify the library class as follows and recompile it but not the client program:

```
public class Words {
    private Words() { };   // Uninstantiable

    public static final String FIRST  = "physics";
    public static final String SECOND = "chemistry";
    public static final String THIRD  = "biology";
}
```

What does the client program print?

Solution 93: Class Warfare

A quick look suggests that the program should print physics chemistry biology; after all, Java loads classes at run time, so it always has access to the latest version of a class. A deeper analysis suggests otherwise. **References to constant fields are resolved at compile time to the constant values they denote** [JLS 13.1]. Such fields are technically, if oxymoronically, known as *constant variables*. A constant variable is defined as a variable of primitive type or type String that is final and initialized with a compile-time constant expression [JLS 4.12.4]. With the benefit of this knowledge, it would be reasonable to think that the client program compiles the initial values of Words.FIRST, Words.SECOND, and Words.THIRD into its class file and prints the null set, regardless of whether the class Words has been modified.

Reasonable, perhaps, but not correct. If you ran the program, you found that it prints the chemistry set. This seems truly bizarre. Why would it do a thing like that? The answer is to be found in the precise definition of the term *compile-time constant expression* [JLS 15.28]. The definition is too long to reproduce here, but the key to understanding the behavior of the program is that **null is not a compile-time constant expression.**

Because constant fields are compiled into clients, **API designers should think long and hard before exporting a constant field.** If a field represents a true constant, such as π or the number of days in a week, there is no harm in making it a constant field. If, however, you want clients to adapt to changes in the field, make sure that it isn't a constant. There is an easy way to do this: If you initialize a field, even a final field, with an expression that isn't constant, the field isn't constant. You can turn a constant expression into a nonconstant by passing it to a method that simply returns its input parameter.

If we modify the class Words to use such a method, PrintWords will print physics chemistry biology after Words is again modified and recompiled:

```
public class Words {
    private Words() { }; // Uninstantiable
    public static final String FIRST  = ident("the");
    public static final String SECOND = ident(null);
    public static final String THIRD  = ident("set");

    private static String ident(String s) {
        return s;
    }
}
```

Despite their name, enum constants, introduced in release 5.0, are *not* constant variables. You can add enum constants to an enum type, reorder them, and even remove unused enum constants without the need to recompile clients.

In summary, constant variables are compiled into classes that reference those variables. A constant variable is any primitive or string variable that is initialized with a constant expression. Surprisingly, null is *not* a constant expression.

For language designers, perhaps it is not such a good idea to compile constant expressions into clients in a language that is otherwise dynamically linked. It is surprising to many programmers and can produce bugs that are difficult to diagnose: The source code in which constants were defined may no longer exist when a bug is detected. On the other hand, compiling constant expressions into clients does enable the use of if statements to emulate conditional compilation [JLS 14.21]. It is a matter of judgment whether the end justifies the means.

Puzzle 94: Lost in the Shuffle

The following shuffle method purports to shuffle its input array fairly. In other words, it purports to generate all permutations with equal likelihood, assuming that the underlying pseudorandom number generator is fair. Does it make good on its promise? If not, how do you fix it?

```java
import java.util.Random;

public class Shuffle {
    private static Random rnd = new Random();

    public static void shuffle(Object[] a) {
        for (int i = 0; i < a.length; i++)
            swap(a, i, rnd.nextInt(a.length));
    }

    private static void swap(Object[] a, int i, int j) {
        Object tmp = a[i];
        a[i] = a[j];
        a[j] = tmp;
    }
}
```

Solution 94: Lost in the Shuffle

Looking at the shuffle method, there's nothing obviously wrong with it. It iterates through the array, swapping a randomly chosen element from the array into each location. That ought to shuffle the array fairly, right? Wrong. There's a big difference between saying "There's nothing obviously wrong with this code" and "There's obviously nothing wrong with this code." In this case, there's something very wrong, but it isn't obvious unless you specialize in algorithms.

If you call the shuffle method on an array of length n, the loop iterates n times. In each iteration, the method chooses one of the n integers between 0 and $n - 1$. Therefore, there are n^n possible executions of the method. We assumed the random number generator is fair, so each execution occurs with equal likelihood. Each execution generates one permutation of the array. There is, however, one small problem: There are $n!$ distinct permutations of an array of length n. (The exclamation point after n indicates the *factorial* operation: n factorial is defined as $n \times (n - 1) \times (n - 2) \times \ldots \times 1$.) The problem is that n^n is not divisible by $n!$ for any n greater than 2, because $n!$ has every prime factor from 2 through n, but n^n has only the prime factors that make up n. This proves beyond a shadow of a doubt that the shuffle method generates some permutations more often than others.

To make this concrete, let's consider an array of length 3 containing the strings "a", "b", and "c". There are $3^3 = 27$ possible executions of the shuffle method. All are equally likely, and each generates some permutation. There are $3! = 6$ distinct permutations of the array: {"a", "b", "c"}, {"a", "c", "b"}, {"b", "a", "c"}, {"b", "c", "a"}, {"c", "a", "b"}, and {"c", "b", "a"}. Because 27 is not divisible by 6, some of these permutations must be generated by more executions than others, so the shuffle method is not fair.

One problem with this proof is that it offers no intuition into the bias induced by the method; it merely proves that a bias exists. Often the best way to gain some insight is to perform an experiment. We ran a program that calculates the expected value of the element at each position when the method is run on the "identity array," where $a[i] = i$. Loosely speaking, the expected value is the average value that you'll see in the element if you run the shuffle method repeatedly. If the shuffle method were fair, the expected value would be the same for each element: $((n - 1) / 2)$. Figure 10.1 shows the expected value for each element in an array of length 9. Note the distinctive shape of the graph: It starts low, increases beyond the fair value (4), and settles down to the fair value in the last element.

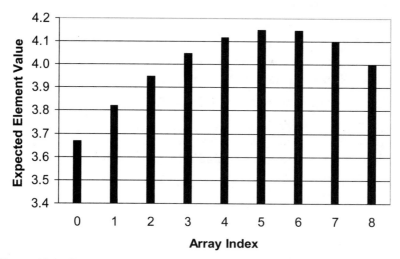

Figure 10.1   Expected values for the `shuffle` method on the identity array.

Why does the graph have this shape? We don't know all the details but we can offer some intuition. Let's restrict our attention to the array's first element. After the first iteration of the loop, it has the correct expected value of $(n - 1) / 2$. In the second iteration, however, there is 1 chance in n that the random number generator will return 0 and the value in the first element will be replaced by 1 or 0. In other words, the second iteration systematically reduces the expected value of the first element. In the third iteration, there's a further 1 chance in n that the first element is replaced by 2, 1, or 0, and so on. For the first $n / 2$ iterations of the loop, the expected value of the first element decreases. For the second $n / 2$ iterations, it increases but never catches up to its fair value. Note that the last element in the array is guaranteed to have the correct expected value, as the last step in the execution of the method is to select it at random from all the elements in the array.

OK, so our `shuffle` method is broken. How do we fix it? **Use the `shuffle` method provided by the library:**

```
import java.util.*;
public class Shuffle {
    public static void shuffle(Object[] a) {
        Collections.shuffle(Arrays.asList(a));
    }
}
```

Whenever the libraries provide a method that does what you need, use it [EJ Item 30]. Generally speaking, the libraries provides high-quality solutions requiring a minimum of effort on your part.

On the other hand, after you suffered through all that math, it seems unfair not to tell you how to fix the broken `shuffle` method. The fix is actually quite straightforward. In the body of the loop, swap the current element with an element selected at random from the portion of the array starting at the current element and extending to the end of the array. Do not touch an element once you've swapped a value into it. This is essentially the algorithm that is used by the library method:

```
public static void shuffle(Object[] a) {
    for (int i = 0; i < a.length; i++)
        swap(a, i, i + rnd.nextInt(a.length - i));
}
```

It's easy to prove this method fair by induction. For the base case, observe that it is trivially fair for an array of length 0. For the induction step, if you apply the method to an array of length $n > 0$, it correctly selects a random element for the zeroth position of the result array. Then, it iterates over the remainder of the array: At each position, it selects an element chosen at random from the "subarray" beginning at that position and extending to the end of the original array. But that is *exactly* what the method would do if it were applied directly to the subarray of length $n - 1$, starting at position 1 in the original array. This completes the proof. It also suggests a recursive formulation of the `shuffle` method, whose details are left as an exercise for the reader.

You might think that that's all there is to this story, but there's one final chapter. Do you suppose that the fixed `shuffle` method generates all permutations of a 52-card deck, represented as a 52-element array, with equal likelihood? After all, we just *proved* it fair. It probably won't surprise you at this point that the answer is an emphatic no. The problem is that we assumed, way back at the start of the puzzle, that "the underlying pseudorandom number generator is fair." It isn't.

The random number generator, `java.util.Random`, takes a 64-bit seed, and the sequence of numbers it generates is fully determined by that seed. There are 52! permutations of a 52-card deck, but only 2^{64} seeds. What fraction of the permutations does that cover? Would you believe 2.3×10^{-47} percent? That is a polite way of saying "practically none." If you use `java.security.SecureRandom` in place of `java.util.Random`, you get a 160-bit seed, but that buys you surprisingly little: The `shuffle` method still fails to return some permutations for arrays with more than 40 elements (because $40! > 2^{160}$). For a 52-element array, you still get only 1.8×10^{-18} percent of the possible permutations.

Does that mean that you shouldn't trust these pseudorandom number generators for shuffling cards? It depends. They generate a negligible fraction of the possible permutations, but they have no systematic bias that we're aware of. It seems fair to say that these generators are good enough for casual use. If you need a state-of-the-art random number generator, you'll have to look elsewhere.

In summary, shuffling an array, like many algorithms, is tricky. It's easy to get it wrong and hard to tell that you did. All other things being equal, you should use trusted libraries in preference to handwritten code. If you want to learn more about the issues discussed in this puzzle, see [Knuth98 3.4.2].

Puzzle 95: Just Desserts

Most of the puzzles in this chapter were quite challenging. This one isn't. What does each of the following programs print? The first two were reported as platform bugs, if you can believe it [Bug 4157460, 4763901]:

```
public class ApplePie {
    public static void main(String[] args) {
        int count = 0;
        for (int i = 0; i < 100; i++); {
            count++;
        }
        System.out.println(count);
    }
}

import java.util.*;
public class BananaBread {
    public static void main(String[] args) {
        Integer[] array = { 3, 1, 4, 1, 5, 9 };
        Arrays.sort(array, new Comparator<Integer>() {
            public int compare(Integer i1, Integer i2) {
                return i1 < i2 ? -1 : (i2 > i1 ? 1 : 0);
            }
        });
        System.out.println(Arrays.toString(array));
    }
}

public class ChocolateCake {
    public static void main(String[] args) {
        System.out.println(true?false:true == true?false:true);
    }
}
```

Solution 95: Just Desserts

If you made it this far, you don't need detailed explanations for these silly puzzles so we'll keep them short and sweet:

A. This program prints 1. It suffers from an excess of punctuation. (Cancer of the semicolon?)

B. This program prints [3, 1, 4, 1, 5, 9] on all implementations that we're aware of. Technically, its output is undefined. Its comparator suffers from "heads I win, tails you lose" syndrome.

C. This program prints `false`. Its typographical layout does not match the precedence of its operators. A few parentheses might help.

The lesson of this puzzle, and of this entire book, is: **Don't code like my brother.**

Catalog of Traps and Pitfalls

Have you done the puzzles yet? If not, go to Chapter 1! Go directly to Chapter 1. Do not pass GO. Do not collect $200. **If you read this chapter before doing the puzzles, it will take all the fun out of the book.** Don't say we didn't warn you.

This chapter contains a concise taxonomy of traps and pitfalls in the Java platform. Each entry in the catalog is divided into three parts:

A short description of the trap or pitfall

Prescription: How to avoid the trap or reduce the risk of falling victim.

References: Pointers to additional information concerning the trap. This typically includes a reference to the puzzle that is based on the trap. Many entries also have *Java Language Specification* and *Effective Java* references [JLS, EJ].

1.   Lexical Issues

This section concerns the *lexical structure* of Java programs: the tokens that make up programs and the characters that make up tokens.

1.1.   The letter *el* looks like the digit 1 in many fonts

Prescription: In long literals, always use a capital *el* (L), never a lowercase *el* (l). Do not use a lone *el* (l) as a variable name.

References: Puzzle 4.

1.2.   Negative hex literals appear positive

Prescription: Avoid mixed-type computation; use long literals instead of int literals where appropriate.

References: Puzzle 5; [JLS 3.10.1].

1.3.   Octal literals look like decimal literals

Prescription: Avoid octal literals. If you must use them, comment all uses to make your intentions clear.

References: Puzzle 59; [JLS 3.10.1].

1.4.   Unicode escapes for ASCII characters are confusing

Prescription: Don't use Unicode escapes for ASCII characters. Where possible, use ASCII character directly. In string literals and character literals, prefer escape sequences to Unicode escapes.

References: Puzzles 14, 16, and 17; [JLS 3.2, 3.3].

1.5.   Backslashes must be escaped, even in comments

Prescription: If you are writing a system that generates Java source code, escape backslashes in generated character literals, string literals, and comments. Windows filenames are a common source of trouble.

References: Puzzles 15 and 16; [JLS 3.3].

1.6.   Block comments do not nest

Prescription: Use single-line comments to comment out code.

References: Puzzle 19; [JLS 3.7, 14.21].

2.   Integer Arithmetic

This section concerns arithmetic on the integral types: byte, char, short, int, and long.

2.1.   Nonzero result of % operator has sign of left operand

Prescription: If you need a nonnegative remainder, process the result of the % operator by adding the modulus if the result is negative.

References: Puzzles 1 and 64; [JLS 15.17.3].

2.2.   Integer arithmetic overflows silently

Prescription: Use types that are sufficiently large to hold results, including intermediate results.

References: Puzzles 3, 26, 33, and 65; [JLS 4.2.2].

2.3.   The sign of the difference of int values does not reliably indicate their order

Prescription: Do not use a subtraction-based comparator unless you are sure that the difference between values will never be greater than Integer.MAX_VALUE. Note that this is a special case of Trap 2.2.

References: Puzzle 65; [EJ Item 11].

2.4.   Compound assignment operators can cause silent narrowing cast

Prescription: Don't use compound assignment operators on variables of type byte, short, or char.

References: Puzzles 9 and 31; [JLS 15.26.2].

2.5.   Integral types are asymmetric: Integer.MIN_VALUE is its own negation, as is Long.MIN_VALUE

Prescription: Program defensively. Use long instead of int if necessary.

References: Puzzles 33 and 64; [JLS 15.15.4].

2.6.   Shift operators use only the low-order bits of their right operand

Prescription: Shift by a constant amount; if you must shift by a variable amount, check that the shift distance is in range.

References: Puzzle 27; [JLS 15.19].

2.7.   When converting between integral types, sign extension is performed if the source type is signed

Prescription: Be careful when working with byte values, which are signed. To suppress sign extension, use a bit mask.

References: Puzzle 6; [JLS 5.1.2].

3.   Floating-Point Arithmetic

This section concerns arithmetic on the floating-point types: `float` and `double`.

3.1.   Floating-point arithmetic is inexact

Prescription: Don't use floating-point where exact results are required; instead, use an integral type or `BigDecimal`.

Avoid floating-point loop indices.

Avoid using the ++ and -- operators on floating-point variables, as these operators have no effect on most floating-point values.

Avoid testing floating-point values for equality.

Prefer `double` to `float`.

References: Puzzles 2, 28, and 34; [JLS 4.2.3], [EJ Item 31], and [IEEE-754].

3.2.   NaN is not equal to any floating-point value, including itself

Prescription: Avoid testing floating-point values for equality. This is not always sufficient to avoid problems, but it's a good start.

References: Puzzle 29; [JLS 15.21.1] and [IEEE-754].

3.3.   Conversions from `int` to `float`, `long` to `float`, and `long` to `double` are lossy

Prescription: Avoid computations that mix integral and floating-point types. Prefer integral arithmetic to floating-point.

References: Puzzles 34 and 87; [JLS 5.1.2].

3.4.   The `BigDecimal(double)` constructor returns the exact value of its floating-point argument

Prescription: Always use the `BigDecimal(String)` constructor; never use `BigDecimal(double)`.

References: Puzzle 2.

4. Expression Evaluation

This section concerns aspects of expression evaluation that are not specific to integer or floating-point arithmetic.

4.1. Mixed-type computations are confusing

Prescription: Avoid mixed-type computations.

When using the ? : operator with numeric operands, use the same numeric type for both the second and third operands.

Prefer constant variables to inline magic numbers.

References: Puzzles 5, 8, and 24.

4.2. Operands of operators are evaluated left to right

Prescription: Avoid multiple assignments to the same variable in the same expression. Especially confusing are multiple compound assignment operators in the same expression.

References: Puzzles 7, 25, and 42; [JLS 15.7] and [EJ Item 37].

4.3. Operator precedence is not always obvious

Prescription: Use parentheses, not white space, to make precedence explicit. Replace inline constant expressions with named constant variables.

References: Puzzles 11, 35, and 95.

4.4. Operators == and != perform reference comparisons on boxed primitive types

Prescription: To force a value comparison, assign or cast one operand to the appropriate primitive type before comparing.

References: Puzzle 32; [JLS 15.21, 5.1.8].

4.5.   Constant variables are inlined where they are used

Prescription: Avoid exporting constant fields unless they represent true constants that will never change.

Use an identity method to make an expression nonconstant.

References: Puzzle 93; [JLS 4.12.4, 13.1, 15.28].

4.6.   Operators & and | evaluate both operands even when used on boolean values

Prescription: Avoid the & and | operators for boolean operands. Document any intentional uses.

References: Puzzle 42; [JLS 15.22.2, 15.24].

5.   Flow of Control

This section concerns statements that affect flow of control, and exceptions.

5.1.   Missing break in switch case causes fall-through

Prescription: Don't fall through from one nonempty case to another: Terminate each nonempty case with a break. Document any intentional fall-throughs.

References: Puzzle 23; [JLS 14.11].

5.2.   It is difficult to terminate an int-indexed loop at Integer.MAX_VALUE

Prescription: To terminate an int-indexed loop at Integer.MAX_VALUE, use a long loop index or write the loop very carefully.

References: Puzzle 26.

5.3.   Abrupt completion of a `finally` block masks pending transfer of control

Prescription: Ensure that every `finally` block completes normally, barring a fatal error. Do not return from or throw an exception from a `finally` block.

References: Puzzles 36 and 41; [JLS 14.20.2].

5.4.   Using exceptions for normal control flow leads to bugs and poor performance

Prescription: Use exceptions only for exceptional cases, never for normal control flow.

References: Puzzle 42; [EJ item 39].

---

6.   Class Initialization

This section concerns class loading and initialization.

6.1.   Order of class initialization is top to bottom

Prescription: Ensure that static fields are initialized in an appropriate order. Use lazy initialization to resolve initialization cycles, which can involve one or more classes.

References: Puzzles 49 and 52; [JLS 12.4.2] and [EJ Item 48].

6.2.   Timing of `NoClassDefFoundError` is unreliable

Prescription: Do not catch `NoClassDefFoundError`. Instead, use reflection and catch `ClassNotFoundException`.

More generally, don't catch `Error` or its subclasses.

References: Puzzle 44; [JLS 12.2.1].

7.   Instance Creation and Destruction

This section concerns constructors, pseudoconstructors, instance initialization, and finalization.

7.1.   Instance initializers execute before constructor body

Prescription: If a self-typed instance field causes recursion during construction, ensure that the recursion terminates.

References: Puzzle 40; [JLS 12.5].

7.2.   Invoking an overridden method from a constructor causes method to run before instance is initialized

Prescription: Never invoke an overridable method from a constructor.

Use lazy initialization to resolve initialization cycles.

References: Puzzle 51; [EJ Items 15 and 48].

7.3.   Failure to null out references can cause memory leaks

Prescription: Null out obsolete object references in long-lived objects. Failure to do so results in memory leaks, more properly known as *unintended object retention*s in garbage-collected languages, such as Java.

References: [EJ Item 5].

7.4.   Failure to add a private constructor makes a class instantiable

Prescription: If you want a class to be uninstantiable, add a private constructor.

More generally, always provide at least one constructor; never depend on the default constructor.

References: [EJ Item 3].

7.5. Finalizers are unpredictable, dangerous, and slow

Prescription: Avoid finalizers.

References: [EJ Item 6].

7.6. Cloned objects can share internal state

Prescription: Avoid implementing `Cloneable`. If you implement it, copy any internal objects that you do not want to share between the object and its clone.

References: [EJ Item 10].

---

8. Other Class- and Instance-Related Topics

This section concerns method invocation, method design, class design, and generic types.

8.1. There is no dynamic dispatch on static methods

Prescription: Never qualify a static method invocation with an expression; always use a type.

References: Puzzle 48; [JLS 15.12.4.4].

8.2. Inner classes are confusing

Prescription: Prefer static member classes to inner classes.

References: Puzzles 80, 89, 90, and 92; [EJ Item 18].

8.3. Failure to make defensive copies destroys immutability

Prescription: Make defensive copies of input parameters and output values as required.

References: [EJ Item 24].

8.4.   Implementing an interface affects the API of the implementing class

Prescription: Do not implement an interface to gain unqualified access to its static fields.

Do not write an interface consisting solely of fields, a so-called *constant interface*.

In release 5.0 and later releases, use static import as a replacement for the Constant Interface antipattern.

References: [EJ Item 17] and [Java-5.0].

8.5.   Using `int` constants as enum values is unsafe

Prescription: Use enum types or, if you are using a release before 5.0, implement Typesafe Enums.

References: [EJ Item 21].

8.6.   Mixing raw and parameterized types weakens type checking

Prescription: Eliminate "unchecked" warnings reported in your code.

Avoid using raw types in code intended for use with release 5.0 or a later release.

References: Puzzle 88; [JLS 4.8].

8.7.   Returning `null` instead of a zero-length array or collection is error prone

Prescription: Don't return `null` from an array- or collection-returning method.

References: [EJ item 27].

9.   Name Reuse

This section concerns the many forms of name reuse possible in Java. The overriding prescription is: **Avoid name reuse except for overriding.** See also "A Glossary of Name Reuse" on page 180.

9.1.   It is easy to overload when you intend to override

Prescription: Mechanically copy the declaration of each superclass method that you intend to override; better yet, let your IDE do it for you.

If you are using release 5.0 or a later release, use the `@Override` annotation.

References: Puzzle 58.

9.2.   Overload-resolution rules are not obvious

Prescription: Avoid overloading.

Provide static factories rather than multiple constructors.

If two methods in your API are both applicable to some invocation, ensure that both methods have the same behavior on the same actual arguments.

References: Puzzles 11, 46, and 74; [JLS 15.12.2] and [EJ Items 1 and 26].

9.3.   Programs that hide entities are difficult to understand

Prescription: Avoid hiding.

References: Puzzles 66, 72, 73, and 92; [JLS 8.3, 8.4.8.2, 8.5].

9.4.   Programs that shadow entities are difficult to understand

Prescription: Avoid shadowing.

Do not reuse names from `java.lang.Object` in public APIs.

Don't try to use static import on a name that is already defined.

References: Puzzles 71, 73, 79, and 89; [JLS 6.3.1, 15.12.1].

9.5.   Programs that obscure entities are difficult to understand

Prescription: Avoid obscuring. Obey the naming conventions.

References: Puzzles 68 and 69; [JLS 6.3.2, 6.5.2, 6.8] and [EJ Item 38].

9.6.   A method with the same name as its class looks like a constructor

Prescription: Obey the naming conventions.

References: Puzzle 63; [JLS 6.8] and [EJ Item 38].

9.7.   Programs that reuse platform class names are difficult to understand

Prescription: Avoid reusing platform class names, and never reuse class names from `java.lang`.

References: Puzzle 67.

---

10. Strings

This section concern character strings.

10.1.   Arrays do not override `Object.toString`

Prescription: For char arrays, use `String.valueOf` to obtain the string representing the designated sequence of characters. For other types of arrays, use `Arrays.toString` or, prior to release 5.0, `Arrays.asList`.

References: Puzzle 12; [JLS 10.7].

10.2.   `String.replaceAll` takes a regular expression as its first argument

Prescription: Ensure that the argument is a legal regular expression, or use `String.replace` instead.

References: Puzzle 20.

10.3.   `String.replaceAll` takes a replacement string as its second argument

Prescription: Ensure that the argument is a legal replacement string, or use `String.replace` instead.

References: Puzzle 20.

10.4.   Repeated string concatenation can cause poor performance

Prescription: Avoid using the string concatenation operator in loops.

References: [EJ item 33].

10.5.   Conversion of bytes to characters requires a charset

Prescription: Always select a charset when converting a `byte` array to a string or `char` array; if you don't, the platform default charset will be used, leading to unpredictable behavior.

References: Puzzle 18.

10.6.   Values of type char are silently converted to int, not String

Prescription: To convert a `char` to a string, use `String.valueOf(char)`.

References: Puzzles 11 and 23; [JLS 5.1.2].

11. I/O

This section concerns the package `java.io`.

11.1. `Stream.close` can throw `IOException`

Prescription: Catch and, typically, ignore exceptions on `close`.

References: Puzzle 41.

11.2. `PrintStream.write(int)` doesn't flush output streams

Prescription: Avoid `PrintStream.write(int)`. If you use it, call `flush` as required.

References: Puzzle 81.

11.3. Consume the output of a process, or it may hang

Prescription: Always consume the output of processes you create.

References: Puzzle 82.

12. Threads

This section concerns multithreaded programming. Multithreaded programming is difficult! The overriding prescription is: **Avoid low-level multithreaded programming where possible.** Instead, use higher level multithreaded abstractions, such as those introduced by `java.util.concurrent` in release 5.0. This is an important special case of the advice in Trap 15.5.

12.1. Calling `Thread.run` doesn't start a thread

Prescription: Never call `Thread.run`.

References: Puzzle 76.

12.2. Library classes may `lock` or `notify` their instances

Prescription: Don't use an instance lock if you extend a library class. Instead, use a separate lock object stored in a private field.

References: Puzzle 77; [EJ Item 15].

12.3. `Thread.interrupted` clears the interrupted status

Prescription: Don't use `Thread.interrupted` unless you want to clear the interrupted status of the current thread.

References: Puzzle 84.

12.4. Class initialization runs with the `Class` lock held

Prescription: To avoid the risk of deadlock, never wait for a background thread during class initialization.

References: Puzzle 85; [JLS 12.4.2].

12.5. Failure to synchronize when sharing mutable state can result in failure to observe state changes

Prescription: Synchronize access to shared mutable state.

References: [EJ Item 48].

12.6. Invoking alien method from within a synchronized block can cause deadlock

Prescription: Never cede control to an alien method from within a synchronized method or block.

References: [EJ item 49].

12.7. Invoking `wait` outside of a `while` loop causes unpredictable behavior

Prescription: Never invoke `wait` outside a `while` loop.

References: [EJ item 50].

12.8.   Depending on the thread scheduler may result in erratic and platform-dependent behavior

Prescription: To write robust, responsive, portable multithreaded programs, ensure that few threads are runnable at any given time.

References: [EJ item 51].

13.   Reflection

This section concerns Java's core reflection APIs.

13.1.   Reflection checks access to the entity and to its class

Prescription: Use reflection to instantiate classes; interfaces to access instances.

References: Puzzle 78; [EJ Item 35].

13.2.   Reflectively instantiating an inner class requires an extra argument

Prescription: Don't use reflection on inner classes.

Prefer static member classes to inner classes.

References: Puzzle 80; [JLS 13.1] and [EJ Item 18].

13.3.   `Class.newInstance` can throw undeclared checked exceptions

Prescription: Use `java.lang.reflect.Constructor.newInstance` instead of `Class.newInstance` if there is any possibility of the constructor throwing a checked exception.

References: Puzzle 43.

14. Serialization

This section concerns Java's object serialization system.

14.1. Making a class serializable introduces a public pseudoconstructor

Prescription: Think twice before making a class serializable.

Think twice before accepting the default readObject method.

Write readObject methods defensively.

References: [EJ Items 54 and 56].

14.2. The serialized form is a part of a class's public API

Prescription: Design serialized forms with the same care that you would design any other API.

References: [EJ Items 54 and 55].

14.3. Using the default serialized form leaks private fields into a class's public API

Prescription: Consider using a custom serialized form.

References: [EJ Item 55].

14.4. Using the default serialized form can cause poor performance

Prescription: Consider using a custom serialized form.

References: [EJ Item 55].

14.5. Maintaining instance-control invariants requires a `readResolve` method

Prescription: Always write a `readResolve` method for singletons, handwritten Typesafe Enums, and other instance-controlled instantiable classes.

References: Puzzle 83; [EJ Items 2 and 57].

14.6. Failure to declare a serial version UID causes fragility

Prescription: Declare an explicit serial version UID in serializable classes.

References: [EJ Items 54 and 55].

14.7. If `readObject` or `readResolve` invokes overridable methods, deserializing cyclic object graphs can cause corruption

Prescription: If a `HashSet`, `HashMap`, or `Hashtable` will be serialized, ensure that its contents do not refer back to it.

In `readObject` and `readResolve` methods, avoid invoking methods on objects currently being deserialized. If you must violate this advice, ensure that no problematic cycles exist in the object graph.

References: Puzzle 91.

---

15. Other Libraries

This section concern various Java platform libraries.

15.1. Overriding `equals` without overriding `hashCode` can cause erratic behavior

Prescription: When overriding `equals`, always override `hashCode`.

References: Puzzle 57; [EJ Item 8].

15.2. Calendar and Date are poorly designed

Prescription: Be careful when using Calendar and Date; always consult the API documentation.

References: Puzzle 61.

15.3. Many classes are immutable, their method names notwithstanding

Prescription: Do not be misled into thinking that immutable types are mutable. Immutable types include String, Integer, Long, Short, Byte, Character, Boolean, Float, Double, BigInteger, and BigDecimal.

References: Puzzle 56.

15.4. Some deprecated methods are toxic

Prescription: Avoid deprecated methods, such as Thread.stop, Thread.suspend, Runtime.runFinalizersOnExit, and System.runFinalizersOnExit.

References: Puzzle 39 and 43; [ThreadStop].

15.5. Using homemade solutions instead of libraries tends to cause wasted effort, bugs, and poor performance

Prescription: Know and use the libraries.

References: Puzzles 60, 62, and 94; [EJ Item 30].

Notes on the Illusions

This appendix contains brief descriptions of the illusions that appear throughout the book. The descriptions are grouped loosely by category. Within each category, the order is roughly chronological.

Ambiguous Figures

An *ambiguous figure* is a drawing that can be seen in two or more ways, though not at the same time. One kind of ambiguous figure is a two-dimensional drawing that can be seen to represent one of several different three-dimensional figures. The *Ambiguous Cube* (page 67) can be seen in three ways: as a large cube with a small cubic region missing from one corner, as a small cube sitting inside a corner of a larger one, and as a large cube with a small cube protruding from one corner.

Another kind of ambiguous figure is the *figure-ground illusion*, which is a drawing that can be seen in two ways, depending on what you perceive as the figure and what you perceive as the background. The drawings on pages 158 and 231 can be seen as black arrows pointing outward against a white background, or as white arrows pointing inward against a black background. The drawing on page 97 can be seen as white letters against a black background, or as black shapes against a white background.

Impossible Figures

An *impossible figure* is a two-dimensional perspective drawing of a figure that cannot exist in three dimensions. The arrangement of cubes on page 122 is based on an impossible figure drawn by Swedish artist Oscar Reutersvärd in 1934. This drawing is thought to be the first impossible figure ever devised. Reutersvärd devoted his career to impossible figures.

The *Penrose Triangle* (pages 36 and 126) is closely related to Reutersvärd's triangle of cubes, but it was created independently by physicist Roger Penrose in 1954. The *Penrose Stairway* (page 63) was created in the mid 1950s by geneticist and psychiatrist Lionel Penrose, the father of Roger Penrose. The Penrose stairway forms the basis of M. C. Escher's famous lithograph *Ascending and Descending* (1960).

The *Three-Stick Clevis* (pages 59 and 200) is also known by many other names, such as *Widgit, Poiuyt,* and *Impossible Trident*. Its origins are unknown, but it dates back at least to 1964, when D. H. Schuster wrote an article about it in the *American Journal of Psychology*. The clevis also graced the cover of the March 1965 issue of *MAD Magazine*, held aloft by a smiling Alfred E. Neuman. The *Ambihelical Hex Nut* (pages 154 and 249) and the *Impossible Ring* (pages 109 and 164) are two more impossible figures of unknown origin.

Geometrical Illusions: Size

The *Jastrow illusion* (page 85) was described by psychologist Joseph Jastrow in 1891. The two shaded areas are identical in size and shape, but most people perceive the top one to be smaller. The *Ebbinghaus* (or *Titchener*) *illusion* (page 137) was described by psychologist Hermann Ebbinghaus in 1897. The two central circles are the same size, but most people perceive the one on the right to be smaller.

The *Shepard illusion* (page 93) is based on a 1990 drawing by Stanford psychologist Roger Shepard [Shepard90]. The two tabletops are the same size and shape, but perspective cues make them look very different. Shepard first demonstrated the effect in 1981.

Geometrical Illusions: Direction

The *Twisted Cord illusion* (pages 13 and 221), also known as the *Fraser figure*, was described by psychologist James Fraser in 1908. The letters "CAFE babe" on page 13 are set straight and true; the perceived tilt is illusory. What appears to be a tilted "Square Spiral" on page 221 is in fact eight concentric squares, set straight and true.

The *Ehrenstein illusion* (page 35) was described by psychologist Walter Ehrenstein in 1925. The sides of the square are straight, but they appear to curve towards the center of the circles.

The *Café Wall illusion* (page 39) was first demonstrated by Fraser in 1908, and named by Richard L. Gregory and Priscilla Heard [Gregory79]. The lines of black and white tiles appear slanted but they are perfectly level. The illusion gets its name from the fact that it was found in a tile pattern on the wall of a café in Bristol, England.

The *Cushion illusion* (page 65) was devised by vision scientist and artist Akiyoshi Kitaoka in 1998. This drawing consists solely of rectangles and squares, set straight and true; the curvature is all in your mind. If you find this hard to believe, you can confirm it with a straightedge. The *Bulge illusion* (page 152) and the *Checkered Flag illusion* (page 169) were also devised by Kitaoka in 1998. They consist solely of squares, set straight and true; the bulging and rippling are in your mind. All three of these illusions are based on the same underlying effect.

The *Turtles illusion* (page 225) was devised by Kitaoka in 2002. The vertical edges appear tilted but they run straight up and down. The underlying effect, known as the *illusion of Fringed Edges*, was described by Kitaoka, Pinna and Brelstaff [Kitaoka01].

Subjective Contours

A *subjective contour*, also known as an *illusory contour*, is a perceived edge that does not exist. The classic example is found in the *Kanizsa Triangle* (pages 146 and 242), devised by Gestalt psychologist Gaetano Kanizsa in 1955. A white triangle appears to float above a black triangular outline, but the lines that form the white triangle don't exist. Your mind constructs them from the contours implied by the "Pac-Man" figures. The variant on page 147 is based on a figure devised by Branka Spehar [Spehar00], and the variant on pages 15 and 168 is based on a figure devised by Takeo Watanabe and Patrick Cavanagh [Watanabe92]. The three-dimensional variants on pages 100 and 101 are based loosely on the *Subjective Necker Cube* of Bradley and Petry, discussed later in this appendix. The *Kanizsa Dot Window* on page 69 is based on a figure drawn by Kanizsa in 1979.

The *Shadow Letters* on page 27 are also a subjective contour illusion. Your mind perceives the letters A, B, and C, when all that is present is the shadows that these letters would cast.

Anomalous Motion Illusions

Anomalous motion illusions are drawings whose components appear to move. The *MacKay's Rays illusion* (page 203) was described by Donald MacKay in 1957. Figure-eight patterns appear to move about the drawing as you scan over it with your eyes. The drawings on pages 47, 192, and 230 are based on the *MacKay's Squares illusion*, described by MacKay in 1961. The figure appears to blink as you look at it. This illusion forms the basis of Reginald Neal's op art prints *Square of Three* (1964) and *Square of Two* (1965).

The *Ouchi illusion* (page 173) was devised by artist Hajime Ouchi in 1973 [Ouchi77]. The inset appears to be on a different plane from the main figure, and to vibrate.

The *Scintillating Grid illusion* (page 161) was discovered by Elke Lingelbach in 1994 [Schrauf97]. Black spots appear to sparkle in the white disks where the grid lines meet.

The drawing on page 96 is based on Kitaoka's *Waves illusions* (2004). Gentle waves appear to undulate through the circles. The *Rotating Snakes illusion* (page 136) was devised by Kitaoka in 2003. If you haven't seen the original, you owe it to yourself to visit http://www.psy.ritsumei.ac.jp/~akitaoka/rotsnakee.html. The effect is breathtaking. Both waves and rotating snakes are based on the stepwise luminance profile variant of the *Peripheral Drift illusion* [Kitaoka03b].

Illusions of Lightness

An illusion of lightness is an image in which we misperceive the lightness (or *luminance*) of some portion of the image. The simplest lightness illusion is the *Simultaneous Contrast illusion*, in which areas of identical lightness appear lighter or darker depending on the background against which they're displayed. This effect has been known since ancient times. It is demonstrated by the images on pages 163 and 165. In both of these images, the central rectangle and the second frame from the outside are the same shade of gray throughout, but they appear to get lighter as the surrounding frame gets darker.

The checkerboard pattern on page 23 is based loosely on the *Craik-O'Brien-Cornsweet illusion*. The top and bottom squares appear lighter than the left and right squares, but all four squares are identical. The lighter corners of the top and bottom squares point inward, while the lighter corners of the left and right squares point outward. Changes in lightness at the edges where the squares meet influence your perception of the relative lightness of the squares.

Logvinenko's illusion (page 189) was devised by vision scientist Alexander Logvinenko [Logvinenko99]. Strange as it may seem, the horizontal cube faces are all the same shade of gray. If you think the horizontal faces in the first and third rows are lighter than the ones in the second and fourth, cover the vertical faces with a mask and prepare to be surprised. The effect underlying this illusion is closely related to the Craik-O'Brien-Cornsweet illusion.

A similar effect is exploited in *Todorovic's Gradient Chessboard illusion* (page 149), devised by vision scientist Dejan Todorovic [Todorovic97]. Though the disks on the checkerboard appear to be of three different shades of gray, they are all the same.

The *Vasarely illusion*, devised by op artist Victor Vasarely, is shown on pages 228 and 229. There appears to be a dark cross on the diagonals of the light version (page 228) and a light cross on the diagonals of the dark version (page 229), but no such crosses exist.

The drawing on page 211 is based on *White's effect* [White79]. The gray bars separated by white bars appear lighter than the gray bars separated by black bars, but all the gray bars are the same.

The drawing on page 135 is based on *Adelson's Illusion of Haze* [Adelson99]. The central diamond, which appears clear, is exactly the same shade of gray as the two flanking diamonds, which appear hazy.

The drawing on page 127 is based loosely on Kitaoka's *Light of Chrysanthemums* (2005), which uses *Zavagno's Glare effect* [Zavagno99]. The center of the flower appears unnaturally bright and an illusory fog appears between the petals.

Compound Illusions

Compound illusions combine two or more illusory effects. The drawing on page 160 is based on *Ehrenstein's figure*, discovered by Walter Ehrenstein in 1941. It combines subjective contours with an illusion of lightness. Your mind perceives circles where the grid lines converge, and the circles are unnaturally bright.

The *Subjective Necker Cube* (pages 33 and 224) was devised by Bradley and Petry [Bradley77]. It combines subjective contours with an ambiguous figure. You can see two cubes, one at a time, but the figure contains none. It merely suggests the edges that comprise these cubes.

The drawing on page 57, based on the *Dahlia Contours illusion* by vision scientist Nicholas Wade, combines subjective contours with an illusion of lightness: Your mind perceives concentric circles at the radii where the arcs cross, and the circles appear brighter than the surrounding page.

The drawings on pages 48 and 49 are based on the *Neon Square illusion* of Marc Albert and Donald Hoffman [Albert99]. This illusion combines subjective contours with the *Neon Spreading effect* [van Tuijl75]. Not only do you perceive squares where none exist, but the squares have illusory color. The illusory square on page 48 appears hazy and the one on page 49 appears dark.

The drawing on page 125 uses an effect similar to the one that Kitaoka used in cushion, bulge, and checkered flag. The drawing looks like a spiral, but it consists of concentric circles. If you move towards the drawing or away from it, it appears to rotate.

The drawing on page 92 combines the "out-of-focus" effect found in Kitaoka's *Earthquake* (2001) with MacKay's squares. The frame appears to float above the defocused grid, and the grid appears to vibrate.

Finally, the front cover illustration combines the Peripheral Drift illusion, the Scintillating Grid, and a third unnamed illusion. The outer ring of fishes appears to rotate clockwise, the inner ring appears to rotate counterclockwise, the white disks at the intersections of the grid lines appear to sparkle, and the grid inset appears to move slightly relative to the fishes.

References

[Adelson99]   Adelson, E. H. "Lightness perception and lightness illusions." In M. S. Gazzaniga (Ed.), *The New Cognitive Neurosciences*, MIT Press, 2nd ed., 1999: 339–351. ISBN: 0262071959. Also available as http://web.mit.edu/persci/people/adelson/pub_pdfs/gazzan.pdf

[Albert99]   Albert, Marc K., and Donald D. Hoffman, "The generic-viewpoint assumption and illusory contours." In *Perception*, Vol. 29 (1999): 303–312.

[Boute92]   Boute, Raymond. "The Euclidean definition of the functions div and mod." In *ACM Transactions on Programming Languages and Systems*, Vol. 14, No. 2 (April 1992): 127–144.

[Boxing]   *Autoboxing.* Sun Microsystems. 2004. http://java.sun.com/j2se/5.0/docs/guide/language/autoboxing.html

[Bracha04]   Bracha, Gilad. *Generics in the Java Programming Language.* 2004. http://java.sun.com/j2se/1.5/pdf/generics-tutorial.pdf

[Bradley77]   Bradley, D. R., and H. M. Petry. "Organizational determinants of subjective contour: the subjective Necker cube." In *American Journal of Psychology*, Vol. 90 (June 1977): 253–262.

[Bug]   *Java Bug Database.* Sun Microsystems, 1994–2005. http://bugs.sun.com/bugdatabase/index.jsp

[Eclipse]   *Eclipse Downloads.* The Eclipse Foundation, 2002–2005. http://www.eclipse.org/downloads/index.php

[EJ]   Bloch, Joshua. *Effective Java™ Programming Language Guide.* Addison-Wesley, 2001. ISBN: 0201310058.

[Features-1.4] *J2SE 1.4.2 Summary of New Features and Enhancements.* Sun Microsystems, 2002. http://java.sun.com/j2se/1.4.2/docs/relnotes/features.html

[Features-5.0] *New Features and Enhancements J2SE 5.0.* Sun Microsystems, 2004. http://java.sun.com/j2se/5.0/docs/relnotes/features.html

[Gamma95]   Gamma, Erich, Richard Helm, Ralph Johnson, and John Vlissides. *Design Patterns: Elements of Reusable Object-Oriented Software.* Addison-Wesley, 1995. ISBN: 0201633612.

[Gregory79]   Gregory, Richard L., and Priscilla Heard. "Border locking and the Café Wall illusion." In *Perception*, Vol. 8 (1979): 365–380.

[Hovemeyer04]   Hovemeyer, David, and William Pugh. *FindBugs—Find Bugs in Java Programs.* 2004–2005. http://findbugs.sourceforge.net

[IEEE-754]   *IEEE Standard for Binary Floating-Point Arithmetic.* Institute of Electrical and Electronics Engineers. IEEE 754-1985 (R1990). 1990.

[ISO-8859-1]   ISO/IEC JTC 1/SC 2/WG 3. *ISO 8859, 8-bit Single-Byte Coded Graphic Character Sets—Part 1: Latin Alphabet No. 1.* ISO 8859-1:1987. 1987.

[ISO-C]   *Programming Languages—C.* International Organization for Standardization. ISO/IEC 9899:1999. 1999.

[Java-5.0]   *Java Programming Language Enhancements in JDK 5.* Sun Microsystems, 2004. http://java.sun.com/j2se/5.0/docs/guide/language

[Java-API]   *Java 2 Platform Standard Edition 5.0 API Specification.* Sun Microsystems, 2004. http://java.sun.com/j2se/5.0/docs/api

[JDK-5.0]   *Download Java 2 Platform Standard Edition 5.0.* Sun Microsystems, 2004. http://java.sun.com/j2se/5.0/download.jsp

[Jikes]   *Jikes Home.* Open Source Technology Group, 1997–2005. http://jikes.sourceforge.net

[JLS]   Gosling, James, Bill Joy, Guy Steele, and Gilad Bracha. *The Java™ Language Specification, Third Edition.* Addison-Wesley, 2005. ISBN: 0321246780. Also available as http://java.sun.com/docs/books/jls/download/langspec-3.0.pdf

[JLS2]   Gosling, James, Bill Joy, Guy Steele, and Gilad Bracha. *The Java™ Language Specification, Second Edition.* Addison-Wesley, 2000. ISBN: 0201310082.

[JVMS]   Lindholm, Tim, and Frank Yellin. *The Java™ Virtual Machine Specification, Second Edition.* Addison-Wesley, 1999. ISBN: 0201432943.

[Kitaoka01]   Kitaoka, A., B. Pinna, and G. Brelstaff. "New variations of spiral illusions." In *Perception*, Vol. 30 (2001): 637–646.

[Kitaoka02]   Kitaoka, Akiyoshi. *Trick Eyes,* Kanzen, Tokyo, 2002. ISBN: 4901782118.

[Kitaoka03]   Kitaoka, Akiyoshi. *Trick Eyes 2,* Kanzen, Tokyo, 2003. ISBN: 4901782169.

[Kitaoka03b]   Kitaoka, Akiyoshi, and Hiroshi Ashida. "Phenomenal characteristics of the peripheral drift illusion." In *Vision* (Japan), Vol. 15, No. 4 (2003): 261–262. Also available as http://www.psy.ritsumei.ac.jp/~akitaoka/PDrift.pdf

[Kitaoka05]   Kitaoka, Akiyoshi. *Trick Eyes*, Barnes and Noble Publishing, October 2005.

[Knuth98]   Knuth, Donald E. *The Art of Computer Programming, Volume 2: Seminumerical Algorithms, Third Edition.* Addison-Wesley, 1998. ISBN: 0201896842.

[Liskov87]   Liskov, B. "Data abstraction and hierarchy." In *Addendum to the Proceedings of OOPSLA '87* and *SIGPLAN Notices,* Vol. 23, No. 5: 17–34, May 1988.

[Logvinenko99]   Logvinenko, Alexander D. "Lightness induction revisited." In *Perception*, Vol. 28 (1999): 803–816.

[MaryBlog]   Smaragdis, Mary. Weblog: *MaryMaryQuiteContrary.* 2004–2005. http://blogs.sun.com/roller/page/mary

[Modula-3]   Nelson, Greg (ed.). *Systems Programming with Modula-3.* Prentice Hall, 1991. ISBN: 0135904641.

[Ouchi77]   Ouchi, Hajime. *Japanese Optical and Geometrical Art.* Dover Publications, 1977. ISBN: 048623553X.

[Schrauf97]   Schrauf, M., B. Lingelbach, and E. R. Wist. "The scintillating grid illusion." In *Vision Research*, Vol. 37 (1997): 1033–1038.

[Shepard90]   Shepard, Roger N., *Mind Sights: Original Visual Illusions, Ambiguities, and Other Anomalies, with a Commentary on the Play of Mind in Perception and Art.* W.H. Freeman and Co, 1990. ISBN: 0716721341.

[Spehar00]   Spehar, B. "Degraded illusory contour formation with non-uniform inducers in Kanizsa configurations: the role of contrast polarity." In *Vision Research*, Vol. 40, No. 19 (September 2000): 2653–2659.

[ThreadStop]   *Why Are Thread.stop, Thread.suspend, Thread.resume and Runtime.runFinalizersOnExit Deprecated?* Sun Microsystems, 1999. http://java.sun.com/j2se/5.0/docs/guide/misc/threadPrimitiveDeprecation.html

[Todorovic97]   Todorovic, D. "Lightness and junctions." In *Perception*, Vol. 26 (1997): 379–394.

[van Tuijl75]   van Tuijl, H.F. "A new visual illusion: neonlike color spreading and complementary color induction between subjective contours." In *Acta Psychologica*, Vol. 39 (1975): 441–445.

[Turing36]   Turing, A. "On Computable Numbers, with an Application to the Entscheidungsproblem." In *Proceedings of the London Mathematical Society*, Series 2, Vol. 42, 1936; reprinted in M. David (ed.), *The Undecidable,* Dover Publications, 2004.

[Watanabe92]   Watanabe, T., and P. Cavanagh. "Depth capture and transparency of regions bounded by illusory, chromatic, and texture contours." In *Vision Research*, Vol. 32 (1992): 527–532.

[White79]   White, M. "A new effect of pattern on perceived lightness." In *Perception*, Vol. 8 (1979): 413–416.

[Zavagno99]   Zavagno, D. "Some new luminance-gradient effects." In *Perception*, Vol. 28 (1999): 835–838.

Index

Symbols

- unary negation operator, 14, 72, 210
- subtraction operator, 154
!= not equal to operator, 70
% remainder operator, 6, 150
%= compound assignment operator for remainder, 22, 68
%n printf end-of-line format, 37
& AND operator, 7, 91
&& conditional-AND operator, 91
&= compound assignment operator for AND, 22, 68
*= compound assignment operator for multiplication, 22, 68
+ addition operator, 26, 30, 66
   precedence of, 31
+ string concatenation operator, 26, 28, 30, 66
++ increment operator, 56
+= compound assignment operator for addition, 22, 68
/ division operator, 6
/* */ comment delimiters, 42
// end of line comment, 36, 43

/= compound assignment operator for division, 22, 68
< less-than relational operator, 70, 74, 237
<< left shift operator, 60
<<= compound assignment operator for left shift, 22, 68
<= less-than-or-equal relational operator, 70
<=> Perl comparison operator, 156
= assignment operator, 22, 24
-= compound assignment operator for subtraction, 22, 68
== equal-to operator, 30, 70, 211–212
   vs. `equals`, 29–31
> greater-than relational operator, 70, 237
>= greater-than-or-equal relational operator, 70
>> right shift operator, 60
>>= compound assignment operator for right shift, 22, 68
>>> unsigned right shift operator, 60
>>>= compound assignment operator for unsigned right shift, 22, 67, 68
?: conditional operator, 19, 237
   operand types and, 177–179
`@Override` annotation, 139